# PALACES OF DISCOVERY

## *The Changing World of Britain's Museums*

Simon Tait

# PALACES OF DISCOVERY

## *The Changing World of Britain's Museums*

Simon Tait

QUILLER PRESS
London

Published by
Quiller Press Limited
46 Lillie Road
London SW6 1TN

First published 1989

Designed by Hugh Tempest-Radford Book Producers
Set in Baskerville by Galleon Photosetting, Ipswich

ISBN 1 870948 009



Printed in Great Britain by Camelot Press plc

# Contents


| | page |
|---|---|
| *Foreword* | vii |
| *Acknowledgements* | viii |
| Introduction | 1 |
| PART ONE | |
| 1. 'Temples where all can worship'. The national museums | 5 |
| 2. 'By the gains of industry . . .' The local museums | 19 |
| 3. 'An absolute necessity'. The independent museums | 33 |
| PART TWO | |
| 4. Hoarders and crackpots | 45 |
| 5. The boffins' cupboards | 58 |
| 6. '. . . and how's thieving?' | 66 |
| PART THREE | |
| 7. What makes them tick? | 81 |
| 8. Discovery | 93 |
| 9. The Water Margin | 100 |
| 10. It's real, but is it true? | 109 |
| 11. Sticky fingers | 118 |
| 12. The whizz-bang dimension | 129 |
| 13. Dead arts | 141 |
| PART FOUR | |
| 14. The Guardians | 155 |
| 15. The Supporters | 166 |
| 16. The Watchers | 173 |
| *Index* | 180 |

# Foreword

by Graeme Farnell, Director General, Museums Association

The number of museums in Britain is at an all-time high. Visitors, and other users, have reached record levels. Media interest in their activities increases daily. In short, our 2,500 museums are now communicating with the public on a scale undreamed of even a few decades ago.

As a result of this, their role can be conceived in a totally new way. As a genuine medium of mass communication. A medium which – unlike any other – brings the visitor face-to-face with three-dimensional reality, and can lend unprecedented vividness, beauty, and even emotional power, to the experience.

How appropriate that Simon Tait should bring a journalist's shrewd eye to bear on this burgeoning medium. His book appears during Museums Year, a celebration not only of the Centenary of the Museums Association as the world's first national museum organisation, but also the world's most extensive festival of, and promotion of, museums.

Museums Year has two aims: to develop a more positive perception of museums; and to encourage investment in them. These two aims are, of course, inextricably linked. For only when those who control the purse strings – whether public or private – appreciate both the popularity and the real benefits (cultural, social and economic) of museums, will museums be guaranteed the resources to enable them both to sustain their growth and reach their full potential.

Simon Tait's lively and attractive book provides both a fascinating insight into the museum world and a significant contribution to the aims of Museums Year.

G.F.
1989

# Acknowledgements

I should like to thank all the museums and museum people who were so generous with their information, advice and time in helping me put this book together, and in particular my thanks are due, in random order, to Dr John Physick, Tim Schadla-Hall, Arthur Jewell, Rona Cole, Commander Richard Compton-Hall, Geoff Preece, Allen Levy, Anthony Burton, Lt-Col. Paul Adair, Michael Ware, Dr Neil Cossons, Giles Waterfield, Robert Opie, Alf Hatton, Mark O'Neill, Julian Spalding, Dr Graham Durant, Peter Longman, and especially to Graeme Farnell for his generous foreword.

This book is dedicated to my wife, Sandra, who worked at least as hard on it under impossible circumstances as I did; to my son, Adam, who raced it into the world and won; to my mother, Alice; and to the memory of my father, Bill, in so many ways the real author of all that I write.

## Picture Acknowledgements

Victoria & Albert Museum; British Museum (Natural History); the Science Museum; the Imperial War Museum; Hull City Museums & Art Galleries; the National Motor Museum, Beaulieu; Beamish; National Museum of Wales; National Museums & Galleries on Merseyside; the Sir John Soane Museum; the British Museum; Birmingham City Council: Museums and Art Gallery; Guernsey Museum and Art Gallery; Eureka!; the Exploratory; Jodrell Bank; Green's Mill – City of Nottingham Arts Department; Royal Air Force Museum; the Tank Museum; Ashmolean Museum, Oxford; Dulwich Picture Gallery; the Wordsworth Trust; Springburn Museum Trust; Glasgow Museums & Art Galleries; British Engineerium (John Maltby); British Waterways Board Photo Library; the Boat Museum; the Royal Navy Submarine Museum; Museum of Advertising & Packaging; the Ironbridge Gorge Museum; Quarry Bank Mill Trust; the London Toy & Model Museum; Leicestershire Museums; Haslemere Educational Museum; Hunterian Art Gallery, University of Glasgow; the Powell-Cotton Museum; Museum of the Manchesters; Wigan Pier Heritage Centre; Chatham Historic Dockyard; Tyne & Wear Museums Service; Jorvik Viking Centre; the Tutenkamun Exhibition; Tate Gallery, Liverpool; Manchester City Art Galleries; National Galleries of Scotland; Dundee Industrial Heritage Ltd; Museum of the Moving Image. TECHNIQUEST; Guards Museum; National Railway Museum; Weald & Downland Open Air Museum.

# Introduction

## *Contemplation and inspiration*

'A museum is like a living organism; it requires continual and tender care; it must grow or it will perish,' wrote the anatomist, surgeon, Crimean War veteran and godfather of the modern museum, William Henry Flower (*Essays on Museums*, Macmillan 1898). He called it the 'new museum idea'. In 1884 he became the first director of the Natural History Museum, and from then almost until his death at the end of the century was genially to gentle through a revolution in the museum world.

South Kensington was the birthplace of the 'new museum idea', its progenitor having been a man of utterly different stamp: the irascible, bullying and visionary Henry Cole, who all but tyrannized the government into the Great Exhibition of 1851, then wrung the South Kensington Museum out of the exhibition's profits. From Cole's creation came the Victoria & Albert and the Science Museums.

The last three decades of the nineteenth century saw a population explosion in museums in Britain, especially in the great provincial cities. In 1860 there were about 90 museums, in 1887 there were 217 (not including a handful of national institutions), and by 1928 when Sir Henry Miers compiled his *Report on Museums in the British Isles*, there were 530 (including national museums). There were 950 in 1973, and about 2,500 in 1988 – even now, statistics cannot keep up with developments.

'Museum' comes from the Greek word for a seat of the muses, *museion*, a place for contemplation and inspiration. In Latin it became *museum* meaning a library or study, and even a venue for philosophical debate.

Mankind has always collected things from the past with varying degrees of intent to educate and to amuse. In Babylon in the sixth-century BC, Nebuchadnezzar collected antiquities, and the archaeologist Sir Leonard Woolley, with his distinguished assistant Max – later Sir Max – Mallowen, digging in the 1930s, discovered that the daughter of another Babylonian king of the era, Nabonidus, had created a museum in a boys' school in Ur with antiquities dating from 1,600 years earlier. They even found a label referring to a nineteenth-century BC inscription as written for 'the marvel of the beholders'. They had uncovered a major clue to the mysterious society of ancient Babylon, and appropriately it was on this excavation that Mallowen met his future wife, the novelist Agatha Christie.

In Athens a hundred years later the Acropolis had a *pinakothekai* – a word which survives in the Munich art museums, the Alte Pinakothek and the Neue Pinakothek – in which a collection of paintings was kept for the general edification of the public (*The Museum Age*, by Germain Bazin, Desoer 1967). Alexander gave his teacher Aristotle money and sent objects for a museum of Alexandria in the fourth century BC. This may have been the beginnings of the museum in the great Alexandrian Library, founded fifty-or-so years later by Ptolemy Sotor and destroyed in AD 391.

Roman temples were festooned with trophies brought back from conquests, and Hadrian had a cumbersome habit of constructing replicas of buildings he had seen on his travels, a sort of forerunner in some respects of our open air museums like St Fagans, Beamish and Ironbridge. Curious finds during excavations of Roman temples in Britain seem to suggest that palaeolithic tools were kept in them for some reason, as at the second century temple at Kelvedon in Essex.

The Medicis created a splendid collection of books, icons, paintings and sculpture in Florence, started by Cosimo (1389–1464) and continued by Lorenzo the Magnificent, his grandson (1449–92), but there is little evidence of collecting on any scale in medieval Britain. Among the learned, though, it was not unknown for private hoards to accumulate. Henry of Blois, brother of King Stephen and Bishop of Winchester for forty-five years of the twelfth century, travelled to Rome at least once and brought antiquities back with him, and 200 years later another king's brother, the learned Duke Humphrey of Gloucester, gave his collection of books to Oxford University to begin what was to become the Bodleian Library in 1611, where complementary objects such as coins and medals later accumulated.

In Renaissance Germany gentlemen and scholars liked to assemble '*Wunderkämmer*', or cabinets of curiosities, and the habit spread, especially in the sixteenth and seventeenth centuries when there was so much from the New World to be curious about.

The word 'museum' entered our language in 1656 with a collection which was to find its way to Oxford too, as the Ashmolean Museum. John Tradescant's *Musaeum Tradescantianum: or, A Collection of Rarities, Preserved at South Lambeth near London* is a catalogue of the extraordinary collections of his extraordinary father, the naturalist and diplomat John Tradescant the Elder who brought lilac and acacia into our lives and opened the first public museum (Chapter 4). The Tradescant collection came into the hands of Elias Ashmole, whose museum was opened by the Duke of York in 1683 as Ashmole's Repository on the upper floor of a new science 'elaboratory', and before long the collecting of curios was to become a social fad.

The Society of Antiquaries, first born in the 1570s but soon abolished by James I, was refounded in 1707, and dozens of versions soon sprang up all over the country. The coffee houses where they met became museums; one of the most famous was Don Saltero's in Chelsea, which boasted such questionable artefacts as 'Pontius Pilate's wife's chambermaid's sister's hat'. In the middle of the eighteenth century Rawthmell's Coffee House in Henrietta Street, Covent Garden, was to see the founding of a society 'for the Encouragement of Arts, Manufactures and Commerce', the Royal Society of Arts, and a century later this body was to play a key part in the history of modern museums.

Founded in 1754 and soon to establish a pre-eminence, the RSA was predated by similar learned clubs in Dublin and Wales, and there was one in Spalding as early as 1709, but the rash of these societies around Britain was mostly between 1770 and 1784, and it was their ethic which was to give museums their accelerating impetus over the next 150 years.

In 1753 the word museum was first used in a statute: The British Museum Act decreed that a 'Museum or collection may be preserved and maintained not only for the inspection and entertainment of the learned and the curious, but for the general use and benefit of the public' (*The Noble Cabinet* by E. Miller, Andre Deutsch 1973). The new museum, which opened in 1759, was notoriously difficult to get into, however. A visitor had to apply for a ticket in writing, return to collect it, then return on the day specified for the tour. Ten tickets an hour were issued, with parties conducted in groups of five; even so, the museum got 10,000 visitors a year from the start.

The British Museum's displays were based on the private collections accumulated and donated by Sir Hans Sloane – the royal physician who founded the Botanic Garden and whose collection was bought by the nation on his death in 1753 – the bibliophile and collector Edward Harley, second Earl of Oxford; and Sir Robert Cotton. Such private collections were invariably the nucleus of the great museums of this early period. Curiously, there are two Hunterian Museums, one each in London and Glasgow: they owe themselves to the private collections of two Scottish-born brothers. John Hunter (1728–93) was a surgeon in London and former Glasgow cabinet maker whose house pupil was Edward Jenner, the discoverer of vaccination. His anatomical collections were bought by the nation and became the Hunterian Museum, first in Leicester Square and then at the Royal College of Surgeons in Lincoln's Inn Fields. His elder brother William (1718–83) was an obstetrician and professor of anatomy at the Royal Academy, who built a house with a lecture theatre, dissecting room and a museum, including a cabinet for coins and medals. The museum was bequeathed to Glasgow University (Chapter 5).

The collections of Sir Joseph Banks, whose botanical researches sent the likes of Captains Bligh and Cook around the world on their adventures, became a museum at Soho, then, after his death in 1820, went to the British Museum and became the nucleus of what is now the Natural History Museum (Chapter 1).

Bequests of collections and objects are still made to our museums, and the potential burden of unwanted legacies became such that many now have it written into their statutes that they need not accept them if they do not want them. Now museums have to be brutally discerning about what is included in their collections and displays. Is it relevant? Can we afford the conservation and the cost of a showcase, and is it worth it against new chairs for the restaurant or a new print run of postcards? Would anyone come and see it?

For scholarly as museums still must be, the non-scholarly visitor has become the prime factor in museums planning. And in 1989 museums were confidently expecting to notch up 100 million visits.

Museums have been developing in this country for 300 years, with two distinct lurches in the upward graph, the late nineteenth century and now, the late twentieth century.

No two museums are alike, any more than any two museum visitors are the same. This book attempts to define the shape of museum development, particularly between the two booms of the 1880s and 1980s, by picking out certain benchmarks in the form of individual museums and some of the people behind them. Without making judgements other than those quoted, I hope to show how important mueums have been in Britain and will continue to be into the future, but to give a clinically accurate picture would mean describing each museum, and since there are at least 2,500 in the United Kingdom this would not only be impossible to compile in the space available, but intolerably tedious to read. Some of the museums I have selected have been chosen not because they are especially commendable or conspicuously unique, but because they are pioneers of their type.

Part One outlines the three broad categories of museums in the country, national, local and independent, in which we find much of the catalyst for the first boom. I have tried to nominate specialities of museums, both in general in Part Two and in particular in Part Three with some of the different kinds of museums we have, to show not only how we have arrived at the present upsurge with the curiously eclectic array that we have but also what we can expect in the coming decades. Part Four looks behind the scenes at those who run museums and care for the objects, those who support museums and those who watch museums and have a vision of their future, and listens to what they have to say. If there were a museum of museums, this could be its guide book.

Montagu House, first home of the British Museum in Bloomsbury.

The main entrance of the Victoria and Albert Museum, its Edwardian glory restored.

The first museum refreshment rooms, at the South Kensington Museum, in a watercolour of 1863 by Anthony Stannus.

The new Natural History Museum's south front in 1880, from The Graphic.

Interior of the Natural History Museum's main hall today.

Sir William Flower, first director of the Natural History Museum and godfather of modern museums.

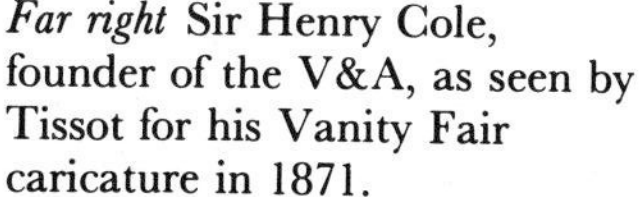

*Far right* Sir Henry Cole, founder of the V&A, as seen by Tissot for his Vanity Fair caricature in 1871.

Dr Evans Hoyle, first director of the National Museum of Wales.

Sir Cyril Fox, creator of the modern National Museum of Wales.

A miniature of James Bissett's 1808 museum in Birmingham's New Street.

# PART ONE

# 1. 'Temples where all can worship'. The national museums

*National museums have been born piecemeal as a result of the government realising its responsibility in individual cases, nearly always as a result of pressure being brought to bear over a period of time. 'National' is a word any museum can claim, and many do, but this chapter looks at truly national ones – those which receive central government funds – and the guiding role they have played at the British Museum (briefly), the Victoria and Albert Museum, the Natural History Museum and the National Museum of Wales.*

THE great collections owe themselves almost entirely to the zeal of wealthy gentlemen with an aesthetic streak, men like Sir Hans Sloane. Born in 1660 he was launched into a glittering medical career by the time the Ashmolean opened in Oxford in 1683, becoming physician to the royal family and president of the Royal College of Physicians. He bought the manor of Chelsea and created the Sloane Estate, with the result that his name and those of his descendants reverberate around this choice piece of residential London.

But he was also president of the Royal Society (for Improving Natural Knowledge, as its full title has it), 'the citadel of rationalism in England',[1] was much travelled – he visited the West Indies, a very enlightened thing to do in the seventeenth century – and was widely read. He inherited the botanical collection of his friend, the naturalist William Courten, whose grandfather's merchant ships had discovered Barbados, and spent the rest of his life building on the collection to create a library and scientific archive of 80,000 objects.

Sloane's archive was to be the core of the British Museum, but George II's parsimony almost prevented it coming to the nation. Sloane left the collection to the state provided £20,000 was settled on his two daughters, a modest sum in terms of the value of what he had accumulated. The king said the Royal Treasury could not afford it, but Parliament instituted a public lottery which not only secured the Sloane Bequest but also the library of Robert Harley, Earl of Oxford. To these was added the library of Sir Robert Cotton, the sixteenth- and seventeenth-century antiquaries, and the British Museum opened in Montagu House, Bloomsbury, in 1759.

[1] Germain Bazin, *The Museum Age*, 1967.

## *The Victoria and Albert Museum*

The British Museum was the first truly national one, and remained so for 100 years, until Henry Cole. Cole was an extraordinary manifestation of the Victorian busy little man who seemed to have a hand in almost everything – the first Christmas card, the first postage stamp, the Public Record Office, the Royal Society of Arts, the Great Exhibition, the Albert Hall and the South Kensington Museum, which was to become the Victorian and Albert Museum, and eventually the Science Museum.

He was the friend of Thackeray, the confidant of Prince Albert and was described by Lord Derby, three times prime minister during the Cole years, as 'the most generally unpopular man I know'.[2] He even achieved Dickensian immortality, turning up in *Hard Times* lecturing on education, his passion: 'A mighty man at cutting and drying he was; a government officer; in his way (and most other people's too) a professed pugilist; always in training, always with a system to force down the general throat like a bolus, always to be heard at the bar of his little public office, ready to fight all England.'

Sir Henry, as he was later to become, was a paradox. As Felix Summerly he wrote the children's picture books, *The Home Treasury*, which sold in their thousands; his friend was the Royal Academician John Horsley whom he persuaded to draw the first Christmas card for him; he persuaded another friend, the sculptor John Bell, to design the famous wheatsheaf breadboard; and he won a prize himself for the design of a tea service.

He delighted in his eight children, who he would take with him wherever he could, and was always accompanied by a little dog. He had a wide and influential circle of friends whom he never failed and who held him in deep affection. But that was his private side. Publicly, he was a hectoring reformer who got his way by skilful manipulation, and was popularly supposed to have lined his own pockets in the process – a lie he never bothered to refute if he ever noticed it – but when he died in 1882 he left an estate worth only £7,000 and Lady Cole had to be given a government pension to live on. Prince Albert used to say to his children, 'If you want steam you must get Cole.'

His friend, confidant and partner in both the exhibition and museums project was Lyon Playfair, who wrote about Cole in his autobiography: 'He was often accused of working from selfish motives. Never was an accusation more unfounded. The public good was always the uppermost – I might say the only – motive in his mind. He was constantly misjudged because his modes of work were not always on the surface. If he came to an obstacle, it was his delight to tunnel under it in secret, and unexpectedly come out at the other side.'

[2] I am indebted to Elizabeth Bonython's 1982 portrait, *King Cole*, for much of my information on Cole, and to John Physick's *The Victoria and Albert Museum: The history of its building*, 1982, for the museum's early history.

Above and below the surface, a century-and-a-half ago, Henry Cole was already testing the tools which museum administrators are having to try now: sponsorship, marketing, publicity, public relations, diplomacy and political astuteness.

Cole was born the son of a recruiting officer in 1808. In 1823 he became a clerk in the Record Commission and industriously made himself almost indispensable while the Commission's reputation of reckless inefficiency and waste grew despite his efforts. In 1835 when a promise of promotion and a salary increase was not kept he objected and was fired, and his true colours were given a viewing. With friends like the critic and poet Thomas Love Peacock and the economist John Stuart Mill he conducted a campaign of pamphleteering and letter writing to expose the simony and corruption of the Commission, a campaign which resulted in a House of Commons Select Committee and Cole's reinstatement in a new grade, to be followed by a complete transformation by him of the department into the Public Record Office. He had discovered the value of public relations and lobbying, which he was to use fruitfully for the rest of his life.

He had thus earned a reputation as a radical, and his circle of friends began to include artists such as Daniel Maclise, Richard Redgrave and William Mulready, some of whom taught in the School of Design and were appalled by the inefficiency there – on which Cole was to bring his skills to bear. Other close friends were C. Wentworth Dilke, the publisher and father of the Liberal Member of Parliament of the same name, and John Scott Russell, secretary of the Royal Society of Arts, which Cole joined in 1846.

By 1850 he was chairman of the RSA, and turned it into what he called 'a society that pokes its nose into everything'. He remained involved until shortly before his death more than thirty years later. Prince Albert, as president, encouraged the RSA to 'improve the condition of the artistic industries of the country',[3] and in 1846 Cole and Russell organised its first exhibition (at which, under his Felix Summerly pseudonym, he won his prize) which became an annual event, with the 1849 exhibition being visited by 100,000 people.

That same year Cole went to Buckingham Palace to suggest to Prince Albert that there should be an international exhibition in London, the Consort heartily agreed and Cole immediately began encouraging businesses to pledge sponsorship, with his royal patron's beaming approval. In 1850 a Royal Commission was appointed by the Queen, with Albert as president, Cole and Dilke on the executive committee and Russell as commission secretary. After many delays, a building was designed by the former head gardener of Chatsworth House, Joseph Paxton, and on 1 May 1851 Queen Victoria opened the Great Exhibition of the Industry of All Nations. It still stands as one of the most popular exhibitions ever, and made an unexpected profit of £186,000. Cole persuaded the Commissioners, with Albert's help, to use the money to buy 87 acres south of Hyde Park in the village of Brompton to create an educational estate with colleges, learned societies and museums. Cole did not like the dull name,

[3] Sir Henry Trueman Wood, *The History of the Royal Society of Arts*, 1913.

Brompton, and pushed to have it changed. It became known as South Kensington.

From the Great Exhibition the government bought a collection of objects for the Schools of Design which Cole had busied himself reforming with his artist friends (these were to become the Royal College of Art). Cole himself was offered the secretaryship of the schools and the post of general superintendent of the new Department of Practical Art, part of the Board of Trade. Straight away Cole persuaded the Prince of Wales to let him borrow five rooms in Marlborough House to display the schools' objects, in what he called the Museum of Manufactures. By 1855 the Prince needed the space for his own apartments, and the collections were moved to South Kensington, to a temporary iron structure known as The Iron Museum and less officially and without affection as 'the Brompton Boilers'; (to Cole it was a 'refuge for destitute collections', and it survives as the Bethnal Green Museum of Childhood).

South Kensington was the first museum to be lit by gas. Cole encouraged not only designers and artists to visit, but the general public too, opening it in the evening. Over the next twenty years he continued to lobby and bully government for funds to expand his museum and its collections. The Royal Engineers architect, Francis Fowke, designed the first permanent buildings, which were erected in two stages between 1856 and 1865, and it had the first museum restaurant, the three refreshment rooms crowned by the magnificent Centre Refreshment Room, now known as the Gamble Room.

By the time he retired in 1873 Cole had established an international reputation for the South Kensington Museum, which, faltering for a while in his absence, continued to grow and prosper. New buildings were designed by the winner of a competition, Sir Aston Webb, of which Queen Victoria laid the foundation stone in 1899 proclaiming a new title: the Victoria and Albert Museum. It was eventually opened by her son, Edward VII, in 1909.

Until 1885 the arts and sciences had coexisted, but the collections of each had been growing separately and that year the science collections were formally called the Science Museum. They were to stay side by side until the opening of the V&A in 1909 when they became administratively separate and eventually, sixteen years after work was begun, the present Science Museum was opened by King George V in 1928. (A more detailed look at the development of the Science Museum and its modern role appears in Chapter 7.)

Henry Cole was knighted two years after his retirement and died in 1882. His legacy was the V&A, the Science Museum, the Imperial College of Science, the Royal College of Art, the Royal Albert Hall and the Royal College of Music, but chiefly the concept of museums as places of learning and discovery for ordinary people, quite separate from the schools of the formal education system.

In 1874 he said, during a speech at the Birmingham School of Art: 'Schools of science and art instruct chiefly the young, but Museums can instruct both young and old . . . they are temples where all can worship in harmony; they teach good habits of order, and cleanliness, and politeness. . . . Museums are antidotes to brutality and vice.'[4]

The V&A has undergone its own new revolution in the 1980s. Along with the other nationals which had been run by government departments, it was 'hived off' and under the 1983 National Heritage Act endowed with a board of trustees to carry on the task previously fulfilled by the government through its Secretary of State for Education. It acquired 'out-stations', or branch museums, as have most of the other nationals with notable exceptions (the National Gallery has none). First its old Brompton Boilers with some of the reserve collections went to bring the spirit of mass education to London's deprived East End in 1872, and this is now the Bethnal Green Museum of Childhood. After the Second World War two great houses on the edge of London were left to the National Trust, with the V&A made responsible for their interiors – Osterley Park House and Ham House. At about the same time, the Duke of Wellington gave his famous forefather's London home, Apsley House at Hyde Park Corner, to the nation and the V&A. The latest branch to be added to the family opened in Covent Garden in 1986 as the Theatre Museum, and by 1989 there were plans for the first V&A branch outside of the home counties, a museum for some of its massive Indian collections to be displayed in a converted mill at Bradford.

The V&A had come through its period of scholarly dignity and its postwar austerity in the 1940s, 50s and 60s, and through a period of being a 'general museum' to which thousands of extraneous and often unwanted objects were left each year, to become, under the directorship of Sir Roy Strong, a place of informed entertainment, with exhibitions which undertook to do something which art museums had seldom ventured to attempt and even less often succeeded in: to thrill.

Trusteeship brought more changes, with the buildings (to which, in 1983, had been added the Henry Cole Wing) requiring massive refurbishments. It was an opportunity to reassess the museum and return it to something of the visual glory which Aston Webb and others had created but which had become obscured in this century. And because the public were still perceiving the V&A to be a general museum, a subtitle was added: the National Museum of Art and Design.

In 1985 the V&A avoided the necessity felt by other nationals to charge for admission by asking visitors for a £2 donation, thereby adopting an American system. A century before there had been a charge, of sixpence on Saturdays only: it was to discourage the general public from going, so that that day could be for serious students of the applied and decorative arts to study the collections, and Saturday became Scholars' Day.

In *The Museum Age*, Germain Bazin wrote:

> Thanks to the talents of its directors who had substantial funds at their disposal, this museum boasts the most beautiful decorative arts collection in the world. However, this aesthetic triumph has not submerged the original educational intentions. From the beginning the Victoria and Albert Museum was distinguished by this very Anglo-Saxon

[4] Elizabeth Bonython, *The V&A Album*, 1982.

trait of being well organised from the pedagogical point of view; it circulated exhibitions, lent books and lecture material to all the Commonwealth countries; in addition public comfort was an early concern; the first museum restaurant was set up in the Victoria and Albert Museum in 1863 in an Anglo-Norman structure.

## *The Natural History Museum*

For some reason, which probably has more to do with bureaucracy than any need for identification, the magnificent cathedral built by Alfred Waterhouse on the corner of Cromwell Road and Exhibition Road opposite the V&A is still doggedly called 'The British Museum (Natural History)'.

It has a completely separate director, staff and board of trustees from the British Museum in Bloomsbury, and until 1987 it was financed by a different government department, with only administrative convenience directing the grant aid for both from the Office of Arts and Libraries thereafter.

But the Natural History Museum it is to us all, and its place in the story of museum development in this country has been assured since it opened on Easter Monday, 1881, and 16,000 people 'of a most orderly and respectable class' set their seal of approval that first day.

The museum did, of course, spring from the collections at Bloomsbury, and as the Montague House museum began to burst at the seams with its burgeoning collections, the debate as to what should be done continued for a large part of the nineteenth century. Something would have to go, but what? 'The pictures have been removed (to the National Gallery), why should not the statues follow? The collections at the museum would then remain of an entirely homogenous nature,' Thomas Watts wrote in the *Mechanics Magazine* in 1837.

The museum's natural history departments were under the direction of the superintendent, the irascible and, to some, reactionary Richard Owen. He was a surgeon who had come to museums through the Royal College of Surgeons' Hunterian Museum. He had achieved considerable fame as conservator of the Hunterian, coining the word 'dinosaur', tutoring the royal children (and getting a grace-and-favour house from Queen Victoria in recognition), supervising the construction of the models of prehistoric beasts for the 1851 Great Exhibition (still surviving and restored in Crystal Palace Park, South London, where the exhibition was moved in 1854), and examining the specimens from Darwin's voyages, though he remained the most implacable opponent to the evolution theory.

In 1856 Owen took over the British Museum's natural history collections, and immediately joined the debate by advocating the removal of them to premises of their own.[5] The matter came before a House of Commons Select Committee in 1860, but it was to be another eighteen years before an Act of Parliament authorised the removal of the collections to what was becoming known as 'Albertopolis', the South

[5] William T. Stearn, *The Natural History Museum of South Kensington*, 1981.

Kensington estate. It was to go on the site of Cole's 1862 International Exhibition, which had been a success but a rather lugubrious one since it opened a few months after the death of Albert.

Francis Fowke won the competition to design the new museum as early as 1864, but he died before he could take his scheme further. That was the first of a whole series of delaying setbacks to beset the project which, in the words of the *Survey of London* (1975), 'was sustained by the ardour of Victorian polemic, the boldness of Victorian exploration and the zest of Victorian curiosity.' Rather than the commission passing to the runners-up in the competition, Fowke's design for a Renaissance building in the mode of the Uffizi in Florence was passed on to Alfred Waterhouse. But he, a Neo-gothicist, decided it was not right and, with Owen, came up with his own plans.

There were many more costly delays, but the 1878 Act allowing the collection's removal from Bloomsbury was a rubber-stamping of the inevitable: by that time the main roofs were already on. Meanwhile Waterhouse had designed Manchester Town Hall (1877) and started work on the National Liberal Club (1884).

Sir Richard Owen retired two years after the museum opened and in March 1884 was succeeded by a man who had followed almost exactly in Owen's footsteps – a surgeon, anatomist, conservator of the Hunterian Museum. But the similarities between Owen and William Henry Flower, the first director of the Natural History Museum (Owen had only been superintendent), ended there. The craggy Owen was powerful, but the gentle Flower was influential to the extent that his 'new museum idea'[6] is still the convention for museums a century after he sprang it on the world.

Almost as soon as he became a member of the Royal College of Surgeons in 1854, at the age of twenty-four, Stratford-born Flower volunteered for the Crimea as an army surgeon. He served at Alma, Inkerman, Balaclava and Sebastopol, survived the winter of 1854 which took so many lives, but was eventually invalided home just before it was too late. After he had recovered he took over the Hunterian and reorganized the collections; becoming more and more fascinated by zoology, he was a convinced evolutionist and opponent of Owen's views. That opposition was to spread out of the scientific domain into the museum gallery.

Owen subscribed to what was then the traditional view of museum presentation: everything should be displayed to see, putting the entire collections on show; he did not see an important distinction between specialist scientific requirements and those of the untutored public, and while the former could go directly to what they needed, the latter's heads would swim. The displays arrangement was of no great importance.

Flower took his theme from Dr John Gray (1800–1875), a former keeper of zoology at the British Museum and, at the end of his career, another opponent of Owen's curatorial style. Flower explained 'the development of what may be called *the new museum idea*' to the Museums Association in 1893: 'Dr Gray [in an address to the

[6] Quoted from the presidential address to The British Association for The Advancement of Science, Newcastle-upon-Tyne, September 1889.

British Association at Bath] laid down the axiom that the purposes for which a museum, was established were two:

> First the diffusion of instruction and rational amusement among the mass of the people, and, secondly, to afford the scientific student every possible means of examining and studying the specimens of which the museum consists. . . . Now, it appears to me that in the desire to combine these two objects, which are essentially distinct, the first object – namely, the general instruction of the people – has been to a great extent lost sight of and sacrificed to the second without any corresponding advantage to the latter, because the system itself has been thoroughly erroneous'.

'This was a remarkable admission,' considered Flower, 'coming from a man who had been brought up in, and had acted throughout the greater part of his life upon, the old idea.'

Not only had the old idea been erroneous, it had destroyed important specimens which could only have survived (as they do now) in the dark and protected from extremes of temperature. The conservation of specimens and objects in museums took many years to become an established part of practice (see Chapter 14), but it was already an important part of Flower's museum philosophy when he took over the Natural History Museum.

Flower was a self-effacing man whose experiences in the Crimea had left a mark, but a mark with a beneficial effect. It taught him that life was too short to create conflicts, and he made it his characteristic to be honest with his colleagues so that when unpleasant aspects arose which, for less trusted directors, might have meant revolt from beneath, there was an implicit understanding that what had to be done was for the ultimate good of the museum. So while he was giving Gray the credit for the 'new museum idea', it was not Gray but Flower, twenty years later, who was to put it into effect, soothing away opposition rather than confronting it. He believed in co-operation and partnership in creating a good museum, but the ultimate architect was the man at the top: 'Some persons are enthusiastic enough to think that a museum is in itself so good an object that they have only to provide a building and cases and a certain number of specimens, no matter exactly what, to fill them, and then the thing is done; whereas the truth is the work has only then begun.'

For, while Owen was content to cover the 12 acres of the museum site with entire natural history collections on public display, then retire to the academic research to which he was most committed, Flower saw his duty to the public first, science second. At Newcastle in 1889 he was chiding the Owenites:

> What a museum really depends on for its success and usefulness is not its building, not its cases, not even its specimens, but its curator.
>
> He and his staff are the life and soul of the institution, upon whom its whole value depends; and yet in many – I may say most – of our museums they are the last to be thought of. The care, the preservation, the naming of specimens are either left to voluntary effort – excellent often for special collections and for a limited time, but never to be depended on as a permanent arrangement – or a grievously undersalaried and consequently uneducated official is expected to keep in order, to clean, dust, arrange,

> name, and display in a manner which will contribute to the advancement of scientific knowledge, collections ranging in extent over almost every branch of human learning, from the contents of an ancient British barrow to the last discovered bird of paradise from New Guinea.

Consignment of valued and valuable specimens and objects to such museums was too often fatal: 'Dirty, neglected, without label, their identity lost, they are often finally devoured by insects or cleared away to make room on the crowded shelves for the new donation of some fresh patron of the institution. It would be far better that such museums should never be founded. They are traps into which precious – sometimes priceless – objects fall only to be destroyed.'

The failure of many museums was their confusion of the two distinct functions, of what became known in the V&A as primary collections in which the interested public could see a story in objects thoughtfully arranged with space to make sense of them, with study collections designed to help experts in their detailed analyses. Flower put it more succinctly: instruction and research.

> To demand, as has been ignorantly done, that all the specimens belonging to our national museum, for instance, should be displayed in cases in the public galleries, would be equivalent to asking that every book in a library, instead of being shut up and arranged on shelves for consultation when required, should have every single page framed and glazed and hung on the walls.

This is not the place to discuss modern museological debates, but a lot of the current arguments were made a century ago, by this man who was described by an eminent German anatomist, Rudolph Car Virchow, as the 'Prince of Museum Directors'.

But Flower took an interest in other aspects of Victorian life as well. Beatrix Potter remarked to her diary in 1896: 'I wonder what Sir W. Flower's speciality is besides ladies' bonnets.' He had campaigned against the slaughter of birds to provide feathers for hats. Earlier, he had written a book (*Fashion in Deformity*, 1881) in which he had shown how the mode for tight-laced corsets and high heels was mutilating the natural shape of women. And he waded into the *Origin of Species* battle, to stand beside Darwin and his mentor in his early career, Sir Thomas Huxley, President of the Royal Society. When the Natural History Museum opened, Owen had gone to the lengths of placing the figure of Adam above the main entrance, in defiance of the evolutionists. When Fowler took over, he did not remove Owen's statement (it fell down during the Second World War) but simply organised a public subscription for a statue of Charles Darwin which the Prince of Wales unveiled on the stairs at the back of the central hall in 1889.

Flower seemed tireless in his work for the museum and the museum movement, but his constitution had never been sound since the Crimea and in 1897 he collapsed. He resigned the following year and died in 1899. He had given his post as head of the institution an authority which his predecessor never possessed and had brought science into the public domain by evolving a display philosophy which is still a template. His successor, Sir Edwin Ray Lankester, wrote after Flower's death:

> There can be no doubt in the mind of any man who is acquainted with the present condition of the public galleries of the great museums . . . that a very great and important change for the better was effected by Flower, who deserves to be considered as an organiser and inventor in museum-work.
>
> . . . energy and patience in the surmounting of obstacles are necessary (in the museum curator), and perhaps as much as or more than any other quality – artistic sense. Sir William Flower possessed this last quality in a remarkable degree.

From its Kensington palace the Natural History Museum continued to grow, adding a new wing in 1975 for its palaeontology department. In 1938 the Rothschild zoological collection at Tring in Hertfordshire was left to the museum, which continues to administer it there, and in 1986 it took over the Geological Museum in South Kensington.

In 1987 the Natural History Museum succumbed to the pressures of decreasing proportions of public funding, becoming only the second national museum to introduce charges (the National Maritime Museum had instituted charging in 1983), not only for admission but also for many of the scholarly services it has always provided. The public's response to this is still being gauged at the time of writing, but the result for the museum is intended to be an expanded service with more access to the accumulated knowledge only the Natural History Museum has in such abundance – an adaptation of the New Museum Idea to conditions a century on, not an abandonment of it.

## *The National Museum of Wales*

To be a national museum has nothing to do with the title. There are twenty-five of them at the end of the 1980s, and they do not include the National Lifeboat Museum, the National Mining Museum or the National Motor Museum. For, although they may all incorporate a British aspect into their specialist collections, they are not directly financed by a central government department.

But, while the 'Big Five' nationals – the British Museum, the Science Museum, the Victoria and Albert Museum, the National Gallery and the Natural History Museum – may have established patterns for others to follow, and while some of the later legitimate claimants to the title 'national' may have a sound basis and abiding characteristic as provincial museums – such as the National Museums of Merseyside (a grouping designed to re-inspire a city centre and the youngest of the the official nationals) – the foundation and survival of national museums was never easy.

The National Museum of Wales was born out of the same ethic created by the dynamic of 100 years ago, and while it was fairly late off the mark it has continued to grow and develop until it is a national network of museums in Wales.

## 'Temples Where All Can Worship'

'There is implanted in the nature of mankind a strong attachment to the land or the country which gave them birth,' wrote an essayist in the 1894 National Eisteddfod, 'and a laudable curiosity to acquaint themselves with the genuine history and antiquities of those people from whom they are immediately descended.' This was not the first call for a National Museum for the Welsh; the matter had come up fairly regularly at the Eisteddfodau and elsewhere from the 1850s on. But it was, once again, a century ago that the bandwagon started to roll, according to a former director, Dr Douglas A. Bassett. He wrote, in his book *The Making of a National Museum* (1983): 'The emergence of a general movement towards the establishment of such national institutions probably dates from the very end of the 1880s and was clearly one of the effects on Welsh culture of the reawakening in national consciousness of the end of the century.'

The university colleges at Aberystwyth, Cardiff and Bangor were federated in 1893 and there was a chorus of calls for a museum, an art gallery and a library, not only from Eisteddfod bards but from town councillors, city fathers and Welsh MPs, who pointed to an annual museums grant for England and Scotland. Why was there none for Wales?

The MPs sponsored a Bill in 1895 which drew only a vague suggestion from the English members that a branch of the South Kensington Museum might be established in Wales. There was another attempt in 1903 and the House of Commons remained unmoved, but the Chancellor of the Exchequer, Austen Chamberlain, did not. He suggested that if the Welsh came up with a properly measured and considered proposal he might be able to help, and a conference was called.

Sir Isambard Owen, of the University of Wales, was asked to draw up a scheme which in 1904 went to Chamberlain, and the Chancellor and Privy Council approved it. 'The museum contemplated by the conference,' wrote Sir Isambard, 'is an institution of interest to all Wales. Its objects are strictly national, and the like of it cannot be found elsewhere.' Cardiff was to have the museum in Cathays Park, next to the new town hall, thanks to an enormous public subscription of £32,500; Aberystwyth was to have the library.

On 19 March 1907 a Royal Charter announced: 'There shall be and there is hereby constituted and founded a museum in the City of Cardiff with the name "The National Museum of Wales".'

But there was no museum, nor a director. The Museum Council first met in March 1908; they decided to find a director and in December they appointed Dr W. Evans Hoyle, curator of Manchester Museum, an authority on museum planning and design. He was sent on a tour of European museums to get some ideas, and while he was away a competition for an architect was organised. It was won, in March 1910, by the London firm of Dunbar Smith and C. C. Brewer, and the foundation stone was laid two years later.

A core collection next had to be established, and the Cardiff municipal museum's was absorbed. But new and more important acquisitions were arriving almost daily to prevent the new museum becoming yet another one of a general nature. This one was to be about Welsh geology and natural history, Welsh art and artists, Welsh industry and manufacture. But it was to be ten years before the collection had the foundations of a permanent home. In the interim there was held a series of exhibitions in a temporary building to maintain interest in the hard-fought-for national museum.

Despite the government's approval of the scheme, the Treasury was to provide less than half the eventual £428,000 cost of the museum (which was not complete until 1932), £231,000 having to come from public appeal. The city organised a massive campaign to attract subscriptions. Building began in 1913 and was halted in 1917, all resources being concentrated on the war effort. Material costs increased, in some cases, a hundredfold.

The 1920s and 30s saw an era of immense hardship for Wales, especially South Wales which was plunged into a depression it had never known before. Nevertheless, building began again in 1918 and the following year objects began to be shifted to it from the municipal museum. But it may have been the prevailing austerity which persuaded Hoyle to drop what had been a pet subject of his, the children's room, which was to have been a special feature.

But in 1922 a small part of the museum was opened to the public, made possible only by a large bank loan. Two years later the strain told on Evans Hoyle whose ill-health forced him to resign, and Mortimer Wheeler, the archaeologist, briefly took the reins before moving to the Museum of London. Cyril Fox (already a famous archaeologist himself) was director by the time George V formally opened the museum in 1927. It was, however, 'little more than a noble entrance hall flanked by a few galleries', according to one commentator, and by the time of the museum's silver anniversary in 1932 only half of the original concept was complete. Even so, in the last ten years annual attendances had doubled to more than 250,000.

Between them Fox and Wheeler had made the museum the archaeological eye for Wales, and important sites such as Caerleon and Caernarvon (sites which took on the status of outstations) were excavated under the museum's aegis, and from 1943 the museum had a statutory right of pre-emption on treasure trove so that important and valuable artefacts thrown up by digs in Wales would not automatically revert to the British Museum, as had happened in the past.

In 1943, too, came the beginnings of the museum's second period of development, after the agonising first one which proceeded only through the determination of the curators and the Welsh people, who gave handsomely despite unprecedented hardship. In 1943 Sir Cyril Fox, as he then was, drew up a memorandum for his advisory council which spelled out more clearly than ever before the functions of the national museum: 'To collect and conserve objects of national regional or local importance . . . to promote awareness, understanding and appreciation of the natural environment and of the cultural heritage to stimulate interests beyond the range of collections normally exhibited.'

There must be exhibitions, circulations of the collections around schools, publications, lectures and 'a well-ordered and arranged museum (which) has a psychological value in the field of adult education' (Bassett). 'No single institution, except perhaps the National museum, can be expected wholly to cover this range of function,' said Fox's memorandum.

Part of the function was to tell the story of the Welsh people in a folk museum, preferably open-air, and Sir Cyril had wanted one for most of his long tenure. In 1946 the Earl of Plymouth offered St Fagans Castle, on the western edge of Cardiff, and it became the Welsh Folk Museum, Britain's first open air museum contrived on the pattern of the Scandinavian originals. It opened in 1948, two months before the retirement of Sir Cyril Fox, with the first transplanted buildings arriving in 1950.

In the course of the 1950s and 60s the museum took on new aspects of museology, such as industrial archaeology (part of the original charter which had never been acted upon). A new wing in 1962 heralded a resumption of capital development of the museum: and a new branch, the Welsh Slate Museum at Llanberis, followed in 1972; new galleries appeared between 1972 and 1976 in the main building; the Museum of the Welsh Woollen Industry at Llandysul opened in 1976; and the Welsh Industrial and Maritime Museum on the site of Cardiff's old Merchants' Exchange in 1977.

By the late 80s the National Museum of Wales had taken on both a national leadership and an international status, illustrated by two exhibitions in 1988: 'Chinese Dinosaurs', the exhibition which showed the unique collection outside China for the first time and was negotiated for entirely by the museum, not the Natural History Museum where the exhibition was later seen – brought an unprecedented half million visitors. And 'Gerald of Wales', organised by the Welsh National Monuments Council, which celebrated the 800th anniversary of the journey through Wales of the Welsh churchman and the extraordinary journal he kept, was an exhibition which reverberated throughout the principality in smaller exhibitions and events throughout 1988.

In 1987 the Welsh Office found £17 million (later increased to £21 million to include a new museum of the north in Llanberis, North Wales) to institute a new expansion programme, which proposed new air conditioning, to be installed in the east wing in 1988, an extension to the wing in 1989 and an increase of the central part by half as much by 1992.

But the London nationals were not the only ones struck by inadequate revenue funding. In December 1988 the main museum followed some of its branches by instituting admission charges to help balance an expected £750,000 overspend.

The national museums and galleries are funded by no fewer than nine different government departments, which may be partly responsible for differing standards. Most of them are in London and there are others in Ulster and Edinburgh; some, like Sir John Soane's Museum, are odd members of the panoply, once included in to fulfill the terms of bequests.

But the national museums have given us not only the pattern for modern museums but collections which cannot be matched. They were created by people of genius, daring, dedication and foresight. Whatever the political reasons for bringing the national collections to the point where they cannot survive without forcing visitors to pay, there is at best a melancholy lack of understanding for what was done for the nation by the likes of Cole, Flower, and the Welsh fathers of their own museum, and what is being done now by the inheritors of their spirit.

# 2. 'By the gains of industry. . . .' The local museums

*By far the fastest growing group of museums in this country is the one run by local authorities, and it is in this community that there has been the biggest sea-change, in both the 1880s when the great neo-gothic repositories arose as testaments to municipal prosperity, and the 1980s when a sense of enlightened self-interest brought fundamental redevelopments. This chapter examines Birmingham Museums and Art Gallery, Guernsey Museum and Art Gallery, Glasgow Museums and Galleries and, briefly, two new phenomena: the county museum service of Leicestershire and the local group made national on Merseyside.*

IF it had an international reputation for anything, mid-nineteenth-century Birmingham was famous for its 'gee-gaws', bits and bobs of cheap jewellery, toys and *papier mâché* ornaments which turned up in all the world's corners thanks to the new mass-market production methods.

Otherwise, today's 'Second City' was slow to get off the mark, not getting its first Member of Parliament until 1832 or a proper town council until six years later.

But it was one of the first provincial cities to have a museum – Bissett's Museum and Picture Gallery, with its gallery of 'the works of savage nations', which opened in 1808 and survived until 1832 when James Bissett died and his collections disappeared. The local Philosophical Institution established one, in 1813 in Cannon Street, which eventually closed in 1849.

By this time, however, the museum habit was established. Birmingham was – and is – very proud of its decorative arts, and was keen to establish a high quality of design for its products. In 1845 the Royal Society of Arts had held its first annual exhibition of 'Art Manufactures', and that year too the Museums Act, allowing local authorities to levy a rate to finance museums, was passed. In 1849 such an exhibition was held in Birmingham and was immensely successful. Meanwhile, a local journalist called J. T. Bunce, for many years editor of the *Daily Post*, was agitating for some permanent influence on the design of Birmingham's products, just as Henry Cole was doing in London.

Cole made the breakthrough by organising the Great Exhibition of 1851, and this was the catalyst to the Birmingham movement which at first resulted, in 1853, in the Birmingham and Midland Institute, one of whose objectives was a museum and 'hall of fine arts', which involved taking over the Philosophical Institution's museum, throwing out large numbers of objects but beginning a picture collection. The Institute opened Birmingham's first public museum in Caxton Street in 1860.

The establishment of a municipal gallery and museum was, however, yet to come and was a subject batted about like a shuttlecock in the political arena of Birmingham Council. The first point to be scored was the passing of the 1850 Public Libraries and Museums Act, which said rate-supported museums should have free entry. But the Act did not allow rate money to be used for establishing a collection. Gradually, this was founded by a series of gifts, starting, appropriately, with a marble bust of perhaps Birmingham's greatest artist, David Cox, given by the sculptor Peter Hollins in 1863.

Hollins led a group of gentleman subscribers who made it their business to create a core collection in the hope and belief that the

> erection of a Gallery of Art, which the Council, with great wisdom and liberality, have sanctioned, seemed to invite such contributions as that we have the honour of presenting; and considering that the occupations of many of the people of Birmingham have a direct connection with the knowledge of the fine arts, it is to be hoped that the Gallery may soon be enriched with a collection of pictures that will not only be a representation of the skills of local artists, but may be the means of educating the tastes of those upon whom the reputation of Birmingham manufacturers chiefly depends.

The city's 'Corporation Art Gallery' was eventually opened in 1867, in a room in the library, with an exhibition of fifty-six paintings of which a dozen or so belonged to the city.

Then, in 1868, Henry Cole's magic touch came to do its trick when his South Kensington Museum lent some armour, jewellery and other items for a seven-month exhibition which was seen by 160,000; its success helped encourage the augmentation of the collections still more. An appeal was launched to start an industrial art museum, and in 1870 the local press was observing: 'To encourage the growth of taste, it is essential that those who are expected to produce the beautiful shall be surrounded by what is beautiful.'

In the 1860s and 70s Birmingham was experiencing something of a civic revolution, and the realization grew that they need not wait for central government to improve the quality of life in their city and that they could do it themselves. 'Sometimes,' wrote Dr Robert Dale, the Birmingham divine, 'an adventurous orator would excite his audience by dwelling on the glories of Florence, and of the other cities of the Middle Ages, and suggest that Birmingham too might become the home of noble literature and art.' One of those orators was Joseph Chamberlain, who led the Liberals to a massive local election victory in 1873. Two years previously a local glass manufacturer, Thomas Clarkson Osler, had begun the Public Picture Gallery Fund with a donation of £3,000, and Chamberlain was made a trustee; a condition of purchase by the fund was that each item should be exhibited in a public gallery free of charge, including Sundays.

Chamberlain it was who revitalized the industrial art fund with the gift of £1,000 in 1875, and by 1878 only a quarter of the money was left, there had been so much acquisition. A new art gallery was proposed in Edmund Street. In 1876 the Corporation was given the Birmingham Gun-Barrel Proof House Museum of Small Arms. Then, in 1879 there was a fire in the library which destroyed a lot of objects, and the corporation itself was stung into matching Chamberlain's £1,000, and collecting became even more in earnest.

In the 1870s there was a fury of municipal development which meant the swelling collections shifting around from one building to another – the library, the Midland Institute rooms in Paradise Street, Aston Hall. Some were even deposited in a bank. A permanent building in the town centre was needed, and the notion agreed in principle in 1880, but no positive action was taken.

Then, in July of that year, John Bunce received a letter about 'the great loss the town sustains in the absence of an adequate Art Collection' from the head of a Birmingham engineering firm, Richard Tangye. He wrote:

> It is all very well for critics to exclaim against Birmingham manufacturers and artisans because of their inferiority to their foreign competitors in the matter of design, and manufacture, but what chance have they of improving these respects? South Kensington is practically as far away as Paris or Munich, while our competitors on the Continent, in almost every manufacturing town, have access to collections containing the finest examples of art, furnishing an endless variety of style and design.

Then came the offer which was to make the dream finally come true: if the corporation would come up with an art gallery and museum, Tangye would provide £5,000 to buy objects, and if this was equalled he would provide another £5,000 as a foundation to provide a purchase fund from the interest.

Action was immediate. By August plans for a new assize court on land fronting Edmund Street, Congreve Street and Eden Place had been pushed aside and the spot allocated to the new museum and gallery. Building work began straight away so that 'the town will, at no distant period, be in possession of a building adequate to its requirements, and second only to the galleries in which the national collections are exhibited.'

More money was raised for collecting, which took on a new urgency. An Art Gallery Purchase Committee was formed, that 'all attainable objects of historic interest, or artistic quality, and of practical suggestiveness, should be included in the Corporation galleries; all indeed, that can extend the knowledge, refine the taste, instruct the judgement, and strengthen the faculty of those who are engaged in Birmingham industries should be provided for the free and constant study of all'.

The Surveyor of the Queen's Pictures, former keeper of art at the South Kensington Museum J. C. Robinson, went to Italy in 1883 to collect pieces for Birmingham, 'embracing a great variety of subjects and styles of treatment, all of which are well adapted for the instruction of designers and artisans in the various trades conducted in Birmingham.' On second thoughts, Robinson added in a mood which is very pertinent a century later:

> If it should be asked what use Italian sculptures, marble saints and madonnas, terracotta busts, carved pilasters and friezes, chimney pieces and cassoni, are likely to be to Birmingham and its working thousands, my answer is that I entirely refuse to admit that art culture in the provinces should be a different thing, or pitched at a lower level, than in London.

In December 1884 a keeper was needed, and Cole's successor at South Kensington, Sir Philip Cunliffe-Owen, suggested the son of his own keeper of art collection, the thirty-year-old Whitworth Wallis, who was to remain in the post until his death more than forty years later.

The new museum and gallery was designed by Yeoville Thomason with all the grandeur the Gothick age demanded, and Wallis was presiding over it when the Prince of Wales opened it as the Birmingham Museums and Art Gallery in November 1885, a tribute to nearly half a century of nagging by the likes of John Thackray Bunce. Stuart Davies, the museum's deputy keeper of local history, remarked in his book written to celebrate the museum's centenary: 'He and many others had always argued that such an institution would be of principal benefit to the artisans of the town, but in the end it was the generosity of manufacturers that secured it for the town. Thus it is that a memorial stone in the entrance hall bears these appropriate words: "By the gains of Industry we promote Art".'

## *Guernsey*

Birmingham is one of the great Victorian palaces of art and science, made in a mood of creativity and capital boom of the 1880s. In the 1970s and 80s building space was at such a premium that when the museum boom struck it was to existing buildings – libraries, great houses, redundant churches, old town halls, warehouses – that museum developers looked for space.

Very few new museums were built in the first stage of this late twentieth century surge, but one exception represents a good example of municipal enterprise against considerable local opposition which was later turned to approbation and national recognition: Guernsey Museum and Art Gallery. One of the most delightful museums in Britain, it is based on a collection which began in the early nineteenth century but which never had a purpose-built museum of its own.

In 1811 Frederick Lukis was a young man of leisure, living comfortably off the fortune made by his father in the wine and spirits trade on the island, and doing very well from his interest in the privateers which operated out of the Channel Islands – between 1790 and 1805 prizes worth £1,800,000 were brought back to Guernsey. Twenty-three-year-old Frederick busied himself around the family estate, but spent much of his time tinkering with scientific experiments. That year some soldiers on military exercises on L'Ancresse Common came across what they called 'an artificial cavern', but what was later identified as a prehistoric tomb known now as La Varde. From it they took some human bones and pieces of pottery, and there was a good deal of local interest and curiosity. One of the onlookers was young Lukis, who went home that day with a human skull under his arm, and the Lukis Museum was born.

Lukis became an archaeolgical pioneer on the island, financing digs and recording their findings. He preserved some of the island's most important monuments, and the series of volumes in which he recorded the archaeological discoveries, *Collectanea Antiqua*, were illustrated by his daughter and are in the present-day museum. Objects filled Lukis House, and he became a compulsive collector of all sorts of curiosities. His four sons inherited his fascination, and spread their family's research to Alderney, Brittany, Cornwall, Wiltshire and even Yorkshire, and Lukis House became a private museum. The collections were bequeathed to the States of Guernsey by Frederick Lukis's youngest son, Francis, and in 1909, two years after his death, Guernsey bought the house and opened it as the Lukis Museum.

Twenty years later the States were left a collection of prints, paintings and ceramics for which there was no room at Lukis House, and it formed a new museum within the Priaux Library at Candie House, a few yards from the modern museum. In the way of museums, both sets of collections, now belonging to the island, grew, and grew out of their premises. In 1938 a military church, St Barnabus's, made redundant by the reduction in the garrison on Guernsey, had been given to the island, and the two sets of collections were amalgamated in it to become the Lukis and Island Museum.

And so it might have continued, a typical Victorian museum of accumulated curiosities in an old building, administered by the island's Ancient Monuments Committee and attracting a few passing holidaymakers during the summer season. But in 1971 the roof collapsed through decay. Something had to be done, and the obvious solution was to shift the whole contents to another old building.

But the Ancient Monuments Committee, belying the image their title provokes, were not satisfied with that solution. The wanted a modern museum, and a museum which was not just the random accumulation of artefacts belonging to long-dead enthusiasts (few of which had much to do with the island), but a representation of the islands's history, nature and geology which local people could identify with and be proud of. They commissioned a report from the Area Museums Service for South-east England and Richard Harrison, later an independent museum consultant, recommended a new museum in Candie Park, and even suggested how the staffing structure should work.

The report was accepted almost without alteration, and the first curator, Mrs Rona Cole, was appointed, almost simultaneously with the architects, Robert Matthew, Johnson-Marshall & Partners of London (the project architect was Ivan Phillips), and a locally resident designer for the interior, Robert Read.

Mrs Cole had spent twelve years setting up a museum in Namibia, South-west Africa, before returning to Britain to study for a Museums Diploma and worked briefly in Edinburgh before coming to Guernsey: 'I had to look it up on the map and panicked when I couldn't find it,' she confessed.

She, the architect and the designer hit it off straight away. 'The whole thing was a model of how a job like this should go,' she said.

> The brief from the committee was simply that the decision had been made that the museum was going to be about the island, which sounds obvious but was a complete turn around from the old museum, which had everything except anything about the island in it. We had to start from the beginning, find out what local material there was and how it could be worked into a viable exhibition.

The vision of the designer, Robert Read, set them off on the right foot. On the top of the hill where the museum was to go he found a run-down old bandstand. 'It had had a 1920s auditorium added which covered more than the ground space of the present museum,' said Mrs Cole. 'It was delapidated and abandoned, a mess – in fact it killed the whole top of the gardens. The bandstand had been glazed between the pillars, which completely destroyed the shape.'

But the bandstand became the theme of the whole design, a design which had to be modest in terms of cost. 'There was very limited finance – £180,000 when the architects started. which with inflation ended up at £320,000, said Rona Cole. 'The architects had to work within that, but they had the concept of restoring the bandstand rather than removing it, and mimmicking the shape in the museum itself.' They wanted to create a series of buildings which blended into the relaxed mood of Candie Gardens and its trees – to avoid destroying one ancient oak, the whole museum was shifted a foot.

There was enthusiastic but firm guidance from the Ancient Monuments Committee. 'We had a brief which laid out certain requirements: environmental considerations, then exactly what was wanted in terms of an entrance foyer capable of being isolated, an assembly point for visitors, a ticket-selling point, a display gallery, an art gallery, an exhibition/lecture room, and a refreshment room, with suggestions as to how big it should be,' said Mrs Cole. 'It wasn't to be a collection-based museum like we'd had in the past, it was a concept museum.'

The museum was ready to be built by mid-1975, but the oil crisis that developed led to the States putting a stop to all capital projects for the time being. When the scheme was approved in August 1977, work began immediately and building was started on 1 October.

'But we weren't twiddling our thumbs for those two years,' said Mrs Cole. 'While we were waiting we did another small museum on the west coast, a maritime museum set in a Martello Tower which we converted under another vote.' So, not only was a museum developing, a museum service was too, for even before the Guernsey Museum and Art Gallery was itself built it had a branch.

Also, while the main museum was under construction, Rona Cole had to create a collection to go into it.

> I came in from outside not knowing anything about Guernsey or its history. The existing collections were in a bad state, and I never saw half of them because they'd already started packing up the old museum before I arrived.

> What I saw was in appalling condition. I was fairly desperate, and I used to have nightmares. There was no material on the historic area at all and very little public support.
>
> The museum went through fairly reluctantly at the time. There was a credibility problem in that the old museum was a typical Victorian one, full of good things but not exciting, so when people thought about a new museum being built that's what was in their minds.

There were letters in the local newspaper objecting to 'the white elephant of Candie Gardens', and one suggested a better use for the space would be for a refuge for battered wives.

The new museum was opened in August 1978 amid muted enthusiasm. 'People quite liked it because they didn't have anything to judge it against so they didn't know if they ought to think it was good or not,' Rona Cole recalled. But they soon made up their minds. In 1979 it won the Museum of the Year Award, a national accolade, and a Special Mention in the European Museum of the Year competition. In 1980 the building got a Civic Trust Commendation. 'Winning the trophy made an enormous difference – if anyone ever needs proof that the Museum of the Year Award is a good idea we are it because there was an immediate turn round of public opinion,' she said.

Objects began to be donated in dozens, then scores, and when it got to hundreds Mrs Cole was politely turning most of it down as duplicate or irrelevant. As well, the museum became the venue for receptions or *vins d'honneur* for important visitors by the States and available for other events, so that it took on a civic role which brought more acceptance and popularity.

As well as permanent displays a busy exhibition programme was written into the overall plan. 'We've got a large local population of 55,000, a seasonal tourist population of about 350,000 and a very small museum,' said Mrs Cole. 'We were very anxious not to be something just for the tourists, but because we were small how were we to attract local people back once they'd been? . . . We decided to have a lively programme of temporary exhibitions.'

Ten years later they had put on over seventy, a significant achievement for a curatorial staff of eleven with the main museum and branches to run, as well as six or seven exhibitions a year. The exhibitions are of three sorts. They are either based on the collections which are not part of the permanent 'Guernsey Story' display, objects normally stored in another building nearby (which the staff are painstakingly transforming into properly catalogued and arranged study collections); they are exhibitions for the community, such as the biennial schools art and craft show; or they are exhibitions brought in to the island 'to broaden the experience' of the Guernsey people.

Celebrating the museum's tenth anniversary in 1988 was 'Renoir in Guernsey', an exhibition of half a dozen paintings by the French master which had been painted in the island's Moulin Huet Bay during a month's stay. They had been borrowed from all over the world, and represented a major breakthrough for Guernsey which had been brought about by a collaboration between its tourist board and its museum. It put attendances up 200 per cent during its busiest eight weeks of the year. 'I think things of excellence will be a draw anyway – the fact of bringing the paintings when they haven't been seen together since Renoir painted them, that they are of Guernsey, that they are by an artist who is top of the pops is a combination we won't get again, but I think it's proved that such things are a draw,' said Mrs Cole, who went on:

> A big name pays dividends. One of the elements of people coming to see the Renoirs was that they couldn't believe they were actually here. I feel very passionately about the local people whose opinion of art is not particularly high because they have no opportunity to see great art. All that people in Guernsey are going to see is our very nice collection of mid-nineteenth watercolours, and there's more to art than that.
>
> So many of us live life second-hand because television is so good. But you can't walk round a painting on television, you look at it from the angle they choose. The opportunity to see the real thing is very important.

But the local history is also the real thing, which can be seen at the museum's two branches, Castle Cornet and Fort Grey, as well as in the permanent gallery in what the locals have taken to calling 'the Candie Museum'.

Guernsey's museum operation is a mixture of traditional tourist appeal with a modern application of Sir William Flower's 'New Museum Idea'. On one hand the swashbuckling antecedants of the island are being capitalized on, on the other the requirements of ordinary local people who simply want to know some more have had a brand-new museum built around them.

Guernsey also represents an essential difference between the fundamental ethics of the 1880s and the 1980s. At Guernsey the requirements of the scholar are given much less consideration than those of the untutored visitor. An attempt was being made to create a study collection of the reserve objects, but not until ten years after the museum had opened. Sir Henry Cole's museum was first for the scholar, artist and designer, second for the public; Flower's for the public and scholar in equal parts; in Candie Gardens, the visitor comes first.

## *Glasgow*

In gardens even lovelier than Candie, but in a place not generally noted for its tranquility, the centrepiece of a network of municipal museums sits magisterially. 'Let's haste to Kelvingrove, bonnie lassie-o,' sang the Glasgow poet Thomas Lyle in the only piece he is known for today, and 800,000 people do that each year, heading for the museum and art gallery.

There was a sharp intake of breath in 1987 when Glasgow was pronounced European City of Culture for 1990. More cultured than Edinburgh? asked the burghers of the royal city, who had rather expected to win the European Commission's nomination. The city of 'fitba', shipbuilding and Billy Connolly?

As if to rub it in, Glasgow mounted a hugely successful garden festival in 1988 with an architectural pastiche at its heart which reminded visitors that Glasgow's cultural provenance was well established a century ago. The city has at least twenty accredited museums and galleries, nine of them run by the city itself. It also has a reputation for festivals and great exhibitions, one of which brought it the Kelvingrove Museum and Art Gallery (in emulation, in the park laid out by the designer of the Crystal Palace, Sir Joseph Paxton, of the Victoria and Albert Museum's conception), another celebrating its opening.

Just like so many other great museum collections, Glasgow's was based on the private accumulation of a local collector. But while other great cities' august institutions may have come into being in predictable and conventional ways, unconventional Glasgow acquired its art collection in an unexpected way. It bought the hoard of a great art lover who had died insolvent, and his house in Sauchiehall Street to keep it in.

Archibald McLellan, coachbuilder, councillor and magistrate, was a connoisseur who amassed a collection of fifteenth-, sixteenth- and seventeenth-century masterpieces and set out his house with the intention of creating a public gallery.[1] But he died in 1854 before he could finish the task, and his estate was found to be, as the first director of the museums to hold the title, James Eggleton, tactfully wrote in 1936, 'heavily involved'. The art collection was reckoned to be worth £15,000, and the house £29,000, when the town council began considering whether, as a tribute to McLellan and his civic dream, they should buy them.

'The Town Councillors of the time,' wrote James Eggleton, 'deemed an expenditure of that magnitude ridiculous excess when it was suggested that the city should liquidate the deceased magistrate's debts and take over the building and works of art.' Nevertheless, probably more to leave McLellan's name to posterity unsullied than to take responsibility for the paintings, both were acquired for £44,500, and in May 1856 'the citizens found themselves in possession of one of the really great art collections of Europe,' Eggleton wrote. The McLellan Galleries officially became the Corporation Galleries of Art.

But the education of the Corporation was a slow affair. The councillors were not really aware of what they had bought, nor how to care for valuable works of art. 'For years they evinced very little interest in its well-being, although public-spirited citizens were donating works to swell the civic art collections,' recorded James Eggleton.

In the 1860s John Ruskin and his social education ideas, emanating from the pastoral magnificence of the Lake District, in which he preached the inspirational value of verdant nature, were influencing the thinking of community leaders in the new industrial cities of Britain, and the Glasgow fathers were not immune – the name is, after all, derived from the Gaelic for 'dear green place'. 'They awakened to the significance of art to the community,' Eggleton wrote some seventy years later.

[1] James Eggleton, *Glasgow's Art Galleries and Museum*, 1936.

'They abandoned their detached air of amused tolerance when they learned that art experts throughout the country were interested in several of the masterpieces . . . and that one of these in monetary values easily exceeded the sum expended by the City for the entire collection and the building.'

At first the building was extended, the collection was conserved, some tenants were moved out to make more exhibition space. 'Gradually,' according to Eggleton, 'with the increase of the collection by donations and bequests, the Councillors realised that the admirable pastime of collecting works of art might be of real and desirable cultural advantage to the citizens.'

Collecting art for the benefit of the citizenry more or less became an organic part of the city, as it did in other nascent industrial centres of the mid-Victorian period – Liverpool, Manchester, Sheffield, Birmingham. With art established in Sauchiehall Street – the McLellan Galleries are still there among the hurly-burly of the shopping centre that has developed around it, now a venue for exhibitions and meetings – Glasgow turned its thoughts to other areas of public education.

In 1870 the Corporation acquired a beautiful, if rather small, Robert Adam mansion in Kelvingrove, beneath the university, to create a general museum, or 'megatherium' as Eggleton put it, and it was a classic Victorian museum.

'The objects it contained promoted wonderment within them – the ring of alum, the model of the brougham, the pulpit, Edinburgh Castle in cork, the nugget of gold, the stuffed birds and the very much alive fish in the aquarium – all contributed delight in the long halcyon days of summer holidays and the brief respite from school of the Saturday forenoons,' enthused Mr Eggleton, clearly remembering his own boyhood in the city.

In 1876 a wing was added – paid for by a public subscription of £7,500 to which the Corporation added £700 – which was a rather unfortunate limb stuck on to what had been a splendid house and was now an ungainly mutant, so that science and technology could have a place. In ten years it had grown to such an extent that a rationalisation of the whole civic collections was decided upon: there would have to be a glorious piece of architecture to rival even South Kensington's recent achievements, and Sir Alfred Waterhouse, creator of the Natural History Museum's, was asked to adjudicate a competition to find the architect.

But first the money had to be raised, and even the fierce civic pride of Glasgow was not going to be capable of stumping up the kind of money the Corporation had in mind. They would copy South Kensington again: they would hold a great international exhibition in Kelvingrove Park, next to the existing museum. The Royal Society of Arts' exhibitions of the 1840s and the Great Exhibition of 1851 had spawned almost a fad for them. Edinburgh had its International Exhibition in 1886, Manchester its Royal Jubilee Exhibition, celebrating the fiftieth anniversary of the Queen's reign, in 1887. Glasgow would outdo them both, and have a prize at least as glorious as South Kensington's.

'Victorian Glasgow possessed all the main attributes of an exhibition city', wrote Perilla and Juliet Kinchin in their *Glasgow's Great Exhibitions* of 1988. 'On a great

*Above* The Industrial Gallery at Birmingham, a typical late nineteenth-century museum display.

*Right* Sir Whitworth Wallis, first director of Birmingham Museums and Art Gallery.

*Far right* Frederick Corbin Lukis, founder of Guernsey Museum.

Sir John Lavery's painting of the great Glasgow Exhibition of 1888, the beginning of Glasgow's Museum and Art Gallery in Kelvingrove.

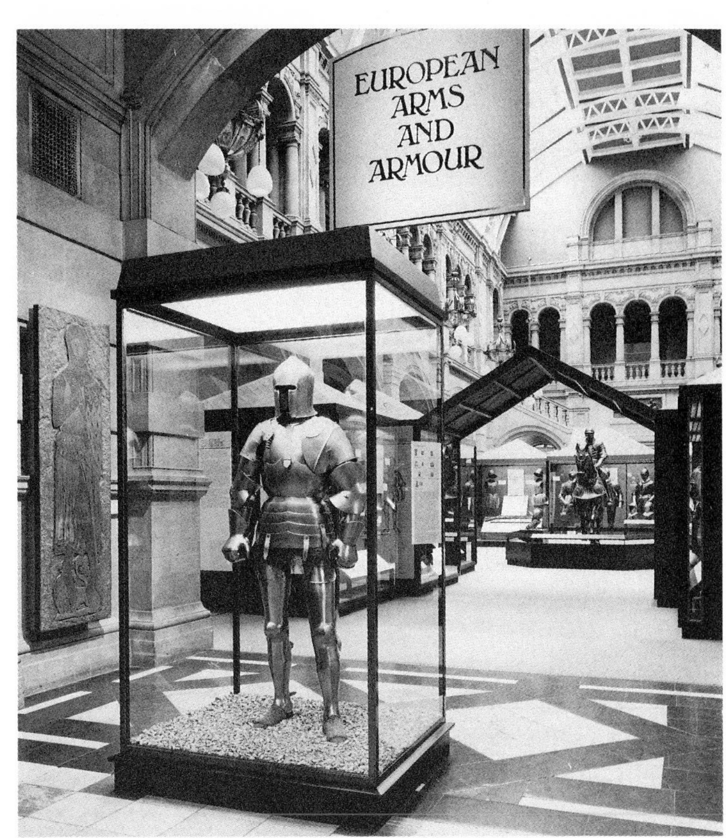


*Right* Glasgow Art Gallery and Museum: entrance to the Armour Court.

*Below* The new Burrell Museum in Pollok's Park, Glasgow.

Mosaic floor at Leicester's Jewry Wall Museum.

Oakham's delightful Rutland Museum; life and work in a former county not forgotten.

river, at the heart of an international trading network, it was one of world's leading manufacturing centres.

'In 1888 its population of 761,000 . . . made it easily Britain's second city, a title claimed since 1811.' Its magnificent municipal chambers were opened by the Queen in 1888, an indication of the stature the city perceived for itself at the zenith of the British Empire.

'Glasgow was ready for a major exhibition, which can be seen in the context of this vigorous municipal activity as another bid for a cultural status to match the city's industrial strength,' said the Kinchins. 'The general aims espoused in the prospectus were a mixture of the altruism and shrewd commercial instinct characteristic of Victorian exhibitions: "To promote and foster Science and Art, by exciting the inventive genius of our people;" and "to stimulate commercial enterprise by inviting all nations to exhibit their products both in the raw and the finished state". . . . Pride and an obligation to match Edinburgh dictated that Glasgow's Exhibition should style itself "international" in the tradition of the Great Exhibition of 1851.'

A total of 5,748,379 visited the exhibition which made £46,000, a quarter of what the Crystal Palace show was able to hand over to the foundation of South Kensington and its institutions more than thirty years earlier. It was not enough, and a committee of 'gentlemen interested in the Arts' was formed as the Association for the Promotion of Art and Music, which raised another £70,000 in five years.

There were sixty-two entries in the competition to build it, and Waterhouse chose John W. Simpson and E. J. Milner Allen as the architects. Work began in 1895, and in 1896 the committee ran out of money so that the Corporation had to step in again. The foundation stone was laid by the Duke of York, later George V, in September 1897, two years before Queen Victoria laid one in South Kensington and declared it to be the seed of what would henceforth be called the Victoria and Albert Museum.

Completed in 1901, the new museum cost £257,000, and the city decided to have another exhibition to celebrate it. 'Almost the entire acreage of Kelvingrove Park was requisitioned for the purpose, the newly completed building being a feature of the place,' wrote Mr Eggleton. At the heart was the museum and art gallery, described in the exhibition's official guide as 'one of the most elaborate edifices devoted to Art in Europe.'

'In every way the venture was a success, as visitors flocked to it from all over the world; and after defraying expenses a surplus of about £40,000 was available for the development of the art and science collections,' Eggleton recorded. One of the principal lenders to the exhibition was a town councillor and member of the organising committee called William Burrell, who lent paintings including works by Manet and Daumier, glass, ivories, enamels, carpets and tapestries. Burrell, later Sir William, was to bequeath his entire collection to the city.

The collections from the McLellan Galleries were moved there, and so were the contents of the old Kelvingrove Museum, which had been demolished in 1899 with only the absurd new wing remaining to be a Japanese gallery, then a library, and eventually it was destroyed to make way for tennis courts.

The museum was formally opened in 1902, but by then the museum bug had bitten the Corporation so severely that they were already acquiring branches. In 1896 Camphill House in Queen's Park was acquired to house temporary exhibitions; the People's Palace, designed by the city engineer, was built for £20,000 on the historic Glasgow Green and opened in 1898, to encourage the working classes to partake of the visual arts on their own doorsteps.

In 1897 the city had acquired the Tollcross Estate and turned it into a public park, with the mansion becoming a children's museum and opening in 1905. That same year another mansion, Mosesfield in Springburn Park in the heart of the locomotive manufacturing suburb in the city's north-east corner, was given to the city and opened as another museum to bring some uplift to the railway workers with ceramics, paintings, silverwork and magazines and newspapers to read. In 1930 came another gift, part of the Aikenhead Estate, which was named King's Park, with Aikenhead itself, the house becoming the King's Park Museum to house period costumes and historical portraits.

Most of these have ceased to operate as museums. The People's Palace does, as a museum of social and political history of Glasgow, and its popularity has never flagged. Camphill House is now the repository for the costume collection, but is only accessible by appointment.

But new branches have been added. In 1964 a Museum of Transport was opened in temporary accommodation in Albert Drive and was moved to Kelvin Hall in 1988. In 1966 Pollok House, the Palladian home of the Maxwell family, was presented to the city and houses the collection Sir William Maxwell was accumulating while the city elders were pondering what to do with McLellan's, and in 1976 Haggs Castle, built by an earlier Maxwell, was opened as a successor children's museum to Torcross House (Chapter 11). The year before, with the local government re-organisations which brought hundreds of museums under the auspices of municipal museums and galleries departments instead of isolated town councils, the little local museum at Rutherglen joined the family and after reorganisation was opened in 1981. Then the fifteenth-century Provand's Lordship, with its permanent and temporary exhibitions of the medieval history of Glasgow, was opened as a museum.

That same year, 1983, the gem in the city's diadem which is the modern era's answer to the Kelvingrove achievement, opened in Pollok Park: the Burrell Collection. Sir William had left his huge and multifarious collection to the city in 1944, and the problem of what to do with this massive compendium of medieval stained glass, furniture, tapestries, Chinese and Indian ceramics and French Impressionist paintings, not to mention antiquities, exercised the city and museum authorities for more than twenty years before it was decided that the only solution was to build an entirely new museum for the collection. It cost £21 million, and the year after it opened it won the Museum of the Year award.

This was the manifestation of a prospect looked forward to before Burrell was even dead. In 1936 the first director, James Eggleton, was bemoaning the lack of space for the burgeoning collection and advocating a new museum: 'But let us consider . . . the essentials of externalities as well as internal design. One in keeping with the spirit of beauty which art, over the centuries, has so nobly endeavoured to keep alive and to preserve for succeeding generations. An edifice in keeping with the chaste restraint of beauty and yet appealing to the majesty of man's conceptions over the ages.

'This prospect,' said Eggleton, 'the separation of the art interests from that of the museum, should not be beyond accomplishment in a progressive community like Glasgow.'

## *Merseyside and Leicestershire*

Local government shifts have been key to the development of museums and museum services, not the least being the 1972 Local Government Act which provided that rate-funded museums could be run both by district and county councils. It meant, for instance, that the important museums in a large county like Leicestershire, which absorbed the old county of Rutland, could be pulled together to create not only a comprehensive series of collections which did not overlap, but a museum service providing centralised education, conservation and exhibition programmes.

In Leicestershire's case the museum service also took on responsibility for archaeology in the county which, with important remains to be found in the city itself and a well-established archaeological museum, the Jewry Wall Museum, within the family, made some more sense.

It also meant that gaps in the county story could be filled without waiting for some enlightened collector to leave his life's hobby to the public, or some inspired entrepreneur to create a heritage centre. In 1988 there were fourteen museums in the family, including Leicestershire Record Office and the museums of former Rutland. There were plans for a hunting museum to celebrate the one sport Leicestershire is probably most famous for – a fox is the county's emblem – and, at the opposite end of the spectrum, to turn Snibston Colliery into a mining and industrial museum, possibly the national mining museum.

In the 1980s the abolition of certain metropolitan counties also had a profound effect, one of which turned a set of local museums into, officially, a national museum in a development which might be repeated elsewhere in the north of England.

Liverpool Free Museum had been built at the expense of a Liverpool merchant, William Brown, in 1860, in the street which still bears his name. It contained the natural history collection of the Earl of Derby, father of the prime minister, who spent a fortune sending expeditions around the world to collect specimens – the first curator of the Liverpool Free, Thomas John Moore, reported that the Derby collection consisted of 18,000 birds, 1,200 quadrupeds and 300 reptiles and fish, 'the greater part of which were stuffed'.

Many more collections were given, and the museum itself collected and grew over the decades. The Liverpool Free, especially under Tom Moore, became a model museum, and it was here that the first annual meeting of the Museums Association was held in 1890. Now the museum became the centre of Liverpool City Museums, and is the headquarters of the National Museums and Galleries on Merseyside, created in 1986 to take over responsibility from the defunct metropolitan county of Merseyside, and funded directly by government as part of its drive to revivify Liverpool.

Merseyside museums and galleries in the group include the Liverpool Museum, as it now is, the Lady Lever Art Gallery in Port Sunlight, the Walker Art Gallery, the Sudley Art Gallery, Merseyside Maritime Museum which opened in 1980 and the 1986 Merseyside Museum of Labour History. Other important buildings, like St George's Hall which was restored and temporarily re-opened in 1988, came under the service's aegis.

It is a matrix which many hope will be used elsewhere to rationalise an important set of museums, and Manchester and Tyne & Wear have both been suggested as ideal candidates. Nevertheless, despite the Department of the Environment's funding, Merseyside's museums are still just that – important local museums.

# 3. 'An absolute necessity'. The independent museums

*There are about 1,300 independent museums in the country and they represent the greatest single influence of the new museums age. But their provenance is as old as most: this chapter looks at the Haslemere Museum in Surrey, the National Motor Museum at Beaulieu in Hampshire, the Weald and Downland Open Air Museum at Singleton near Chichester, Quarry Bank Mill at Styal in Cheshire and the Wordsworth Museum at Grasmere in Cumbria.*

THERE is no such thing as an independent museum, say curators in publicly funded museums. No public museum survives now without some kind of government funding, central or local, so 'independent' is a misnomer.

But that is a semantic which does not go far enough, say the independents – and, in fact, there are some which do survive with no public bounty at all. Independence refers to the individual spirit of enterprise which establishes and maintains a museum irrespective of the policies and budgeting of national or local government, they reply. But then, many local-authority museums owe their existence to the independent enterprise of curators like Elijah Howarth of Sheffield Museum and Gallery or Tom Sheppard of Hull Museums and Galleries (Chapter 6) who worked all their lives on a corporation salary but could hardly have been freer spirits.

Independent museums, goes a harsher opinion, are the slightly distasteful entrepreneurial side of the business, in it for profit and to capitalise on the heritage craze, with scholarship a poor second. The truth is that by the 1980s the distinctions between independent museums and publicly funded ones have become blurred with independents adopting a sense of responsibility for the local heritage while local authority museums are borrowing from the experience of independents to bring marketing skills and other non-traditional museum management disciplines to bear. In the eye of the beholder there is no difference.

## *Haslemere Education Museum*

The Haslemere Education Museum, for instance, fits no easy definition, but it is the focal point of the community and an educational resource not only for local people but, with its microscope laboratory, for scholars from all over the country who come to study the botany and geology of this spot tucked into the Surrey countryside. Yet it is fiercely independent, set up by Sir Jonathan Hutchinson in 1888 and, now expanded into its third building since then, proudly upholding the tradition he set in an age of different prevailing values. Although it now receives modest grants from the county and borough councils, its largest source of income is its own fund-raising.

'Museum teaching may easily be made to interest all classes,' wrote Sir Jonathan in 1893 in a report for the Museums Association, of which he was later to become president. His benediction would be put differently today, but the sentiments are very much the same for his museum and scores like it:

> Whether, however, we regard the acquaintance of a general knowledge of natural facts and of the history of nature as easy or difficult, I unhesitatingly assert its priceless value, and, apart from its collateral advantages, its absolute necessity. It is that which will make our lives cheerful and rational; it will enlarge our sympathies, diminish our superstitions, and fit us for our duties towards each other.

The extent to which the vocation which founded this particular independent museum survives is eloquently testified to by the fact that 1988, its centenary year, saw the retirement of only its third curator, Arthur Jewell.

Mr Jewell spent forty years at Haslemere, twenty-five as its curator. He made many of the models in his geology gallery, established a laboratory with a range of microscopes, including a projecting microscope, and raised essential funds himself by such ploys as playing piano duets with Miss Laura Ponsonby, sister of Lord Ponsonby and one of the museum's staunchest supporters. He also had the rare distinction of being president of the local Women's Institute, among a sheaf of other local dignities. He raised his family in the tied cottage which goes with the museum.

Haslemere Museum was founded by a Lincolnshire man to whom considerable fame had come in the field of medicine. The role of medical people in the growth and development of museums in the eighteenth and nineteenth centuries is intriguing: Sir Hans Sloane, whose collection was the basis of the British Museum, was a royal physician, and the Hunter brothers and W. H. Flower were also famous examples, their mission – which was only partly connected with their professional skills – being to maintain collections for others. Sir Jonathan Hutchinson, Hunterian professor of surgery at the Royal College of Surgeons and president of the Royal College and the father of modern dermatology, was another of those doctors whose hobby became almost more of a memorial to them than their distinguished careers.

In 1866 Sir Jonathan bought Inval near Haslemere as his country home. In 1868 he was suggesting to the British Medical Association that at their annual meeting they should set up a temporary museum of objects collected by members over the previous year, and this became a popular feature for BMA members for many years.

As well as being a famous surgeon Hutchinson was something of a polymath, as Victorian gentry was encouraged to be, who believed that some knowledge of astronomy, geology, zoology, botany, natural philosophy, human history and so on were essential to all, and that museums had a vital role to play in disseminating this knowledge.

'It is to be hoped that the time will soon come,' he told the medical department of Yorkshire College, Leeds, in 1885, 'when every town, however small, and every school will have its educational collection of objects illustrating the history of man and the natural sciences,' and he saw the museum as 'a richly illustrated book which those who would might read'.

Three years later he wrote the first chapter of the Haslemere Museum book by establishing it in a series of barns and sheds at Inval. When he invited the Museums Association to see it in 1893, he told them modestly: 'The thing has been in truth a personal experiment in which I have been trying in various directions how a museum for the instruction of the general public might be inexpensively constructed.'

He organised weekend lectures on such subjects as the elephant's skull, Hebrew history and Wordsworth, and distributed lists of important historical events. Members of his family were given corners of the museum to look after, and the catalogue of 221 objects he produced was printed by his two nephews on the printer they used to make museum labels.

Haslemere and its surrounding countryside became a haven for celebrities from all walks, and the museum recorded their visits: W. E. Gladstone, Bertrand Russell, Rudyard Kipling, Sir Arthur Conan Doyle, Marie Stopes, the cartoonist Bruce Bairnsfather, and latterly broadcasters such as Freddie Grizewood and Richard Dimbleby.

In 1895 the museum moved to a new building in East Street with which Hutchinson hoped to encourage other museums to fulfil his ambition declared ten years before – which it did, to an extent. More and more specimens were being acquired – though not the 75-ton whale he enquired about which had been washed up on Blackpool beach and which was being offered for £700 – and some were beginning to deteriorate. Sir Jonathan decided he needed a curator, and in 1897 E. W. Swanton was appointed the first; he was to stay for more than forty years.

'In 1898 and 1899,' recalled Swanton in his book published in 1947, *A Country Museum*:

> Hutchinson frequently came to his museum at weekends, walking over from Inval, arriving about 11 o'clock and occasionally staying late. He brought sandwiches and wine, sometimes a bottle of Camp Coffee, which he put, in winter time, on the top of one of the stoves to warm, and more than once forgot it with disastrous results! He kept a pair of easy slippers in the bookroom, and a large white pinafore with sleeves and a capacious front pocket, in which he carried dusters and also a small sweeping brush when spring-cleaning operations were going on. He bought many specimens and books at London salerooms. . . . The natural history purchases were sent down by road in a two-horse van. The books came by rail in large packing cases, sometimes so large that four men were needed to lift them from the railway van and carry them in.

Hutchinson introduced 'space-time' schedules for history as an easy *aide-memoire* based on simple cross-references, local schools began using the museum as part of their curriculum – they were even set examinations by the museum – and the Haslemere's reputation spread so that new museums such as Newbury's were set up on the Haslemere pattern.

In 1913 Hutchinson died, but his museum continued to expand, and in 1921 there were over 14,000 visitors. East Street became too small, and in 1926 the museum opened in The Lodge in Haslemere High Street, a sixteenth century house which had been the home of the Hesse family of local notables since the 1750s, and was now enlarged and adapted by public subscription to be the museum as it more or less remains today.

Swanton retired in 1948 and John Clegg was curator until 1962, when Arthur Jewell succeeded him. It continued to expand gently, in the Hutchinson idiom, explaining in time-honoured fashion the relationship between man, natural history and geology in the context of the particular area, the progress of mankind and the development of more prosaic subjects such as transport, agriculture and domestic life. There are reconstructions of a local cottage kitchen and a blacksmith's forge, and a gallery dedicated to peasant crafts in northern Europe. 'Haslemere was a favourite for the Fabian sort of gentry,' Mr Jewell explained, 'and they appreciated this kind of display.'

The museum is still a centre of village life: where elsewhere on Saturday morning 'the pictures' has been the highlight of the week for children the country over, here it has been Saturday morning at the museum, where lectures, activities, and rambles have been organised. Objects are constantly arriving, for no better reason than someone from the village or a friend of the museum had thought it right for the museum.

On the day of my visit a phonograph had arrived and was sitting on Mr Jewell's desk with dozens of cylinders waiting for his attention. 'I don't know where it'll go, but we'll find somewhere for it.' There is an incomparable photographic archive of Haslemere in a roll-front cupboard, waiting to be sorted; on a table is a photographic enlarger 'which I got for a pound at a jumble sale; matter of fact, I got this jacket there for a pound too: you have to support local charities.' His pride and joy has been his microscope laboratory, which is in constant use by visitors and local students.

Some acquisitions can be an embarrassment. Shortly after taking over, Mr Jewell found an Egyptian mummy in an appalling state of decay which was long past being conserved and could only be destroyed in the interests of public health. Later the son of the donor arrived to know where it was, and Mr Jewell had to put him off repeatedly in the hope that he would give up, without being told the awful truth – eventually he was.

'You see, our best asset is good will. You have to keep it going.'

## *The National Motor Museum*

What has become almost an icon for independent museums today and one of the most persistently successful of the present generation, is now called the National Motor Museum at Beaulieu, Hampshire. The enterprise of one man, Lord Montagu, it is now a vast concern attracting a consistent half million visitors a year.

Its creator, the third Baron Montagu of Beaulieu, became renowned for his achievement and a sought-after consultant in the boom which is own museum was in at the start of; he was the first chairman of the Historic Buildings and Monuments Commission for England, or English Heritage, and has been president of the Museums Association and of the Historic Houses Association. But at the beginning Lord Montagu had not intended to create a museum, he merely wanted to reflect the enthusiasm his pioneering father had had for motoring, the father whom he succeeded to the title at the age of only three.

The second Lord Montagu had foreseen the future of the invention when it first began to appear on the Continent in the late 1880s. Soon after he became MP for the New Forest and later, in the House of Lords, he was campaigning for the motor car at a time when it had many opponents; it was a noisy, smelly, dangerous contraption, they argued, which frightened the animals and sprayed dust over crops. It was in 1896 that the law was changed and there was no longer any need for a man to precede a self-propelled vehicle on the public road with the statutory red flag that had disappeared in 1878. At the same time the speed limit was raised to all of 12 m.p.h., a major victory because it gave the motor car the freedom of the open road for the first time.

Lord Montagu bought his first car in 1898 and a year later added the first four-cylinder Daimler to be produced in this country. He was the first Englishman to race an English car on the Continent, and toured his Rolls-Royce Silver Ghost in Europe before the First World War. He was a man of considerable influence, and both Kaiser Wilhelm II and King Edward VII were guests at Beaulieu at different times. When the king was still Prince of Wales, in 1899, Lord Montagu gave him his first long motor drive on a public thoroughfare.

Although motoring was seen as a rich man's hobby, by the early years of the century the car's commercial potential was already being exploited, and the De Dion Bouton, for example, was being sold to doctors and commercial travellers; Montagu was to acquire his own 1903 De Dion in 1912 in payment of a bad debt.

But Montagu was not a collector – in fact he gave his 1899 Daimler to the Science Museum in 1912 (it is now back at Beaulieu), and a horse-drawn fire engine from the estate went to Hull Museum when he no longer had a use for it. He died in 1929 and the 10,000 acre estate was held in trust for the new Lord Montagu until 1951, when he turned twenty-five. Beaulieu had been much used in the war as a training ground by the Army and Special Operations Europe; there was also an airfield on the edge of the estate. It was a mess.

Lord Montagu, who had a successful career in public relations to pursue if he wanted it, had a dilemma. 'He had to make up his mind whether to stay behind and look after the estate which was run down, underfinanced, undercapitalised,' said the museum's curator Michael Ware, who has watched and, with Lord Montagu, planned the growth of the museum since the mid-1960s. 'He decided to stay and sold off 2,000 acres to raise initial funds, then to open the house to the public and use the funds to restore the estate. . . . It was not the first stately home to do so, but the first to do it with a flare for publicity and public relations.' Montagu brought his professional training to bear on his inheritance.

The thirteenth-century Cistercian Abbey around which the original estate had been established had been a ruin since the Reformation, but it had been opened regularly since the beginning of the century with thirty- to fifty-thousand annual visitors. That could be improved upon, and Lord Montagu also turned his attention to the family seat itself, Palace House. He created tableaux to tell the story of Beaulieu and its inhabitants, and the entrance hall was to be dedicated to his father and his great love of motoring. He did not know it then, but the beginning of the National Motor Museum was just five old cars, mostly borrowed: an 1899 Daimler, an 1895 Leon Bolleé Tricar, the De Dion, a Lagonda Tricar and an 1898 Benz, chosen to represent the sort of cars which were around in the early days when his father was taking such an interest. The De Dion had been quietly rusting in the stable having been pensioned off from its duty as a hack car around the estate.

The house was opened in April 1952, with two-and-sixpence as a cover-all charge for both the house and the abbey, and with Lord Montagu promising: 'If we have a hundred visitors today we'll have champagne for dinner.' He had champagne for lunch.

'He never intended to start a motor museum,' said Mr Ware. 'In the 50s you just didn't find old cars in the same way you do now. The Veteran Car Club only had about 300 members in those days, and now you can see old cars at nearly every fête and function in the country. The visitors were interested, Lord Montagu saw that and decided to start a collection of old cars.' He began with a 1906 Renault and has also gathered some of his father's favourites – he traced his Rolls-Royce Phantom I towing mowers on a Somerset cricket field, and later the car he had taken to India during the First World War was discovered by the museum in Australia where it is now being restored. The present baron's own 1909 Rolls Royce Silver Ghost, still available for hire and surely the most photographed one outside of the factory model, was a breakdown lorry when he found it. Recently the museum traced the son of the original chauffeur of the 1909 Silver Ghost, who has added a lot of detail to their knowledge of its history – including the fact that it was once a hearse.

Lord Montagu moved the cars into a wood shed, then built a second shed. 'He explained to me that as the first shed was filled up and the second was built,' said Michael Ware; 'he used a courtyard in Palace House in which he put motorcycles overflowing into the old dairy, with bicycles in the kitchen, and the whole house smelled of oil.'

By 1955 it was the Montagu Motor Museum, and by 1959 he needed a building big enough to take the 100 vehicles he had accumulated – and built it. It was an immense success, and within a year Montagu was considering the next development. At one point he was venturing beyond motor cars to please a growing public, with the first hovercraft, a train, even a Spitfire aeroplane, but these were experiments which did not earn a permanent place.

'All the time,' Michael Ware said, 'it was run by a commercial company, the

Beaulieu Development Company, along with the rest of the estate. In the 1960s Lord Montagu felt someone ought to be doing a museum of motoring for Great Britain; he made inquiries in the motor industry and the Science Museum, and no-one was prepared to take it on. Had there been no national motor museum ten years ago, it seems pretty logical that there would be a motoring out-station of the Science Museum, but not in those days.'

So Lord Montagu decided to do it himself, meaning a major enhancement of the status of his collection which would have to include a much larger building and many more public facilities. But he knew that it needed industrial support and to get that he would have to create a charitable trust. Planning went on through the 60s and by 1970 he was ready to begin. The Duke of Kent opened the National Motor Museum in 1972.

Back in 1960, when the place was beginning to get an international reputation, an increasing number of inquiries were coming in, and a library was established, followed by a photographic library in 1962. In 1963 Michael Ware joined Montagu to run the photographic library, and was the museum's curator by the time the National Motor Museum came into being nine years later. In 1979 a film library was added. This, sponsored now and known as the BP Library of Motoring, is probably the best free-use reference source of its kind in the world – the only charge is for photocopying. Open seven days a week, it has 25,000 sales catalogues, 9,000 instruction books, 11 journals and books. 70,000 written inquiries a week, 80 telephone inquiries and 50 personal visits.

Today the National Motor Museum has 310 vehicles and half a million visitors a year. With the blessing of the Charities Commission there is a management agreement between a private limited company, Montagu Ventures, successor of the Beaulieu Development Company, and the National Motor Museum Trust; the company provides the management services on a day-to-day basis, leaving the Trust to look after all the curatorial aspects of the museum. Lord Montagu is chairman of the Trustees of the National Motor Museum and, with the exception of his two elder children, all the other Trustees are entirely drawn from the motoring and allied industries.

For many years it has been the policy at Beaulieu to have a one-price admission ticket (£4.75 in 1988) to all attractions: the Motor Museum, Palace House, Beaulieu Abbey, the grounds, gardens and a choice of the special features. The management agreement contains within it the formula for remitting part of the aggregate receipts for the National Motor Museum Trust. All trading at Beaulieu, such as shops and catering, is controlled by Montagu Ventures Ltd.

Michael Ware told me more about how the museum balances its budget:

> Once overheads are taken out, there is nearly enough to run the museum on a day-to-day basis, but not enough for us to have big new displays, buy important new acquisitions or do major restorations, which is why we go for sponsorship help from outside. We have two sponsorships of £1m each running at the moment, down to covenants and donations of several hundred pounds a year, and that's what keeps us going.

> Even so, it's very hard to contemplate buying expensive cars. If we're looking for a project we wish to put in the museum, say for example the history of the family car which in round terms would be a £100,000 display, I've got to find a firm to come up with that and more.

So, unlike most other independent museums, Beaulieu is one which does not benefit from trading. Trading income is retained by Montagu Ventures Limited, but they provide a guaranteed and increasing annual income to the Trust, which has obvious and considerable advantages.

A former chairman of the Association of Independent Museums and a great traveller on behalf of the museum movement, Michael Ware knows how different it is: 'What normally happens is this: somebody wants to preserve a beam engine somewhere; a group of people get together, and forming a charitable trust is the obvious thing to do because then they can benefit from grants and so forth; they find they have to raise money so they form a development trust, but they particularly want to sell things so they start a trading company. Beaulieu was the other way round: the commercial company spawned the charitable trust.'

Despite being called the National Motor Museum – and there is nothing to stop any museum calling itself the 'national' collection, no matter how small – Beaulieu gets no direct government grant in the way that statutory national museums do. There is no government indemnity to cover insurance, as with nationally owned collections, and with the soaring costs of collectable cars now insurance costs are high. The insurance value of the collection in 1988 was £3,500,000.

Beaulieu happily defends its national role. 'From an early stage we had a collecting policy: motoring on the roads of Great Britain,' said its curator. 'It was a collection of vehicles which you would normally have seen on the road and race tracks in this country, but not necessarily made in Britain – we're not a museum of the British motor industry. So you would get Bugattis, Delages, Mercedes Benz, but we don't have to go and buy a Holden in Australia because the Holden has never been marketed in this country at all.'

The museum has an exhaustive guidance document on what will and what will not be collected. Lord Montagu's personal collection is on loan to the trust for sixty years from 1972 and is almost static. The museum likes to have temporary loans from private sources, which means that the display automatically changes without enlarging the permanent collection.

A new £2.3 million block, open in 1989, contains all the administration and libraries, a 230-seat lecture theatre, an education department together in the same place for the first time with a working classroom, plus a new store for seventy vehicles.

'We do collect and keep up to date, and we have no cut-off point,' said Michael Ware. 'But we do not intend to increase the size of the National Motor Museum because we believe we are at the optimum for our average visitor – we could easily bore them stiff. Remember our visitors are really only coming once in the year, perhaps once in five years – we have a 45 per cent return in a ten-year period.'

Nevertheless, there is a modest shopping list, top of which is the 1935 Bluebird in which Sir Malcolm Campbell broke the world land speed record. It is currently in a museum in Alabama, but at the time of writing the price was beyond reach.

The next item on the list, though, was obtained in 1988 thanks to a national appeal which secured the Britain's oldest surviving racing car, the 1903 Gordon Bennett Napier, half the £300,000 cost being met by the National Heritage Memorial Fund.

'We know who our visitors are, and we probably know more about them than any other leisure complex in Great Britain knows about theirs,' said Mr Ware. 'We know that 68 per cent are staying away from home at the time of their visit and are tourists, and you've only got to look at them to see that they are an average married couple with two kids. We deliberately aim our museum right at them, not at the academic: our captions are written to be understood by an intelligent fourteen-year-old child, but I hope we don't talk down to our visitors.'

But what about the aficionado who wants something more than a bright teenager seeks? He must look beyond the caption. 'The enthusiast may think we're superficial but the enthusiast will know a lot of it anyway and will gain from lots of things that we don't print out in the caption. Our enthusiasts are about 10 per cent of our visitors. In many cases they don't like museums – it's anathema to many enthusiasts that cars are in museums, they should be out being driven.'

Beaulieu has an education officer, Graham Carter, who has the added job of understanding the visiting public and what the museum should be saying to them. The kind of research done in the quest for acceptable interpretation has led to some of the latest developments in the museum, including 'Wheels', its ride through a hundred years of motoring history, and the new commercial vehicle section which has been presented as a period film set, a street in which various deliveries are being made, complete with street noises, smells and video explanation.

The museum also has an advisory council. 'It's very easy for a museum like this to be the museum of the curator of the time – or in this case of Lord Montagu and the curator,' said Mr Ware. 'A long time ago we set up the advisory council of experts within the motoring movement, which meets every nine weeks, where we sit and look at offers, talk about displays and ideas, and they are a think tank. Comments are sent to Lord Montagu as chairman of trustees, but it works as an informal valve and stops us making expensive blunders.'

The competition for museums such as Beaulieu is increasing all the time, not necessarily from other museums but from other mass entertainment facilities such as theme parks, one of which opened near Beaulieu in the mid 1980s. It means constant vigilance for what the public want and enjoy, and a finger on the pulse of developments elsewhere. Today there are rides in open-topped buses, opportunities actually to drive a 1920s Bullnose Morris, and actors performing cameo scenes from the history of motoring. Possibilities for the near future involve a facility representing the internal combustion machine in which visitors would be asked to imagine they are the fuel and travel around the workings of a giant engine; another ambitious project is for a display detailing the development of roadways from Roman times to the present; and there are plans to create a period garage. These will need sponsorship, but are being developed as a direct response to visitor surveys.

'I'm so aware that the majority of motor museums in this country are private collections containing five vintage Bentleys or seven Austin Sevens, and that is not, in my mind, a true museum,' said Michael Ware. 'What we're trying to be is the best thought-out motor museum in the world, and I think we're there.'

## *The Weald and Downland Open Air Museum, Quarry Bank Mill and Biographical Museums*

Open-air museums began in Scandinavia in 1885 when a twelfth-century church was shifted from central Norway to save it from being demolished and re-erected on a peninsula in Oslo Fjord. Another museum of buildings followed at Lillehammer, Norway, and then the famous Swedish one at Skansen. The Welsh Folk Museum at St Fagan's in 1947 was strictly Britain's first, and was followed by a rash of them, including Beamish and Ironbridge Gorge, whose purpose was essentially, if not wholly, to preserve important buildings by transporting them from the original sites where they were scheduled for destruction.

The Weald and Downland Open Air Museum at Singleton near Chichester, Sussex, was launched in 1967 by enthusiasts led by the museum's founder, J. R. Armstrong. A site was offered to them by a charitable foundation, and it opened in 1971 with four buildings from the immediate region – a treadwheel from Catherington near Brighton, a base-cruck cottage from Fareham, a market hall from Titchfield and an early granary from near Winchester.

'The main purpose of the Museum,' wrote Mr Armstrong in the first guide book, 'is to rescue good examples of vernacular architecture, that is humbler buildings such as farmhouses, which are threatened with destruction and to re-erect them at the Museum.' He added, 'It must be emphasised that the Museum is primarily a preservationist body and in the first instance will always fight to keep buildings in situ.'

In the 1987 guide his successor as director, Christopher Zeuner, said: 'So far more than thirty buildings have been re-erected, but a similar number are in store, and others will be rescued. If public support continues, the Museum will be able to maintain its development not only by re-erecting buildings but also by expanding its educational, recreational and research facilities.' Public support did not seem to be slacking: that year there were 175,000 visitors. They had come to see not only ancient English architecture but old working buildings at work: the watermill makes flour which you añ buy, the stable has horses in it and charcoal is made in the kiln at the charcoal burner's camp.

* * *

While Singleton is a beacon of agrarian architecture through our past, Quarry Bank Mill at Styal in Cheshire represents a spotlight on an industrial phenomenon from the eighteenth and nineteenth centuries. It is one of the finest surviving cotton spinning mills of the first generation, said its director until 1989, David Sekers, who was also chairman of the Association of Independent Museums.

Founded in 1784 by an Irishman called Samuel Greg (the wife of one of whose descendants was to be a patron of museums in the mid-twentieth century), it was prosperous during his lifetime, but was overtaken by newer technology in the second half of the nineteenth century. Fortunately, although cotton spinning ceased there in 1904, the mill kept running until 1959 by which time it and most of the estate had been given to the National Trust.

In the 1960s the buildings needed urgent and costly repair, and several options – a trading warehouse, a hotel, a craft centre – were discarded in favour of a museum. The mill was leased by the National Trust to the Quarry Bank Mill Trust, who opened it as a museum in 1977.

'The period which Styal can uniquely well represent,' wrote David Sekers in 1984, 'is the pre-urban era, when the mills were located in the countryside and the business of spinning cotton could be tempered with a certain enlightened self-interest in the establishment of reasonable facilities for the work force.' Which is what it does, both in the mill itself and in the village Greg created for his workers and which the museum also has care of now. With local authority help a working water wheel was installed in 1986, and in 1988 the Apprentice House was restored and opened, as much as an educational vehicle as a museum feature.

> The site is a very significant chunk of prime English history, where you can see what's left of the textile revolution and which will give you a complete feeling for it. So we really have a major part to play, particularly in the GCSE syllabus. We do it without any subsidy, which is very hard for us, but it works and we're helped largely by volunteer guides and a dedicated staff.
>
> In furtherance of all this we've opened the Apprentice House. We have thirty children a day, spending it as apprentices. It's immersion in history which is possible in these places. It's about much more than monuments now, much more than machines, it's about people and the monuments are a backdrop.

Largely in the independent sector there is a great corps of biographical museums, ones which are built around the story of an individual whose work and life radiate knowledge in the areas of endeavour or interest with which they were associated. Almost invariably they are founded on the subject's birthplace or home.

There is the Brontë Parsonage Museum which has made the home town of this extraordinary family, Haworth in West Yorkshire, a magnet for tourists with increasing power. Charles Darwin's house at Downe reveals not only the way in which Darwin arrived at his thesis of man's development by natural selection, but the atmosphere in which he worked and brought up his large family of brilliant children.

London is blessed with at least twenty biographical museums including the homes of Freud (where he lived for the last two years of his life), Keats (where he lived for the most productive two of his), Dickens, Thomas Carlyle, the Duke of Wellington, Florence Nightingale (from 1989), Anna Pavlova, Dr Johnson, William Hogarth, Baden-Powell, John Wesley and Sir John Soane.

Elsewhere Jane Austen, Alfred Lord Tennyson, Robbie Burns and, of course, Shakespeare are celebrated, and some have been expanded beyond being mere three dimensional biographies.

The Wordsworth Trust was set up to do more than describe the poet and his circle of friends. It began as a private charity in 1890 created to buy William Wordsworth's home, Dove Cottage at Grasmere in the Lake District 'for the eternal possession of all those who love English poetry all over the world'. The Wordsworth Museum was established in 1934.

Under the guidance of Dr Robert Woof, an English lecturer at Newcastle University, the moribund museum was revived in 1981. Dove Cottage was restored, Wordsworthian archives were rescued and a library created which has more than 90 per cent of the poet's surviving manuscripts. 'Where else in the world can a comparable proportion of a great writer's manuscripts be examined by scholars on the spot where the work was originally composed?' said Dr Woof. 'And no writer has a closer relation than Wordsworth with the area in which he lived.'

Wordsworth himself had a famous circle of friends, including the poets Southey, Keats, Charles and Mary Lamb, Leigh Hunt, the scientist Humphrey Davy. and Coleridge. At Grasmere Keats would fret, Coleridge disappear into his hallucinations, Dorothy Wordsworth would manage and her brother would preside.

But the influence of Wordsworth, his family and his coterie was so great that it coloured their era for posterity as the Age of Romanticism, and that is what Dr Woof's Trust – chaired by a descendent of the poet's, the Oxford don Jonathan Wordsworth – have made not only Dove Cottage but the village of Grasmere the Centre for British Romanticism.

Wordsworth was Sir Jonathan Hutchinson's favourite poet, and the founder of Haslemere Museum would often quote *The Prelude* to those who mustered for his Saturday lectures:

There is
One great Society alone on earth,
The noble Living and the noble Dead:
Thy consolation shall be there, and Time
And Nature shall before thee spread in store
Imperishable thoughts, the Place itself
Be conscious of thy presence . . .

# PART TWO

# 4. Hoarders and crackpots

*Some of our best loved museums are the results of obsessions and passions of collectors who either had a missionary zeal to carry their message to the rest of the world or whose collections became so large there was simply no recourse but to turn them into public curiosities. We look at the first of them in this chapter, the Ashmolean Museum, then at the Sir John Soane Museum, the Powell-Cotton Museum, the Museum of Advertising and Packaging – formerly called The Pack Age – and the Bakelite Museum, which has no museum.*

## *The Ashmolean Museum*

'A wonderful variety and incongruous juxtaposition of . . . objects', was how Sir William Flower described John Tradescant's collection.[1] Reading the collection's catalogue must have been almost as entertaining as going to the museum which first brought the word into our language. The catalogue, *Musaeum Tradescantianum: or, A Collection of Rarities, Preserved at South Lambeth neer London*, was written by Tradescant to describe the extraordinary collections of his extraordinary father, also John Tradescant, which was to become the Ashmolean Museum in Oxford. It is still one the world's most stunning museums.

John the first came from obscure Suffolk origins where he embarked on a career as a gardener. He was to become a gardener to kings, and the most widely travelled horticulturalist until, perhaps, Joseph Banks 150 years later.[2] Horticulture led to botany, and to journeys to Europe to acquire species. He hitched a ride with a diplomatic mission to Russia in 1618 from which he brought back not only plants but items of clothing which had caught his imagination. Only two years later he joined a group of 'gentlemen volunteers' sent by Charles I to Algiers to suppress piracy, but his was an ethnographic adventure rather than a maritime one.

Working for the Duke of Buckingham four years later – he was in the duke's ill-fated expedition of 1627 to relieve La Rochelle – Tradescant's circle of friends and

[1] Presidential address to The British Association for the Advancement of Science, Newcastle, 1889.
[2] R. F. Ovenell, *The Ashmolean Museum 1683–1894*, Clarendon Press, 1986.

correspondents grew vast. One was Captain John Smith, rescued in legend by Pocahontas to become the first Governor of Virginia, and the star exhibit of the Tradescant 'Cabinet of Rarities' is the cloak said to have belonged to the princess's father, Powhatan.

In fact the collection had grown to such an extent, thanks to his own forays and to contacts with diplomats and merchants, that he had to lease a large house in Lambeth in 1625 in which to keep them and display them, and he was to spend the rest of his life there.

By 1630 Tradescant was Keeper of His Majesty's Gardens Vines and Silkworms at Oatlands, Queen Henrietta Maria's house, and was wealthy and respected. His collection had become a curiosity in itself, a tourist attraction which, for a small fee, anybody could visit, and his rarities became known as Tradescant's Ark, our first public museum. John the second's catalogue – the first museum catalogue – lists

> Divers sorts of Egges from Turkie, one given for a Dragon's Egge . . . The Claw of the bird Rock, who, as Authors report, is able to trusse an elephant . . . Dodar from the Island Mauritius; it is not able to flie, being so big . . . Garments, Vestures, Habits and Ornaments' [including Edward the Confessor's woollen gloves] Mechanick, Artifical Workes in Carvings, Turnings, Sowings, and Paintings.

Tradescant the elder died shortly after becoming keeper of the Physic Garden at Oxford and John the second took over the Ark, also succeeding his father at Oatlands. Although not the *picaresque* figure his father was, he certainly travelled to America and brought back specimens of Indian weaponry and clothing.

The second Tradescant seems to have restricted admission to the Ark, but one of those who became a regular visitor from 1650, often staying with the family, was Elias Ashmole (1617–92), a polymathic astrologer and antiquary. It was Ashmole who, with the physician Thomas Wharton, helped Tradescant compile the *Musaeum Tradescantianum*, published in 1656. The list was a curious mixture of painstaking accuracy on some subjects, and hopeless generalisation – such as 'Severall curious paintings in little forms, very antient' – on the other. But it was the first museum catalogue, and a serious attempt to classify a collection.

Perhaps in remorse at the death of his son, the third John, Tradescant bestowed the collection on Ashmole. He himself died in 1662, and he and his father are both buried at St Mary-at-Lambeth (next to the Archbishop of Canterbury's Lambeth Palace) which is now the Museum of Garden History.

Elias Ashmole, philosopher, soldier, lawyer, tax collector, mathematician, astrologer, botanist, anatomist, alchemist, founder member of the Royal Society and inveterate collector, had to fight Tradescant's widow for the collection, however. According to the deed of gift, made in 1659, the Ark was to be held in trust for Ashmole by Mrs Tradescant while she lived, but since it was not mentioned in her husband's will she contested the deed before the Lord Chancellor, Lord Clarendon himself, in 1664, who found for Ashmole that the 'Books, Coynes, Medalls, Stones, Pictures, Mechanicks and Antiquities' should come to Ashmole on Hester Tradescant's death.

Intermittent skirmishes continued over the next fourteen years. Then Ashmole bought the house next door to Mrs Tradescant's, who inexplicably handed over the rarities, except for the pictures, forthwith. She died in 1678, mysteriously drowned in her garden pond, and a few days later Ashmole recorded in his diary: 'I removed the pictures from Mrs Tredescants House to myne.'

In fact, Ashmole had already decided to give the Tradescant collection and his own to Oxford, and wrote to the Bodleian Librarian confirming this and 'to propose the building of some large Roome, which may haue Chimnies, to keep those things aired that will stand in need of it.' So, even while he was still squabbling with Mrs Tradescant, Ashmole was not only thinking of the collection's future, but of its conservation and the foundation of a museum to keep it in.

The offer came at exactly the right time. Oxford had been a dynamo for scientific progress in the mid-seventeenth century, and the value of research had been recognised since Francis Bacon's day in the early years of century. With the Restoration came an academic flowering which was thirsty for new learning, and Ashmole's suggestion had the support of enough men of influence to ensure its manifestation.

His 'Roome' was to be part of a building devoted to the study of science and philosophy, built in Broad Street next to the Sheldonian Theatre – and rather too close to the Exeter College lavatories, Rev. Thomas Dixon reported in a letter: 'In digging they undermin'd ye said necessary house & caused such an inundation that some of them had much ado to escape with ye safety of their lives, & were glad to leave their clothes swimming behind them.'

Ashmole's gift was formally ratified in 1683, five days after the future James II opened the museum. If Tradescant's Ark was the first museum to open to the public, Ashmole's was the first institutional museum to allow general admission.

Despite his anxiety for the conservation of the objects, many did not survive. The dodo remains only in fragments, now transferred to the Pitt-Rivers Museum. But the museum flourished under a succession of enlightened curators and benefactors, and eventually moved to its present Beaumont Street neo-classical building in 1845. Today the Ashmolean has grown from the eclectic Cabinet of Rarities gathered together by the John Tradescants, and switched its emphasis to become one of the world's leading art museums: antiquities from Egypt, China and Greece; paintings by Titian and Giorgione and breathtaking drawings by Raphael and Michelangelo; later work embracing van Dyck, Rubens, Rembrandt, Gainsborough, Rowlandson, Constable and Turner; a Stradavarius violin, and The Alfred Jewel, the little Anglo Saxon pendant which, more than any other object, grasps visitors' gaze.

## *Sir John Soane's museum*

In London's Lincoln's Inn Fields there are two gems for the museologist. One is the Royal College of Surgeons' Hunterian, whose story is told in Chapter 5. On the opposite side of the square is the Sir John Soane Museum.

John Soane was born near Reading in 1753, the son of a mason called – according to the *Dictionary of National Biography* – Swan, although the museum itself has his father as a bricklayer called John Soan. At the age of fifteen he entered an architect's office, that of George Dance, winning a Royal Academy silver medal four years later and a gold one in 1776, when he was introduced to George III.

In 1781 he opened his own practice, and in 1784 married the niece of a wealthy builder. By this time the name was Soane, and his future was assured with the appointment as architect to the Bank of England in 1788. In 1790 his wife inherited substantial property and John made his first purchases of works of art, two lions and two vases from the sculptor John Flaxman, and two years later he built Number Twelve Lincoln's Inn Field for himself. From then, as the commissions came in the collections grew: casts, engravings, paintings, commissioned family portraits. In 1800 he bought a country home, Pitshanger Manor at Ealing, to help with the education of his sons whom he hoped would become architects, and converted it to his own comfort – an unusually satisfying exercise, probably, since the original architect had been his first master, George Dance. Pitshanger Manor is now a museum itself.

The collecting became more ambitious. Antique marble sculptures came to Lincoln's Inn Fields, then Hogarth's comic series, *The Rake's Progress*, then a Turner, then a Canaletto. By 1808 he was getting pushed for space, and he bought Number Thirteen. In 1810, when there seemed no chance of his sons following into the architectural profession, he sold Pitshanger so that the collections there came to Lincoln's Inn Fields as well. In 1823 he bought Number Fourteen and rebuilt it, adding a picture room, and the same year bought the remarkable Belzoni Sarcophagus, the coffin of the Egyptian king Seti I, which the British Museum had unaccountably turned down. It is one of the great treasures of the museum now, and although he paid the enormous sum then of £2,000, Soane does not seem to have been altogether clear about what he had got. He wrote his own inscription for it:

> This marvellous effort of human industry and perseverance is supposed to be at least three thousand years old . . . and is considered of pre-eminent interest, not only as a work of human skill and labour, but as an illustrative of the customs, arts, religion and government of a very ancient and learned people. The surface . . . is covered externally and internally with hieroglyphics, comprehending a written language, which it is to be hoped the labours of modern literati will render intelligible.

To be sure, they did, but not until 1908.

John Soane was knighted in 1831 and presented his collection to the nation in 1833, with the 'Act of the settling and preserving of Sir John Soane's Museum' becoming law that April. The Soane Bill, introduced by the Radical John Hume, caused a brief maelstrom of controversy. Sir John's novelist son George protested that 'his father had been "improperly importuned and persuaded" to take a step which would leave himself and his family destitute.'[3] William Cobbett opposed the

[3] G. Soane's evidence to House of Commons Committee, reprinted in 'A New Description of Sir John Soane's Museum', Appendix II, 1986 edition.

bill on the grounds that 'it is morally wrong for a man to divert his estate from his family'[4], and Sir Robert Peel thought Soane ought to give it to the British Museum instead of making a separate burden on the nation. Nevertheless it became law, with trustees being appointed and obliged to give free access 'to Amateurs and Students in Painting, Sculpture and Architecture' and, even more important, they 'shall not (except in Cases of absolute Necessity) suffer the arrangement in which the said Museum . . . shall be left . . . to be altered.'

And so we have the house and its contents more or less just as Soane left it on his death in 1837. Sir John is said to have declined a baronetcy to spite his son, and his grandson, John, was to be allowed to live in the house only if he followed his grandfather's profession, which he did not. In 1838 the family tried to get the museum back and failed.

Over the years cleaning and redecoration has taken place, some ill-advised conservation was done in the last century, electric light was installed, curators came and went (including one called Wyatt Angelicus Van Sandow Papworth, who, alas, died the year after his appointment). The trustees successfully got the Underground diverted from running beneath the museum, and unsealed a bath in which some papers of Sir John's had been hidden. In 1939 the best pictures were evacuated, and in 1940 bombs caused some minor damage.

The present curator, Peter Thornton, formerly keeper of furniture at the Victoria and Albert Museum, has instigated a programme of restoration for the museum.

Number Fourteen backs on to what had once been a monastery cloister, and under the new picture room Soane built a room which he called the Monk's Parlour. In his original guide of 1830 he wrote: 'The interest created in the mind of the spectator, on visiting the abode of the monk, will not be weakened by wandering among the ruins of his once noble monastery.' This was his own epitaph – the Monk's Parlour was also known by Soane as the 'parloir of Padre Giovanni', or Father John's Parlour (Soane, his wife, who died in 1815, and their elder son are all buried at St Giles-in-the-Fields). He also wrote 'The stone structure, at the head of the monk's grave, contains the remains of Fanny, the faithful companion, the delight, the solace of his leisure hours'; Fanny was the name of Mrs Soane's pet dog.

## *The Powell-Cotton Museum*

The first object to greet the visitor entering the Powell-Cotton Museum at Birchington on the east Kent coast is a portrait of a white hunter. He sits in a camping chair in the shade of his tent porch, wearing an old and torn bush jacket and clutching his trusty hunting rifle. At his feet is the head of a bull, blood still oozing from its nostrils.

This is the founder of the museum, Major Percy Powell-Cotton. In the case which

[4] Petition presented in House of Commons by William Cobbett opposing Bill, reported in 'A New Description of Sir John Soane's Museum', App. II, 1986.

holds the large painting there are a number of other objects connected with it, particularly the old jacket. This, explains the didactic, was worn by the major when he was mauled by a lion in Central Africa in 1906. He had took seventeen claw wounds before a courageous native porter and a headman attacked the lion, just in time to save the major's life. The lion is in the next room, stuffed and mounted.

So the image we have of Major Powell-Cotton is of a Victorian big game hunter, and the host of animal heads stuck on adjacent walls confirm the image. It is a completely false one, for this man was a David Attenborough, pre-television. In his day he was more travelled in Africa and Asia than anyone else, and created a collection which is unique and was of primary scientific importance when he put it together.

'Although he was a man of his time, definitely a hunter, which he greatly enjoyed, there was always at the back of his expeditions a collecting element to a much greater extent than in the cases of others of the time – say the Theodore Roosevelt expeditions,' said Christopher Powell-Cotton, who is the honorary director of his father's museum. 'He was anxious to build up collections here, not only a collection of near record heads but also a study collection: he made a major series of primate material which was used extensively for research.' Lord Zuckerman, when he was professor of anatomy at Birmingham University, cleaned the whole of the primate collection for the museum so that he could also study them at close quarters in his laboratory.

'He was a gentle sort of man, and he was also – though it's quite difficult for people in this day and age to take the point – quite concerned about the conservation of species. All our mammal collections were made before the last war in circumstances which were very different from today,' said Mr Powell-Cotton.

The major perfected a style of writing in extremely small characters so that he could record copiously in his diary or on small scraps of paper what he observed while he was in the bush. He observed not only animals in their habitats, but the natives of what we call the Third World, and befriended them. He was the first white man to survive a Tibetan winter.

Percy Powell-Cotton was also a white hunter who was eager not only to preserve his victims as trophies, but to use them to help educate those who could not find out about them as he had done. When he began there was no television, film was in its infancy and black-and-white photography was a cumbersome and unreliable craft. 'The only way people in this country could get any idea of wild life was either in zoos or museums like this,' said Christopher Powell-Cotton. 'He was much more interested in the animals and the peoples amongst whom he travelled than the average white hunter was.' Aware that species were in danger at a time when the phrase 'endangered species' was not in our vocabulary, when wholesale slaughter for the skin and ivory trades had not reduced bush creatures to the point of extinction, his solution was to make his kills selectively, embalm the corpses and ship them back to England to be stuffed and mounted.

Up to this point there is nothing about his enterprise which marks it out as anything but the private fixation of an obsessive amateur zoologist and ethnographer, creating an archive interesting of its sort but vastly inferior to the great natural history collections in South Kensington and other, publicly-owned museums.

But what the major did was to put his specimens, mostly stuffed and mounted by Rowland Ward who is credited with turning the craft of taxidermy into an art, into re-creations of the habitat scenes in which he had found them, even repeating the incidents he had witnessed. Some of these dioramas contain more than thirty animals, depicted in poses appropriate to the scene. In one, two little duiker deer take on a python which is squeezing the life from a third, a scene which he had witnessed. An African elephant, apparently as big as any brought out of the bush, could only be installed by lowering the gallery floor and building out at the back. The white rhinoceros family, now close to disappearing for ever, is of a species named after Major Powell-Cotton, and the lion which almost killed him is seen in a central scene attacking a buffalo from Central Africa which was also named after him.

Percy Powell-Cotton was not only concerned with wildlife, however. 'He was essentially an avid collector,' said his son. 'In the late nineteenth century you couldn't collect everything but he made a good shot at it.'

Born in 1866 to a family which had made its fortune in the East India trade and had bought the estate at Birchington in 1777, Powell-Cotton inherited Quex House which had been built in 1808. In 1887 he had begun his travels – twenty-eight expeditions in all, the last one being in the year before his death in 1940 – and as soon as the house came into his possession he built a museum in the grounds, one room of which he opened in 1896.

His life revolved around his expeditions, and even his marriage in 1905 was in Nairobi with the honeymoon a safari through Uganda and the Congo. Nearly all the specimens, both of animals and of ethnographic items, were collected by Powell-Cotton himself, a few being bought at auction.

It was a collection which seems completely alien to the rest of the museum but which he acquired in 1910 which gave the museum international notice in 1988: a few days before it was due to go to auction, Major Powell-Cotton bought ninety-three pieces of Imperial Chinese porcelain, the largest single collection of Imperial china outside China.

'He completely refurnished the main rooms of the house with antiques which he purchased, and he had an interest in a Canterbury antique shop whose best stuff I suspect he bought – he had a fine eye,' said Mr Powell-Cotton. 'The Chinese porcelain fitted into a general pattern, but why be bought this particular collection I don't know, except I think he thought it was attractive, something of a bargain, and went for it.' It had simply been part of the household decoration in the oriental drawing room. 'We knew that they were nice pieces, but not that they were important,' said Mr Powell- Cotton. 'We'd built a small gallery in the early 70s to bridge a gap between the museum and the house in order to be able to open part, and that gallery was to house the oriental decorative arts collection including a substantial slice of the porcelain, Japanese netsuke and so on.'

When the present curator and assistant curator, Derek and Sonja Howlett, arrived in 1982, Mrs Howlett, a lifelong collector of ceramics, could not believe that the pieces were genuine. 'When I went into the gallery and saw a lot of yellow ware, very rare because deep ochre yellow is reserved for the emperor, masses of them mixed in with Japanese and Chinese export wares,' said Mrs Howlett, 'I just couldn't believe they could be genuine because I didn't think anybody could treat them that way.' A specialist from Sotheby's was invited to see them and confirmed that they were genuine, unique and of great importance. Mr Powell-Cotton and the other trustees agreed to the trust financing a catalogue of the Powell-Cotton Imperial China and to new cases being made to do them justice. Publication and opening coincided in 1988.

Odd as the Imperial porcelain story seems to be, it is far more reflective of the man responsible than the portrait at the entrance. Before he bought the china – from a mysterious R Pope whose story neither Sotheby's nor the museum had been able to uncover in time for the publication of the catalogue – he sought the advice of the soundest brains he could, and bought only the most valuable in terms of their beauty and importance. And he bought them at a time when western connoisseurs knew almost nothing about such pieces, having had only export china to study before.

The major's one-room museum has been enlarged six times since he opened it in 1896. Places he visited are still given the names he would have known, such as British East Africa and Abyssinia.

It is a museum run by a private charitable trust, set up when Powell-Cotton died, and the costs of staying open are so great that it is only able to do so for a maximum of four days in a week during the height of the summer – in fact a costing exercise showed that it would be more cost-effective for the museum not to open to the public at all. Under such circumstances, for the museum to spend £30,000 on cataloguing a very small part of its collection may seem at best quixotic. But the fact that today a minor museum of great charm and interest can devote such a large sum of money to future scholarship without the certain knowledge that such costs can be recouped shows that the spirit of dilettante learning in which Powell-Cotton's and hundreds of other museums were created a century ago not only survives but is being built upon.

## *The Museum of Advertising and Packaging*

Perhaps Robert Opie is a bit of a crank. Only a crackpot would have collected 250,000 items of the extraneous rubbish which we and our forefathers have been throwing away without a thought. His collection and his museum in Gloucester Dock are enormously entertaining, comic, pathetic, outrageous, martial. But beneath the coverlet of jolly crankiness, they represent the finest ethic of the specialist museum.

'The museum idea had started almost from the word go,' he said. 'I was always aware of that part of life, having really grown up with a museum in the house, and having collected stamps and stones and coins and the Lesney Matchbox series, I

Upper Horseshoe Gallery, Liverpool Museums in Victorian times.

Albert Dock, Liverpool, with the Merseyside Maritime Museum, one of the National Museums on Merseyside.

Pictures arrive for the children's art exhibition at Haslemere in 1932.

Inside Haslemere Educational Museum in the 1970s.

The Montagu Motor Museum before its new building helped turn it into the National Motor Museum.

*Below* Sir Jonathan Hutchinson, the surgeon who founded Haslemere Educational Museum.

*Below* Quarry Bank Mill, now a highly distinctive and successful museum at Styal, Cheshire.

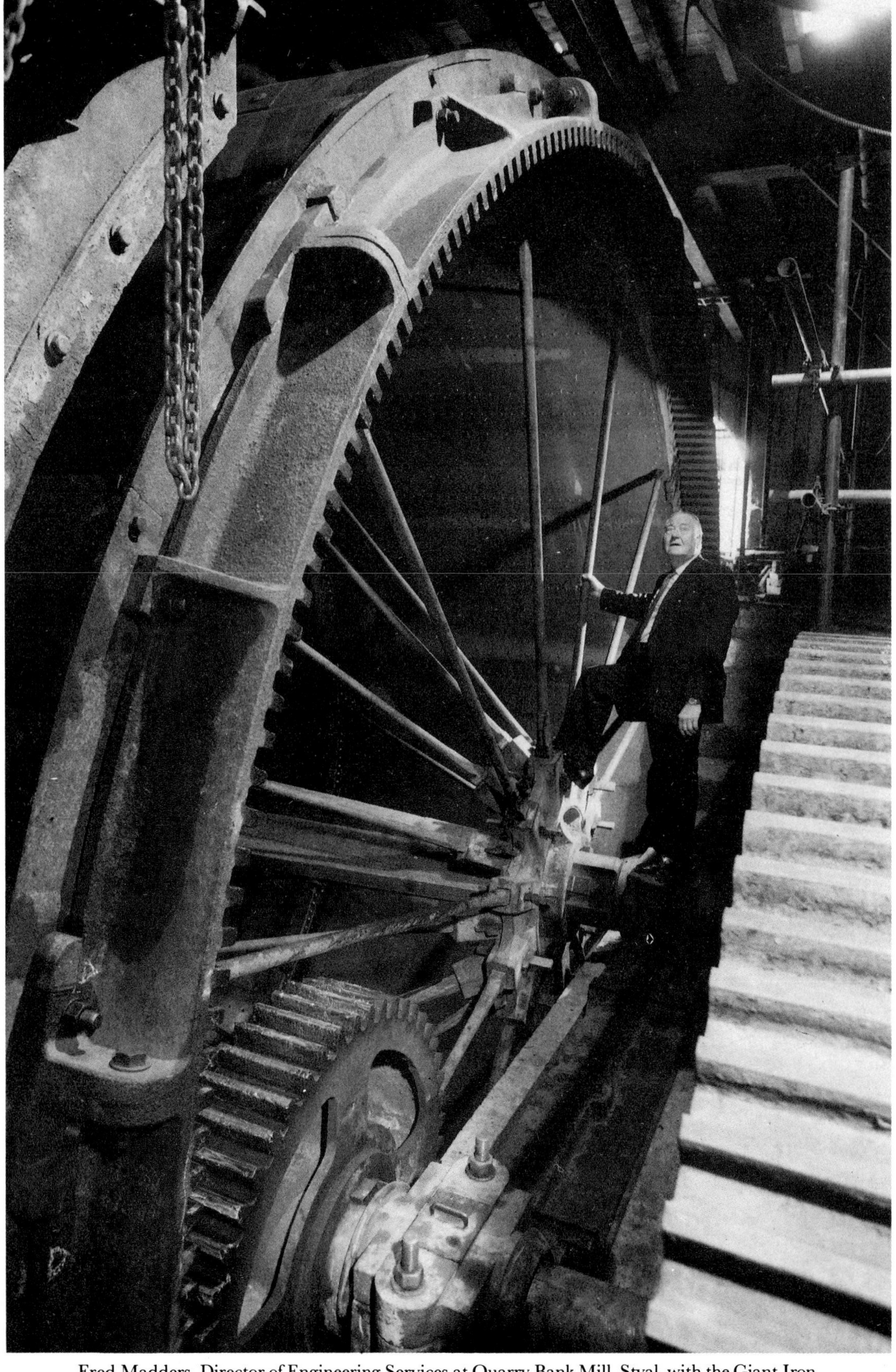

Fred Madders, Director of Engineering Services at Quarry Bank Mill, Styal, with the Giant Iron Water Wheel.

knew that you could get a whole load of packs and make it interesting. What I hadn't realised was that you could find the earlier things, going back in time, and the museum idea was a gradual realisation.'

What he collects is the packaging and advertising detritus of everyday life since marketing first began to draw the consumer to particular brands. It proves that one can be nostalgic about things which one has never seen before, and as such Robert Opie's collection is the ultimate trip down memory lane. The bottles, packets, cartons, hoardings, posters and tins create an almost tangible image of domesticity of bygone times, some of them within our memories but most of them decades beyond.

'Whether or not the social historian of the future will look back on the past hundred years as being the Pack Age in the way archaeologists today refer to an earlier period in our history as belonging to the the Beaker People remains to be seen. Certainly they would be justified in doing so,' he said in a handlist for a temporary exhibition of his collection in 1976.

'The throw-away carton, the labelled tin, the jar, the bottle, the food wrapper of paper, foil or polythene, have become indispensable to our way of living. Yet the probability is that the future historian will be unaware of the extraordinary part that retail packaging plays in our daily lives.'

Born in 1947, Robert Opie is the son of the educationalists Peter and Iona Opie, editors of the *Oxford Dictionary of Nursery Rhymes* and compilers of probably Britain's most comprehensive collection of children's books, with the possible exception of the Bethnal Green Museum of Childhood's Renier Collection. What he discovered was a kernel in the current museum romance, the urge to freeze time past in order to savour it and ordinary life which was being lived in it. Journalists found him good copy.

His obsession began with some sweets which he bought in 1963 when he was still a sixteen-year-old schoolboy and found himself on a deserted Scottish railway station on a Sunday evening. 'I couldn't find anything to eat except for the contents of a vending machine which had this packet of Munchies and a packet of McVities gingernuts. I purchased these two items and it was actually while I was eating the Munchies that this whole thought came that we were literally throwing away our social history. If the manufacturers changed the packaging or went out of business, the 1960s Munchies packet would vanish for ever. From that instant I have saved everything.'

It led inexorably on to 'cereal packets, coffee jars and every type of toiletry. I even remember going into a chemist and buying every kind of toothpaste they stocked.' A dozen years later the collection was a house-full, and had become well enough known for the V&A to mount an exhibition of it which he called 'The Pack Age – A century of wrapping it up', which was one of the most successful small shows the museum has mounted in postwar years.

Robert Opie found the inventiveness of the packaging and design fascinating, and felt compelled to trace its development. 'Technical progress in the nineteenth century made possible not only cheap packaging but packaging that was splendidly colourful,' he wrote in the handlist. 'Bold lettering, image-making designs, and on occasion the likenesses of attractive ladies or trustworthy gentlemen, added cheer to the product.'

'The Duke of Wellington long graced Oakey's Knife Polish. The jolly cook, who relied on Edwards' Desiccated Soup was drawn by Louis Welerter about 1900. The two kids who savour the aroma of Bisto were immortalised by Will Owen. Other artists of enduring renown whose work is to be seen on ephemeral containers include John Hassall (Veritas Mantles), Louis Wain (Mazawattee Tea), and Heath Robinson (Peek, Frean's Biscuits).'

He had researched every item and spent most weekends at auctions, jumble sales and junk shops. But it was not the unexpected high class of the 'commercial artists', as they used to be called, of some of the products, nor their graphics nor the bare-faced cheek of borrowing the likenesses of famous people – even royalty – which attracted Robert Opie's abiding fascination with commercial ephemera. 'I tend to look at it as a collection of the way we live, but I also tend to collect things that no one else has collections of. What I tried to do was collect things that other people hadn't taken seriously enough,' he told me for another newspaper article, about another temporary exhibition which this time went on at London's Trocadero Centre in 1986 and was called 'That British Feeling'. 'I look at every item in half a dozen different ways. It may be exactly the same item, but it's the perspective that you put on it that makes the difference.'

By 1988 Gloucester Dock was threatening to become a creditable rival to Liverpool's Albert Dock and Bristol Dock as a waterside attraction moulded around a heritage theme for tourist interest, with the new Waterways Museum enjoying its first season and a progression of new leisure points springing up around the estate. But in 1984, when Robert Opie opened his own museum there, it was a near-derelict range of gaunt and empty warehouses, their glassless windows staring gloomily like sightless eyes. Just one of them was alive, on the ground floor, with 'The Pack Age' – the title was too good not to revive.

'Now it's the Museum of Advertising and Packaging. The Pack Age was fun but not understood by the public at large. We had to call ourselves a museum, which we wanted to get away from initially. "Centre" didn't give the historical perspective.'

It began modestly, with a few hundred visitors trickling through the unsophisticated displays, but the visitors gradually became more numerous and the show more ambitious until by its fourth season it was entertaining 40,000 a year. Curiously enough, it was an audience built up by the museum itself, without a publicity budget, with the Waterways Museum accounting for no more than a 5 per cent improvement. Robert Opie explained, 'We have relied entirely on leaflets and the press and media to get the story over, and word of mouth, one of the key elements. We borrowed money from banks, but there was no sponsorship – we felt that we needed to prove the point and then go for sponsorship later.'

Opie had other interests though, ones which did not fall appropriately into 'The Pack Age' theme. In 'That British Feeling' in 1984 he was able to incorporate things like magazines, postcards and comics. One cameo tableau he created then was

'Granny's Attic, an apparently random jumble of trunks, clothes, riding boots, pots and pans, topis, vases, Hoovers, shooting sticks, bread bins, croquet mallets – not necessarily Victorian things, anything up to the present day because Granny was stuffing things into her attic all her life,' he said. 'I might make an appeal for people to send me photographs of their attics, because nobody ever takes photographs of their attics. Any photographic album is a complete bias of history because you're always wearing your best clothes or you're on holiday, or they're photographs of Christmas time or special occasions. You never have photographs of mother washing up or shopping.'

Robert Opie has uncovered a wealth of social historical matter, a demographic science, which has passed most people by: a study of essences of the domestic so familiar that they are disregarded and discarded by us, but which create a weighty portrait of our lives and those of our recent ancestors.

Only about 5 per cent, 8,000 items, of his vast collection is to be seen at Albert Warehouse in Gloucester Dock. Much of it is stored at his London home, and some aspects are to be seen in an exhibition in Chatham Historic Dockyard. The museum does not pay for itself, but it is supported by the hiring of objects to television, stage and film companies and advertising agencies to help them create period sets.

Opie's stylish displays of his throwaway treasures are a shameless pandering to our current collective mood of wistfulness for the past, but they are deeply researched and seriously catalogued. His 1985 book *Rule Britannia: Trading on the British Image* was a scholarly if thoroughly readable examination of a particular phenomenon in early marketing in this country. It was followed by *The Art of the Label* and *Sweet Memories*, whose 1988 publication coincided with the launch of his plan to expand the museum to double its size and give it a national title. He said then:

> We need to get everybody pulling together, the industry as well, for something which the nation deserves and must have. There's no facility for looking at our industrial processes on that level, the consumer level, as such.
>
> I'm looking at it in totality, which is mind-boggling, but nothing happens in isolation. You need to look at advertising, for instance, in the context of how we live; it's only then that you realise why it's necessary to have advertising. There are so many prejudices all the way along the line. I'm trying to make not only shopping more exciting and interesting, but also to build up the status that people working in the industry should have.
>
> If they have their roots shown not only to themselves but to everybody else, they themselves have the esteem and everybody sees them in a better light.

## *The Bakelite Museum*

Robert Opie's has been a qualified success story. He has got his museum open and is expanding it, but its future is by no means assured. It relies on his own enthusiasm and commitment, and on his persuasive powers to keep the museum operating in a situation which barely pays its way.

Some do not. There are sage watchers of museums who believe that the future is in the specialist collections, the one-subject museums, but perhaps not the very small ones relying on one collector's devotion and dedication. There are museums such as the House of Pipes at Bramber in West Sussex, the collection of what its creator, Anthony Irving, calls 'smokiana'. There is now a teddy bear museum, a shoe museum, a fan museum, a plasterwork museum, a wireless museum, a cinema museum, a bagpipe museum, even a taxi museum. Everybody's favourite crazy museum, Potter's Museum of Curiosity, isn't Arundel created by the Victorian naturalist and taxidermist Walter Potter whose animal tableaux of nursery rymes like *Who Killed Cock Robin?* which were so romantic in the 1860s and rather grotesque in the 1980s.

One that did not survive and may be lost to Britain if a new venue for it is not found is the Bakelite Museum, the plastic collection of sculptor Patrick Cook, whom I met just as his collection had been rescued from almost irreparable damage while it was in store.

'Yes, it's a long way from Mundania,' he reflected as he sipped tea from his urea-formaldehyde Linga-Longa Beatle mug and surveyed some of his 7,000 'plastiquities', spread around his studio to dry: radios, lamps, flasks, cameras, toys, jewellery, TV sets, sculpture copies, clocks, an electric hot water bottle made of Bakelite but looking like the rubber version, only with a flex coming out of the spout, razors, combs, an ingenious nail buff, a tie-press which winds your tie up and spits it across the room, perfectly ironed. It is hard to see it now, but this could be the nucleus of a very serious National Plastics Museum.

Until May 1986 it had been one of the most delightful little museums to be found, decorously crammed into a south London art-deco flat in a block called Mundania Court. Every inch was covered with the collection – 300 wireless sets alone, forty telephones, not one connected. Even the toilet was a gallery. Not just Bakelite, but its earliest ancestors from Vulcanite (1830s), Parkesine (1850s), shellac from which early phonograph records were made, *bois durci* – made from blood, egg white and sawdust – to casein made from dried curds and formaldehyde.

Some safety-conscious museums might have baulked at the diabolical celluloid, sought after jewellery in the 1980s but notoriously combustible in the 1890s: 'For instance, a farm worker was sitting in the sunshine having his lunch when his artificial leg exploded,' said Mr Cook. 'The sun had reflected off his spade on to the celluloid. Bang.' Gun fights would be started in seedy dives by billiard balls going off, stiff shirt fronts would make a conflagration from a cigar spark.

Then Mundania was to be renovated and the museum had to go. It lay in a container in ICI's Welwyn Garden City car park until October when Cook found it rotting in a sauna of condensation, bubble wrapping wringing wet, cardboard boxes sodden, Bakelite oxidising into a kind of plastic measles.

'I had nowhere else for it to go, I just knew I had to get it out of there as quickly as possible.' Gradually Patrick Cook had all the items brought to the studio, a converted Edwardian stable block not far from Mundania.

But Mr Cook, a sculpture graduate of the Royal College of Art, is no more a crank than Robert Opie, and he has become one of our leading experts on the development and use of plastics. There are frequent calls from the Science Museum, the V&A, the Museum of London, even more frequent ones from writers around the world wanting to know about Charles Goodyear's first real plastic, or Alexander Parkes's invention of a cheap substitute for tortoiseshell, or Leo Baekeland who changed the world when he created the first wholly synthetic plastic out of phenol-formaldehyde and called it Bakelite.

'I've got to convert all the information that I have into either a serious job or it stays a hobby, and I don't think it is a hobby any more,' he said. 'Collecting is a serious job – I want to improve on all the damaged pieces, there are early chunks of the collection which are missing and I want to get packages for modern items because in any exhibition I put on it's important to be able to conclude with that side of it. I'm not making any effort to collect industrial pieces. These things here are what the true consumer ends up with and not the disguised pieces hidden inside lorries and so on.'

Like Mr Opie, Patrick Cook has to make his collection earn for him. The other calls he gets are from film companies, advertising agencies and theatres wanting to hire pieces for period productions. But while the museum has been bubble-wrapped and sweating to death in Welwyn Garden City he hasn't been able to respond. 'I need to have everything readily available, as it was in Mundania, for when people want to hire it so that the collection can start paying for itself again.'

Stephen Bayley, director of the Design Museum at Butler's Wharf near Tower Bridge in London, would like the collection – 'But as an archive so it would just be shut away till someone wanted to see something and then it would be pulled out,' said Mr Cook. He got a letter from the National Plastics Museum at Leominster asking if he would take his collection there. He went to find it and discovered it was Leominster, Massachussetts: 'It hasn't opened yet, and anyway I think it ought to be in Britain.'

Idiosyncratic as the Cook collection may be – 'I'm interested in the traditional trappings, pack-away pieces, ordinary domestic items of novelty and humour. I repeat items to make the point that they were mass-produced, and not valuable' – its absence from any national plastic collection would leave it incomplete.

But in the end it will probably have to stand alone, as the collection continues to grow. Patrick Cook is a leading member of the Plastic Historical Society which meets monthly to bring the industry and collectors together and plan a National Museum of Plastics. 'What worries me about the "National Museum of Plastics", in inverted commas, is how industry sees museums. I don't think they have the vision to see it as not only entertainment, but as a fantasy palace where you are totally enveloped by the theme of plastics for a day, and you get a whole sense of the history of the objects as well as finding out how the stuff is made. It has to be a kind of Crystal Palace of Plastic.'

# 5. The boffins' cupboards

*Our universities used museums as teaching aids, and many of them remain fulfilling that role. Some were founded by the universities, others were taken over by them, some have remained within the confines of an academic resource, others have become public institutions. In this chapter we look in particular at the two Hunterian museums, archetypes, and at the Manchester Museum in which 'town and gown' still collaborate.*

THE universities have always collected specimens for instruction, sometimes notoriously – in the 1820s the murderers Burke and Hare sold the corpses of at least fifteen victims to Dr Knox, an Edinburgh anatomist so eager to study physiognomy that he asked no questions. The official collections were mostly scientific ones which became full-blown museums, but they were not always: the Fitzwilliam Museum in Cambridge, based on the fine arts collections of the Irish peer and scholar Viscount Fitzwilliam which came to the university on his death in 1816, and the Ashmolean in Oxford are both university museums. The Courtauld Institute Galleries is one of several London University museums, which include the recently refurbished Petrie Museum, drawn from the Egyptian excavations of the archaeologist Sir William Flinders Petrie and his successors in London, the Percival David Collection of Chinese porcelain, and the Flaxman Gallery which has the models and drawings of one of the greatest English monumental sculptors, John Flaxman, who died in 1826. There are something over 150 of them in Britain, and they represent a link with the first manifestation of museums in this country, often the only tangible link with our most glittering scholarly achievements. Some are not open to the public, some are so familiar to us it is a surprise to know that they constitute an academic faculty as well as a public museum.

## *The Hunterian museums*

Not all physicians were as unscrupulous as Dr Knox of Edinburgh, and it was often physicians who created the most comprehensive museums. Two eighteenth-century Scottish brothers, born in Lanarkshire in 1718 and 1728, each rose to the top of the medical profession, and each founded a museum, but they could hardly be more different. They were William and John Hunter.

William Hunter was thirteen when he went to Glasgow University, later taking up medical studies and, ten years later, moving to London to study surgery and do some tutoring. Teaching developed into a series of lectures which won him some fame and a sizeable income: students accustomed to dry monologues which were illustrated at best by a dog's corpse to represent the human anatomy were delighted to have humorous lectures delivered by a natural entertainer who gingered them up with anecdotes and practical demonstrations. He became the first great teacher of anatomy, saying that he 'conceived that a man may do infinitely more good to the public by teaching his art than by practising it', becoming professor of anatomy at the Royal Academy. But he turned from surgery to midwifery to do the first serious studies of obstetrics, becoming physician-extraordinary to Queen Charlotte.

But he was also an almost manic collector. His wealth grew thanks to some shrewd market speculation and in the mid-1750s he was buying pictures, books, fossils and in 1755 an Egyptian mummy. After essaying several schemes, including setting up a school of anatomy in London and then a medical school in Glasgow, both of which came to nought, he decided to use his fortune to build up a museum. He collected anatomical preparations, minerals and coins, and had a house built in Great Windmill Street with domestic quarters, a lecture theatre and 'one magnificent room fitted up with great elegance and propriety as a museum', and he moved in in 1768.

Between 1770 and 1782, according to C. H. Brock's 1980 essay 'Dr William Hunter's Museum, Glasgow University', at least £22,664 was spent on coins, and £1,500 on minerals. He bought paintings through agents throughout Europe, and developed a natural history collection which almost certainly included specimens from Captain Cook's first voyage to the South Seas. Queen Charlotte gave him a white robin, and the corpses of a zebra and an elephant which had died in her menagerie.

In 1784 the scientist Thomas Martyn described Hunter's museum as a 'repository wherin is treasured, for the instruction and wonder of the present as well as of future ages, an assemblage of literature, antiquities, natural history and anatomy, far exceeding any yet formed and reflecting an honour on the country as well as the name of the immortal founder.'

But he was unmarried and left no heir, and he had to consider what was to become of the Hunterian. Oxford University is thought to have been offered it and turned it down, and Dr Johnson is credited with having persuaded Hunter to leave it to Glasgow University. This he did, together with £8,000 to provide a building and a foundation, but it was not until twenty years after his death in 1783 that the new museum was built.

'So,' wrote Dr Brock, 'in 1806 there was built in Glasgow the first of the British Greek Temples to Arts and Science which, through the nineteenth century, were built up and down the country to house national, municipal and institutional collections.' The collections were moved up from London in 1807, in a massive operation which involved academic experts on the various subjects being sent to pack each section.

But it was not treated much like a temple. Because the Hunter bequest was badly mishandled, the foundation did not provide enough money for adequate curatorial and supervisory staff, and the museum was available only to a few. The public were required to pay an admission fee, and students were allowed in once a year 'as an opportunity of witnessing an exhibition of curiosities rather than an auxiliary of study', according to the Scottish Universities Commission report of 1826. Free admission did not come until 1907.

Dr Brock found minutes of the museum's trustees which 'show a concern for the inadequacies of the heating system, designed by James Watt – the dampness of the building, its lack of adequate light, theft of lead from the roof and of minerals by the under-keeper's daughter – but the collections themselves receive scant attention.' In 1839 the commission reported that the anatomical collection was badly decayed, twenty years later they were told that the museum 'had not kept pace with the advance of science and did not afford those means of instruction which are desirable and which appear to have been contemplated by its donor,' and in 1877 the museum was being described in the university senate as 'buried treasure'.

In 1870 the university had shifted from the High Street (having sold the land to a railway company), re-established itself on Gilmorehill, overlooking Kelvingrove in a building designed by Giles Gilbert Scott, and the museum was rehoused within it. But the university could not afford the removal costs. They decided to sell the coin collection – reckoned in 1807 to have been second only to the French royal collection, and still one of this country's four finest – and the library, with the approval of the University Commissioners who said they 'could not be considered for use for educational purposes'. There was an outcry, and the funds were found partly from a public subscription without having to sell either collection.

Although Hunter himself kept meticulous accounts of his collection, nobody much bothered in the nineteenth century so that the identification of original material is difficult now, but with notable exemptions – his mummies have gone, a Stubbs painting he had has disappeared – the Hunter collection is more or less intact.

The museum still suffers from financial privation, but it is a museum of the present with its galleries gradually recast, and now there is refreshment at 'William Hunter's Coffee House'. The remarkable collections of geology, coins, anatomy, ethnography and natural history which Hunter put together still form the backbone, and have been added to. The art collection was so important that it was made into a separate art gallery, which now holds a re-creation of the house of Glasgow architect Charles Rennie Mackintosh. For a boffin's collection of curiosities, the Hunterian has a remarkably wide appeal; over 100,000 people visit the museum and gallery every year.

The other Hunterian Museum gets less than a tenth of that number of annual visitors, and as a teaching and research collection is normally only accessible to interested members of the public by appointment. But John Hunter's collection, buried on the first floor of the Royal College of Surgeons in Lincoln's Inn Fields, London, opposite the Sir John Soane Museum, is no less fascinating.

John Hunter was the youngest of ten children, and ten years younger than his brother William. As a boy he was much more interested in the countryside than school, and started his career as a cabinet maker in Glasgow. Then he went to London to assist this brother with his anatomical dissections, astonishing the elder Hunter with his skill. He learned surgery, and in the early 1750s began assisting William with the lecturing, but he was not as gregarious and preferred to study. He gave up a place at Oxford University because he did not want to 'stuff Latin and Greek at the university' and thirty years later when this was held against him he wrote: 'Jesse Foot accuses me of not understanding the dead languages; but I could teach him that on the dead body which he never knew in any language dead or living.'

In 1760, he left the anatomy school because of his poor health, and some months later he became an army surgeon serving in France and Portugal, where he had ample time to study flora and geology, which he brought back to form a collection. On his return he created his own anatomy school in London and, far from being disenchanted by surgery in favour of another branch of medicine as his brother had been, he rose in eminence and in 1768 he became Surgeon at St George's Hospital. He began to take pupils, among whom was Edward Jenner, the discoverer of vaccine, who was to be a lifelong friend.

Far from 'making do', as conventional lecturers did, with animal carcases as substitutes for the human body, Hunter made important discoveries with his animal experiments – in toxicology for instance (he admitted to having 'poisoned some thousands of animals').

In 1776 John Hunter was appointed surgeon-extraordinary to the king, and about this time was making the first studies of dentistry, but all the time he was collecting, and at about the time of his brother's death, 1783, he built a museum to house them. He spent a fortune, perhaps only a little more modest than his brother's, on collecting, and sent explorers to bring back specimens.

'Hunter's museum differs from others in existence during the latter part of the eighteenth century,' wrote Elizabeth Allen, curator of the museum, in 1974, 'as it was not merely a collection of exhibits but an illustration of his theories and, in particular, of the constant adaptation in living things of structure to function. It was, in fact, John Hunter's unwritten book.' He was the opposite of William in that he preferred to demonstrate than to expound, and some of the most famous surgeons of the day came under his tutelage – Astley Cooper of Guy's Hospital and John Abernethy of St Bartholomew's were among them.

After Jenner had returned to his beloved countryside in 1773, Hunter carried on a fascinating correspondence with him until his own death in 1793, letters which spoke of experiments, curious medical cases and discoveries. 'I am obliged to you for thinking of me especially in my natural history,' Hunter wrote. 'I shall be glad of your observations on the Cuckow and upon the breeding of toads; be as particular as you possibly can.' Hunter nagged on about 'cuckows', and eventually Jenner did a study on their habits, proving that they squatted in other birds' nests, an observation which got him elected a Fellow of the Royal Society but which was not finally accepted until the 1920s.

Jenner would send specimens for experiments, and also items of country fare which he knew Hunter enjoyed. Sometimes, though, he would forget to add a letter to the parcel: 'I thank you for the Fish but I should thank you more if you had let me know who it came from,' chided Hunter. 'Somebody sent me a cheese with a Fish upon it, it was perhaps you; you know I hate to be puzzled.'

John Hunter's collection was unique and of incalculable scholarly value, and he decreed in his will that it should be kept as an entity after his death. To be conservator of the Hunterian became a major stepping stone in the career of a Victorian science curator. Sir Richard Owen became the second conservator before moving on to the British Museum's natural history department, and the fourth was Sir William Flower, who followed Owen to the Natural History Museum to become its first director and one of the greatest Victorian innovators in museum thinking.

The museum itself was badly damaged by bombs in 1941, and more than half of the physiological specimens were destroyed. It took more than twenty years to piece the museum together again, but it was restored as exactly as possible to the arrangements laid down in Hunter's original catalogues.

Hunter was interested in people of unusual stature, and the museum has the 7 foot 7 inch skeleton of the Irish giant Charles Byrne – also known as O'Brian – who had come to England to be exhibited as 'the tallest man in the world', but died suddenly in London in 1783.

'There is no verified account of how Hunter came by O'Brian's body, but there are shades of Dr Knox about it, the most popular version being,' wrote Miss Allen, 'that Byrne, knowing that the anatomists were anxious to acquire his body, arranged on his death to be placed in a lead coffin and buried at sea. However, Hunter bribed the undertakers with £500 to deliver the body to him, and then prepared the skeleton in the large boiler in his Earls Court home.' Byrne's skeletal feet can be seen in Reynolds's portrait of Hunter.

The two Hunterian museums are quite different, as were the two men, but any possibility of them coming together dissolved in 1780. The experiments of the brothers overlapped from time to time, and when John Hunter was studying the development of human foetuses and claimed to have discovered the nature of the placenta's circulation, William claimed to have discovered it earlier. They spoke again only once, when William was on his deathbed.

## *The Manchester Museum*

The Manchester Museum had its foundation, like hundreds of municipal ones, in the zeal of a local society, this time the Society of Natural History. But instead of the local authority stepping in when it ran into difficulties, it was Manchester University which came to the rescue, and one wonders how different it would have been had the Corporation taken it over, as it did the Manchester City Art Gallery in 1882.

The collections began in 1821 with the foundation of the natural history society. Industrial Manchester may seem an odd place for a love of flora to be nurtured, but botany was, after all behind the great wealth the town was enjoying: its prosperity was due to the cotton plant, which was turned into cloth with the use of fuel provided by fossilised organic matter, coal.

Manchester was, in fact, something of a botanical centre, with the university making a speciality of it and wealthy enthusiasts making such contributions as Leo Grindon's herbarium, with which he pioneered adult education in the subject and from which he distributed seeds and plants to bring colour to the yards of the miserable back-to-backs which still characterize the place for us, even though most of them are long gone.

The botanical collections developed an international reputation and a collection to go with it. In 1835 one of the ubiquitous neo-classical buildings which announced the enhanced status of industrial revolution towns was built for the museum in Peter Street, and fifteen years later the natural history specimens were joined by those of the Manchester Geological and Mining Society.

It was in 1862 that the Manchester Society for Natural History and their museum struck the financial rocks, and the city itself turned down the collections when they were offered. It was Owen's College, which was to become the nucleus of the university, which saw the potential for students in the museum, and took it over in 1867 with the pledge that it should also be available for the general public as before.

The same names keep appearing through the museums' story, particularly the names of architects – Soane, Barry, Fowke. In 1888 a new building by Alfred Waterhouse, architect of the Natural History Museum, was built for the museum in Oxford Road to make it an integral part of the university, which is also there.

Archaeology too was becoming something of a speciality for the museum by the 1890s, particularly Egyptian archaeology. University College London received probably the finest finds of one of the greatest Egyptologists, Sir William Flinders Petrie, which form the Petrie Museum mentioned earlier. He was sponsored by a Manchester textile magnate called Jesse Howarth. Howarth made sure that a lot of Petrie's finds came Manchester way. The first sites to be excavated were towns, rather than the burial sites which had caused such a stir and were to create a sensation in the 1920s when tombs such as Tutenkhamun's were opened, and Manchester got many fascinating items of everyday life from up to 5,000 years ago.

By the turn of the century there were also tomb finds coming – such as the compete tomb-group of the 'Two Brothers' at Rifeh of about 1900 BC, and cartonnage masks and portrait panel covers which covered the faces of the buried dead – so that by 1912 the museum needed an extension. This was designed by Alfred Waterhouse's son, and another extension, to house the oriental and ethnological collections, was built in 1927 by a third generation of Waterhouses.

So popular did the archaeological collections become beyond the university's own faculties that annual public lectures were given by Professor Flinders Petrie himself, and the Manchester Egyptian Association was formed. But it was also a centre of research, which university museums inevitably are, and it was at Manchester, under the first curator of the Egyptology collection, Dr Margaret Murray, that the first major multi-disciplinary investigation of mummified remains was undertaken when the mummies of the 'Two Brothers' were unwrapped. It took an hour and a half, and was watched in complete silence by an audience of 500 – each of whom was allowed to have a piece of the wrapping as a memento.

In 1973 the Manchester Egyptian Mummy Research Project was begun, led by Dr Rosalie David, and the museum made headlines two years later when another mummy was unwrapped, under the scrutiny of medical scientists as well as archaeologists this time. The team discovered a great deal about disease, dietary habits, living habits and causes of death, and established an International Mummy Data Bank at the museum collating information from around the world.

More recently, the same methodology was applied to the study of the earlier Petrie finds of Kahun, the town where the workmen who built the pyramids lived. The work of the Mummy Project came to a natural conclusion with a book, an international symposium, and an immensely popular exhibition, 'O, Osiris, Live For Ever'.

Following the local government reorganisation of 1974 the city council, which, despite its unwillingness to take full responsibility in the 1880s had given annual grants to the museum since 1895, handed over its financial commitment to the Greater Manchester Council, and this led to more important developments. A long-held hope to build a brand new museum foundered in the financial crises of the mid-70s, but the GMC and university became partners in renovating the former dental hospital next to the museum, which was opened as a new administration block in 1977.

The collections were becoming vast, and a travelling exhibition programme was begun to give reserve objects and specimens an airing outside the confines of the museum, and even abroad. 'The Manchester Museum is a rich storehouse of treasures and not even the museum display galleries, less still the contents of this exhibition, can hope to indicate more than a fraction of the wealth of the collections,' said its present director, Alan Warhurst. 'In total there are about nine million specimens collected between the museum's foundation in 1821 and the present day. The scale of these collections presents considerable logistical problems, both in orderly storage and information retrieval.' Using the university's computer centre, the museum has now established the information on a database.

All university museums suffered in the late 1980s from lack of funds. Manchester lost a bulwark with the disbanding of the Greater Manchester Council in 1985, and further pressures on university grants made life difficult for all these boffins' cupboards – to the extent that one university, Newcastle, sold its unique collection of oriental art and ethnography.

But Manchester Museum has continued to develop despite the difficulties. It was the focus of national attention when Lindow Man, the Iron Age body found preserved in the Cheshire peat, came here for initial examination. In 1987 it won the Museum of the Year award, and thanks to sponsorship got new mammal galleries in 1988 – in which the boffins of the future could try out their skills by building their own mammals on a computer.

The university museums often suffer from being considered only another department of the university in funding, so that a university which has little interest in its museum will allocate meagre funds to it. The Museums and Galleries Commission had hopes that it would persuade the government to change the funding system so that their essential scholarship would remain the central method, but their survival would depend on being popular with the university senate as it shared out its grant from the University Grants Committee. Some of these museums, like the incomparable Ashmolean, have had to draw in their horns and even lose curatorial posts; others, such as Wales's oldest museum, the Royal Institute at Swansea, may even be lost completely.

Some, such as Reading University's Museum of Rural Life, which is the public face of its Institute of Agricultural History, may make partnerships with other museums, non-university-based and less beleaguered, to create money-making diversifications. But such museums and their deep roots of learning are the kernal of British museum life now as much as they were in 1683 when the Ashmolean opened.

Alan Warhurst's remarks about his own museum ought to be a definition for all university museums: 'The Manchester Museum is now, at one and the same time, an integral part of University teaching and research and a free educational and entertainment centre for anyone who cares to enter its doors.'

# 6. '. . . and how's thieving?'

*Faced with recalcitrant councils, baulking bureaucracies or just apathy, creators of museums have often had to resort to picaresque means to establish their collections in their rightful places. The chapter salutes some of the museum pirates who succeeded, at Hull, Beamish, Wigan and Springburn in Glasgow.*

THE great tradition of municipal collections, reflecting the town or city and its people, seems almost as much a part of our community as the parish church itself. But the great municipal museums grew from the boom of a century ago, no more, and owe their existence to a civic enthusiasm for historical identity which blazed then as it does now, and in many cases to individuals who combined antiquarianism, often self-taught, with a brand of swash-buckling determination to establish their museums.

## *Tom Sheppard: Hull City Museums and Art Galleries*

Tom Sheppard was such a man. Single-handed he took the collections of Hull's Literary and Philosphical Society and, over forty years, created a collection which was spread among nine different museums, and if not the first municipal collection became one of the finest. His story is not unique; there have been many Tom Sheppards – in fact, he was very much in the mould of Sir Henry Cole who gave us the national museums' cradle, South Kensington.

Twelve months after Sheppard retired and four years before he died, almost the whole of his life's work was destroyed in a single bombing raid on the town in 1941. But his chief accomplishment, the establishment of museums in the personality of Hull, survived and, far from dying, has been consolidated and built upon.

Thomas Sheppard was born the oldest of ten children in 1876, the son of a schoolteacher. He left elementary school at thirteen to become a railway clerk, eventually at the Dock Offices which were to become the Town Docks Museum almost a century after his birth. An amateur geologist, he joined the Hull Geological Society in 1893, began writing papers on geological subjects in 1895, became secretary of the Hull Scientific and Field Naturalists' Club in 1898 and was elected a Fellow of the Geological Society in 1900.

In 1901, at the age of twenty-four, with no experience of running museums at all, Sheppard was appointed the first curator of Hull's Municipal Museum. The corporation did not see his lack of experience as a serious handicap: what they were chiefly interested in was the new art gallery which would go on top of the museum. For the Literary and Philosophical Society had, in the manner of such clubs formed over the previous century or so, established its own museum in Albion Street. The child Tom himself had often paid his penny to visit, frequently the only visiting soul there in the ramshackle old place. The city had acquired it as a cheap, central building in which they could put the art gallery.

Public subscription had provided the money for the art gallery, little was spared for the museum. In fact, on his appointment Sheppard was told 'that the museum was merely a means to obtaining an art gallery, that [he] could come at ten, smoke [his] cigar, leave when [he] liked, answer any enquiries that were necessary, look after the specimens, but on no account spend money, as it was required for the pictures.'

He seems to have been paid £150 a year ('In those days the salary did not encourage the cigar-smoking habit,' he later remarked) and the total expenditure for wages, rent, fittings, heating and lighting was no more than £100. He did not believe in overstaffing, and in 1906 when he opened his second museum he had a total staff of four, including himself; by 1938, when he was working on his ninth museum, the full-time staff had risen to five. Nevertheless, Sheppard managed to be in debt to the tune of another £250 in the first year, 'a habit which has been more or less chronic ever since excepting on one memorable year when, as very occasionally happens, the question of an increase of salary arose,' he related towards the end of his career.

> I was told by my chairman that if I had the money in hand at the year end there would be no difficulty. By holding over rent accounts, and by other temporary measures, we actually had a balance in hand on the following year, but as I did not get my advance of salary and the balance in hand was lost to the committee and put in the general melting pot, I received a lesson I have never forgotten.

When Sheppard took it over the 'Lit and Phil' was badly run down. His first action was to close it, reopening on 2 June 1902, eighteen months later, completely recast, labelled and catalogued. It was also free, and instantly popular. In the first week there were 1,700 visitors, and by the end of the first year there was an average attendance of 2,000 a week. For two winter evenings a week he opened from 7.30 to 9.30, and from 1908 opened on Sunday afternoons as well.

The museums' primary role in the community was an instructing and improving one, Sheppard believed, and he gave hundreds of lectures to schoolchildren. He saw museums as a means of reflecting the city's pride in itself, and of attracting visitors from beyond. His collecting policy was clear: all the objects must be of scholarly importance, be relevant to the community and have educational value for the museum users. 'A chinaman's hat, a lion's claw, a piece of Queen Elizabeth's walking stick, a double-headed pig, a stone from Jerusalem, etc., etc, are all very well in their way, and may amuse a certain class of the community for the time being,' he once wrote, 'but what good can a glance at scores and scores of such miscellaneous objects, crowded together in cases do to those who have the fortune, or misfortune, to pass through the building?'

Sheppard made it plain that he believed objects should come from within the district whenever possible: 'There is now no good reason why valuable objects found in the neighbourhood should be sent to museums and collections elsewhere . . . within recent years many specimens of altogether exceptional interest have been forwarded to London and other places, some even out of the country altogether and irrevocably lost, so far as bringing them back to Hull is concerned,' he said at the opening of his museum. He made his catchment area the East Riding of Yorkshire, and spent many frustrating years trying to get items from, for instance, the British Museum which he felt belonged in Hull.

But he had a buccaneering style of acquisition. Most of the society's objects had been labelled as 'lent' by certain benefactors, a situation which Sheppard found unsatisfactory. While the art gallery was being built on top of the Albion Street museum 'the elements played havoc with the specimens below. I suppose during that time the "lent by" labels were washed off; and when I finally rearranged the collection there was not one left, and I will say that it is to the credit of the people of Hull to report that, with one exception, there has never been an application for any object said to have been on loan.'

It was during those early days that Sheppard was approached by a professor of Leeds University with the words: 'Well Sheppard, and how's thieving?'

In a 1923 after-dinner speech he was described as using the techniques of Viking raiders:

> . . . having, like William the Conqueror, an ingrained habit of annexing objects first and asking, or not asking, permission as seemed expedient afterwards . . . a habit which is believed to have reduced to despair authorities of other museums within Mr Sheppard's sphere of influence who, with a due respect for red tape and the conventions, found themselves handicapped in the race for the acquisition of rare finds and valuable ethnological specimens.'

He bought when he had to, but would negotiate long and hard on a price and even longer if there was the hope of a gift. He developed a network of contacts throughout Yorkshire and Lincolnshire, and his first job of the day was to scour the newspapers for new finds. If a flint axe was reported as having been turned up in the region, an offer by telegram would often have the object on its way to Hull before the local museum even knew of the discovery.

He was a passionate believer in free museums, and attacked the art gallery for its initial policy of charging. The only section of the community excluded from the Albion Street museum was small, scruffy boys with dirty shoes, a policy rigorously implemented by the first museum attendant, Edmund Raper.

Sheppard bullied, cajoled, persuaded, pleaded and begged on behalf of his collections, but perhaps his greatest triumph was the acquisition of the Mortimer Collection, comprising 66,000 objects, mostly archaeological, gathered together by two brothers, local corn merchants who were immensely successful archaeologists as well. The collection was kept at their home in Driffield, some 15 miles north of Hull, and its importance was famous, so famous that even before the Albion Street museum came under Sheppard's control there was a good deal of interest in acquiring the collection the Mortimers were concerned that it, like so many other collections, would disappear south or even abroad.

'Surely,' wrote J. R. Mortimer in 1900, 'the East Riding possesses some governing body which, before it is too late, will see the wisdom of permanently possessing the collections, and handing them down to future governing bodies as a source of education and a treasure of permanent value to the district.'

When Mortimer died in 1911 Hull had a year to buy the collection, and the price set by the Mortimer trustees was £3,000. The city would not pay, and Sheppard roundly attacked the councillors in the local paper for their meanness. But rather than give up he renegotiated with the Mortimer trustees, and his policy of attrition ground the price down to £1,000, provided the Mortimer Collection was exhibited in its own building. While the corporation was pondering on this, another friend of Sheppard's, Col. G. H. Clarke, broke the deadlock: in May Sheppard truculently wrote to Reginald Smith of the British Museum, 'Did I tell you we had the Driffield Collection offered for a thousand pounds and a Hull gentleman has found the money?'

Nevertheless, it took him another sixteen years to get the collection catalogued and on display in its own building, formerly a second art gallery superseded by the present Ferens Art Gallery which brought the whole municipal art collection together in the gift of a local MP.

The 1909 story of the Brigg Boat illustrates even better Sheppard's mixture of tenacity and swiftness at the crucial point. The largest logboat ever found in Europe was excavated in Lincolnshire and placed by its owner in a specially built exhibition shed at Brigg. Sheppard had repeatedly asked for the boat to be shifted to Hull Museum, and the owner had declined. For a brief moment, though, he relented, and Sheppard had the boat on the road to Hull in hours. The next day the owner had changed his mind and sent a telegram demanding 'DO NOT MOVE BOAT'. Tom Sheppard wired back 'BOAT ALREADY IN HULL'.

But Thomas Sheppard collected museums as avidly as he did specimens. More, he invented museums to suit a purpose. The first Hull Municipal Museum opened in 1902, and in 1906 Wilberforce House, dedicated to the local-born abolitionist William Wilberforce, opened. In 1910 the vacated Art Gallery above the museum became the Natural History Museum. That same year the original 'Lit and Phil' collections had been so much augmented by his own additions that Sheppard realised he needed a new museum for them and persuaded a local trawler owner and philanthropist, Christopher Pickering, to build him one in Pickering Park which opened in 1912.

In 1925, in what was the Corn Exchange and is now the Archaeology Transport

Museum, Sheppard opened what he described as 'the first permanent commercial museum in the country', the Commerce and Transport Museum, to tell the story of local firms and their processes (mostly paid for by the firms themselves), and complemented by a small fleet of motor cars from the early motor museum in London (which the Science Museum eventually took control of), cars which are still there but whose presence in Hull has never been fully explained.

Following the achievements in Scandinavia with open air museums in which buildings themselves became specimens and objects of curiosity, Sheppard created a social history museum in the Easington Tithe Barn which opened in 1928, filled with Hull Corporation's objects supplied by the Municipal Museum's curator and run by the East Riding Antiquarian Society.

Behind the City Hall had been a second art gallery whose collections the new Ferens Art Gallery had taken over, and in it Sheppard put the Mortimer Collection of Prehistoric Antiquities which opened in 1929.

A railway worker at the start of his career, Tom Sheppard never lost his enthusiasm for it. At first his railway collection fitted into the Commerce and Transport Museum, but before long it outgrew it and in 1933, in Paragon Station, he opened the Railway Museum. Almost immediately after the opening the words 'Railway Museum' was added to the heading of his notepaper, on which he lost no time in writing to the North Eastern Railway Company suggesting that, as an official collector of railway memorabilia, he ought to have a free rail pass.

The now-famous street in York's Castle Museum, opened in 1938, is widely credited with being the first authentic reconstruction of a bygone thoroughfare. Sheppard's 'Old Time' street museum behind Wilberforce House was, he claimed, first, but it was never officially opened to the public. He reconstructed a local pub, the King's Head, a tobacconist's, a smithy, a wood turner's shop, a pharmacy, a hotel called the White Lion and even acquired a shop front from Lewes in Sussex.

Much of what Sheppard created was lost to the World War II bombs of a single raid though some of his collections were being excavated in 1989, but his battles, his frustrations, his triumphs will be recognisable to many modern curators of local authority museums.

How familiar this sounds: 'There is little wonder that at the end of the first year the expenditure exceeded income. This has been a chronic complaint with us ever since, though just now the chairman is probably effectively putting the screw on by threatening to knock it off.' Sheppard was talking about his first year, 1901, and speaking at the 1913 Museums Association conference at Hull, adding: 'This year we shall probably be better off as I am not having any expenses for attending a museums conference.'

Talking then of how he got his job, he said: 'After what seemed a very long delay applications were invited for the post of curator and one of our experts and myself were selected as candidates. Possibly because I knew the least about museums I was appointed.'

His unfailing enthusiasm made him many friends, among whom he numbered celebrities of such diversity as Colette and Marie Stopes. He wrote prodigiously on a wide range of antiquarian subjects whose common feature was the East Riding. He retired in 1941 and died in 1945.

His *modus vivendi* – the search for sponsors, donors, 'angels', friends in high places, friends in auction houses, friends in other museums, the over-riding belief in the educational vocation of his creations, the creative element of never giving up on an idea until it has had a chance to succeed, as well as shortage of grant and the need to not only preserve the integrity of the collections but enhance them with new acquisitions – are the same as distinguished successors among Britain's museums of all classes, and Hull's museums have continued to develop.

The Redcliffe-Maude report of the early 1970s, which brought the birth of so many of our municipal museum services, was not the catalyst for the foundation of the Hull City Museums and Art Galleries, just the formalising agent. That year, 1975, the Town Docks Museum opened, and with the Sporun Light Ship opening to the public in 1987 and the Old Grammar School opening as a community museum in 1988, the family now consists of seven museums. The first phase of a new transport museum was due to open in August 1989.

'In Hull,' Thomas Sheppard said, 'we take second place to none for the opinion we hold of the value of the work our museums are doing.'

## *Frank Atkinson: Beamish and Cherryburn*

Frank Atkinson is almost a natural successor to Tom Sheppard, although there is nothing piratical about the creator of the North of England Open Air Museum, Museum of the Year in 1986 and European Museum of the Year in 1987, and better known as Beamish. The dream was the same, and he developed the notion of transplanting buildings to a controlled setting where they could be made to tell an historical story. But Mr Atkinson went several steps further. His museum is a regional one, financed by eight different local authorities instead of one, three counties, three cities and two districts.

Beamish could have been doomed by success to stagnate, and the stern approval which Geordies gave it in the early days could easily have tempted Mr Atkinson to modify his dream, much as Tom Sheppard could have modified his because of funds starvation, and opted for the easy life which he was offered.

Before Beamish was even open it had a weekend exhibition, called 'Museum in the Making', which attracted 50,000 visitors, and on the bank Holiday Monday before Lord Eccles, then the Arts Minister, cut the ribbon in May 1972, Beamish was attracting more visitors than all the other museums in the region except for Mr Atkinson's former charge, the Bowes Museum.

'Piled on shelves in once elegant rooms are prewar wireless sets, a clutch of miners' lamps, a dustheap of vacuum cleaners, four lines of ancient typewriters, a spinning wheel and a group of old gramophones,' Ronald Faux reported in *The Times* at the time of the opening. 'Out of doors, the collection becomes even more awesome,' he continued. 'There are redundant fire engines, a dismantled railway station, and a steam navvy set on vast caterpillar feet – 100 tons of wheezing strength with a bucket that can take seven-ton bites at the ground.'

Beamish was the country's first open air museum, Frank Atkinson told Faux, who seemed no less impressed than those early visitors, describing it as 'A place where people can look into the past and see how things worked.' In fact it was not quite the first open air museum, which had been common enough in Scandinavia since the late nineteenth century. The Welsh Folk Museum had been going at St Fagans since 1947, the Avoncroft Museum of Buildings, Bromsgrove, opened in 1963 and the Weald and Downland at Singleton, West Sussex, in 1969. But when he was just twenty-three, at the very start of his career, Frank went to Norway. 'I remember standing on a steepish hillside at Lillehammer in central Norway, overlooking a lake, a large area where they'd rebuilt quite a lot of wooden buildings, and I remember leaning againt this bridge thinking "We must do this in England".'

At twenty-five he was already the youngest museum director in the country, first at Wakefield, then at Halifax, and in 1958 he took control of the almost bankrupt Bowes Museum at Barnard Castle, got Durham County Council to take it over from the beleagured trustees and transformed it. Durham was one of the first counties to be given power to run a museum, after an Order in Council, and while they were at it, suggested young Atkinson, 'the county council surely would want to do something about its country history as well; now they had the chance, and there was nothing preserved anywhere. Why not do something in parallel with this beautiful fine and decorative arts museum. They said "Great, let's do it".'

He created a travelling exhibition called 'Museum With A Difference', which would go to different towns and villages each Saturday, with him giving a talk in the evening, and next day two vans would come, one to take away the exhibition, the other to take away the objects which had been given. But nothing more happened for some years; Frank Atkinson continued to transform the Bowes Museum, and his social history collection grew in its store, an ex-barracks at Brancepeth.

Then there was a sudden scare that more local authority reorganisation was in the offing, and he persuaded the county council chairman and a local MP to get all the county authorities in the north of England round a table. More than a dozen representatives came and pledged support, some dropping out later, but a working party was set up and Mr Atkinson used its report to outline his ideas:

> An open-air museum serves to illustrate vividly the way of life, the institutions, customs and material equipment of the ordinary people. It is an attempt to make the history of a region live, by showing typical features of that history as accurately as possible.[1]

There was another scare in 1968 when a new Conservative administration at Newcastle cut the project from their budget. 'We practically collapsed again, but by various means we clawed back and eventually Newcastle decided to come in again,

[1] *Policy for a Regional Open-Air Museum*, 1966.

which made it once more possible.' In 1970 the agreement was signed and Frank Atkinson was appointed director and began work getting his collections to Beamish. He had seen the site years before and watched it: his working party had made a list of thirty, Beamish was at the top and the owners, the Coal Board, were persuaded by him to hang on to it until the museum was ready to buy it.

At first it was no more than the collection in Beamish Hall described by Ronald Faux with such enthusiasm, which is now the administration block, with a 200-acre empty canvas, but gradually the enormous dream of twenty years before materialised.

What he created was a microcosm of the community of North-Eastern England, Geordieland. There is Old Town with the Georgian Ravensworth Terrace, brought from Bensham, Gateshead, in which a mayor of Gateshead, Alexander Gillies, once lived. Now a solicitor has his practice there, based on the offices of a great Tynesider and reformer of the early twentieth century, Robert Spence Watson – on whose shelves can be seen the file relating to the affairs of Sir Robert Shafto, the Bobby Shafto who was the subject of an electioneering song of the 1760s which entered into nursery lore. It is a nice irony that the heiress of Brancepeth, where the Beamish collection was in gestation for its first twelve years, is alleged to have died for the love of Bobby Shafto.

Next door is the dentist's of the 1920s, complete with a typical waiting room display of skulls and jaws which must have been enough to convince many a sufferer that toothache was preferable to the horrors beyond the surgery door; then comes a typical family home of the same period, a fire blazing perpetually in the front parlour.

The Sun Inn came from High Bondgate in Bishop Auckland, and sells Newcastle's famous Federation bitter, and behind the pub is the 'livery stables where four mighty shires live and are cared for. I found Barron (*sic*), 17.2 hands high and six years old, being combed by a girl groom of about eight hands' height and standing on a bench. 'How far shall I go?' she asked the head groom who was standing over her. 'Till you run out of hair,' he said.

The stationer's and printer's is a shop downstairs, while upstairs is a collection of printing equipment which produced everything from handbills to newspapers during the fifty years represented at Beamish.

Across the street is the Co-op, once the centre of thousands offender communities which may never have survived without them in the bitter 1920s. This one came from Annfield Plain and has a grocery, a drapery and a hardware shop in it.

There is also a working drift mine, with a row of colliers' cottages (from Francis Street, Hetton-le-Hole, near Sunderland) filled with the actual furnishings and household necessities from four decades, each cottage representing a different one, in which housewives bake and sew for the benefit of tourists now as they did then to keep a poor family in health and dignity. Home Farm has rare breeds of animals being husbanded.

The railway station comes from Rowley, near Consett, and its iron bridge from Howden-le-Wear, Crook, and the whole ensemble is linked by a 1925 tram from Gateshead and, in the summer, a 1913 open-top bus.

Frank Atkinson retired in 1987, but not before he had pulled off a remarkable development. Beamish needed a visitors' centre to provide a focus for the whole museum, and it needed a substantial car park to accommodate the vehicles bringing 300,000 visitors a year. The first was provided by the acquisition of a Georgian stable block from Greencroft Hall Estate near Lanchester, but the car park was a considerable problem. The space needed for it would cost £30,000 to prepare, money he had not got, and it was sitting on two seams of coal. He solved it by making a deal with the National Coal Board (as British Coal was then called), who took enough coal to pay for the car park. He opened the visitors' centre and car park on the day he retired.

Frank Atkinson's successor, Peter Lewis, was a surprise choice, but he had come from another remarkable success in the realm of local authority museums. He had initiated and presided over the unebbing popularity of Wigan Pier, which was to provide another gear change in the progress of museums in the 1980s. In a restored nineteenth-century canal warehouse, Wigan Pier tells the story of the town's social and industrial life in the first decade of this century, and was the first museum to get Equity approval for its cast which acts out life in a typical schoolroom of the time.

Wigan Pier has shown that a museum can revive a moribund urban centre by attracting people into it and the transport, catering and shopping services they will require. It has become a template for communities to revive themselves, and a keystone to build inner city developments on, for Wigan is now attracting new industry to its area because its appeal can draw management staff who see it is a pleasant place to live, a bizarre twist of fate in the shadow of the mill and canal workers whose bitter way of life the museum celebrates.

Peter Lewis had already had an unconventional background before he was appointed by Wigan's education committee – he had been a manager for Littlewoods stores, then marketing director for a Manchester theatre company. He began his Wigan project in 1983, opened it in 1985 and in 1987 was stepping into Mr Atkinson's shoes. Those shoes had belonged to something of a legend in museum circles, but Mr Lewis wares them comfortably. He sees his role – and role-play has much to do with his own vision of museums – as a new dynamo for the Atkinson Mark I engine. He gave the Co-op store as an example:

> It is wonderful re-creation of the past, with demonstrators – not actors – 'serving' behind the counters, but their merchandise is information, having been intensively schooled in the kinds of goods people bought, what was available, what everything was for. I understand why Frank wanted to build a Co-op and show it as we do. I think my role as the second man in is to find a way of explaining what the Co-op was about, why it was formed, why it collapsed and the people that were anti the Co-op at the time. I might have to do it with publications or with a separate display area, I could do it by moving away from the present demonstrators and use actors instead. What I'm not going to do is take a third of the artefacts away and replace them with information labels.

Beamish has an enormous collection of objects, of which perhaps 5 per cent is on display, and one of the museum's long term projects is to show them, in Mr Lewis's words, 'in such a way as to do away with the wretched rope and brass hook. It operates on Frank's "green spot" system – stuff which we have a lot of or are particularly solid and it wouldn't be upsetting if they wore out, are marked with a green spot. They don't have to be nailed down or put under glass.'

In the late 1980s museums such as Beamish and Wigan Pier were being severely criticised for presenting an idealised view of history, one which obeyed the call for nostalgia but did nothing for the demand in education circles for realism. Peter Lewis debated this point:

> Is it just nostalgia? I'd commit suicide if I thought it was. It's been promoted for the value of nostalgia – for or five years ago the leaflet had as its headline '200 acres of nostalgia, come and step into the past at Beamish'. That isn't the intention, but I think it was part of the marketing.
>
> The problem is that over the few years words have got debased and nostalgia is one of them, just as 'heritage' is being debased. Nostalgia actually means 'returning home with pain', and if it means that now I'm not ashamed for Beamish to be about nostalgia.

Purists fear that the obvious enjoyment of the people who flock to the likes of Beamish and Wigan Pier may be obscuring not only the research that goes into the displays (and, in the case of Wigan, performances), but also the information which is being absorbed. Are the customers getting the full value from the resource, or encouraged just to scratch the surface? Peter Lewis came from a background where clarity and an understanding of the audience/customer were the key to success, and he applied a good deal of both to his first museum venture. They had artefacts, they were going into period settings, but there was a new dimension:

> We wanted to convey, for instance, without masses of statistics, the idea that for us to live so long and for infant mortality to have gone, is very recent, and things like sulphur drugs and penicillin didn't come into practical use until the 1930s. But if you do the statistics in the standard way you look at the average death age and its twenty-four, and the average marriage age is twenty-six – so people got married two years after they were buried.

So, instead of explaining all this in labels which would never be read, he brought in actors and incorporated it into their scripts which brought an element of realism as well as a much more easily assimilated distribution of facts. But research still provided shocks:

> Let's suppose that these people survived to the age of twenty and we took their lives on from there; in women's terms we found that you go to work, you keep working as well as having children, and life expectancy from twenty was through to forty-two or forty-three, during which you might have had sixteen pregnancies of which nine might have been successful and have never stopped working. Throughout the 1900s there were more women working in the cotton industry and the mines than there were men – male unemployment was far greater.

Much of that ethic is being incorporated into the new Beamish features. Old Town is to get a sweet shop, a chemist's and other shops, there will be another farm; while Pockerley Farm was opening the tramway was being extended, and there was to be a resource centre costing £1,350,000. Half the total cost of £3,500,000 was coming from an appeal run by a development trust – a local authority museum by now indistinguishable in its mode of operations from successful independents like Quarry Bank Mill or Ironbridge Gorge.

Also in the plan is a chapel in the mining community, due to open in 1989. 'We ought to be saying something about its life, how it served the community,' said Mr Lewis. 'In this part of England we ought to be saying something about how Methodist chapels in particular trained trade unionists and Labour politicians.'

A school of about 1880 from nearby East Stanley was also due to open its rolls in 1990, with a rebuilt classroom, a lesson going on in a second, and a third for the schools' own role-play use. 'It isn't Peter Lewis changing what Frank did, it's Peter Lewis coming in and doing what Frank would have had to do.'

Frank Atkinson had started with a staff of five – himself, Rosemary Allen, now keeper of social history, a technician, a labourer and a secretary. When he retired early there were 200 staff. 'I felt I'd done everything I'd set out to do at Beamish, and there were lots of other things I wanted to do, so I moved on.'

He had already been appointed to the Museums and Galleries Commission, but he had another museum in his inside pocket. The birthplace of the great eighteenth-century naturalist and engraver Thomas Bewick was only two miles from Frank's own home. 'We'd set up a trust a year or two earlier to save his birthplace when the whole of the six acres plus the house came up for sale, and it wasn't even listed. Anyone could have bought it and knocked it down, and it seemed a pity – Thomas Bewick is probably the most important artist in the north-east, and the least one could do was try to save his birthplace and put him on the map.' They raised £85,000 and bought the place in 1986, then had to wait for more money to come in to restore it. Eventually it did, and his friend the Queen Mother – a frequent visitor both to 'dear Bowes' and Beamish – opened Cherryburn, Bewick's lifelong home, in June 1988. An extraordinary piece of luck had come the Birthplace Trust's way when one trustee, Ian Bain of the Tate Gallery, called at the Hancock Museum in Newcastle which had been bequeathed a lot of Bewick documents:

> In 1987 Ian had been coming up for a trustees' meeting, and he called in at the Hancock to look at some papers. He opened a box which had been brought out, and discovered this drawing by Robert Bewick, Thomas's son, of the interior of the first cottage. It looks as though, after they built the new house in the 1830s, they probably kept on Bewick's old cottage for farmworkers, and in the 1840s presumably changed it into a stable. Robert must have heard of this plan and gone up to make a sketch before his father's cottage was destroyed. Up to then we had no idea what the interior of the cottage looked like, and we were able to reconstruct it exactly according to the drawing.

Bewick's personality is used in this small way to do what the buildings of the Geordie worker had done at Beamish: to mirror the life of the region.

Frank Atkinson wanted to show the regional community of the industrial north-east of England its recent, largely unsung past, and there was a good deal of the

The old Ashmolean Museum, before it moved to its present Beaumont Street building.

The de Critz portrait of John Tradescant the Elder, whose collections, the first to be opened to the public, formed the nucleus of the Ashmolean Museum in Oxford.

Elias Ashmole, who acquired the Tradescant Collection and used it to found the Ashmolean Museum at Oxford in 1683.

Sir John Soane by Sir Thomas Lawrence.

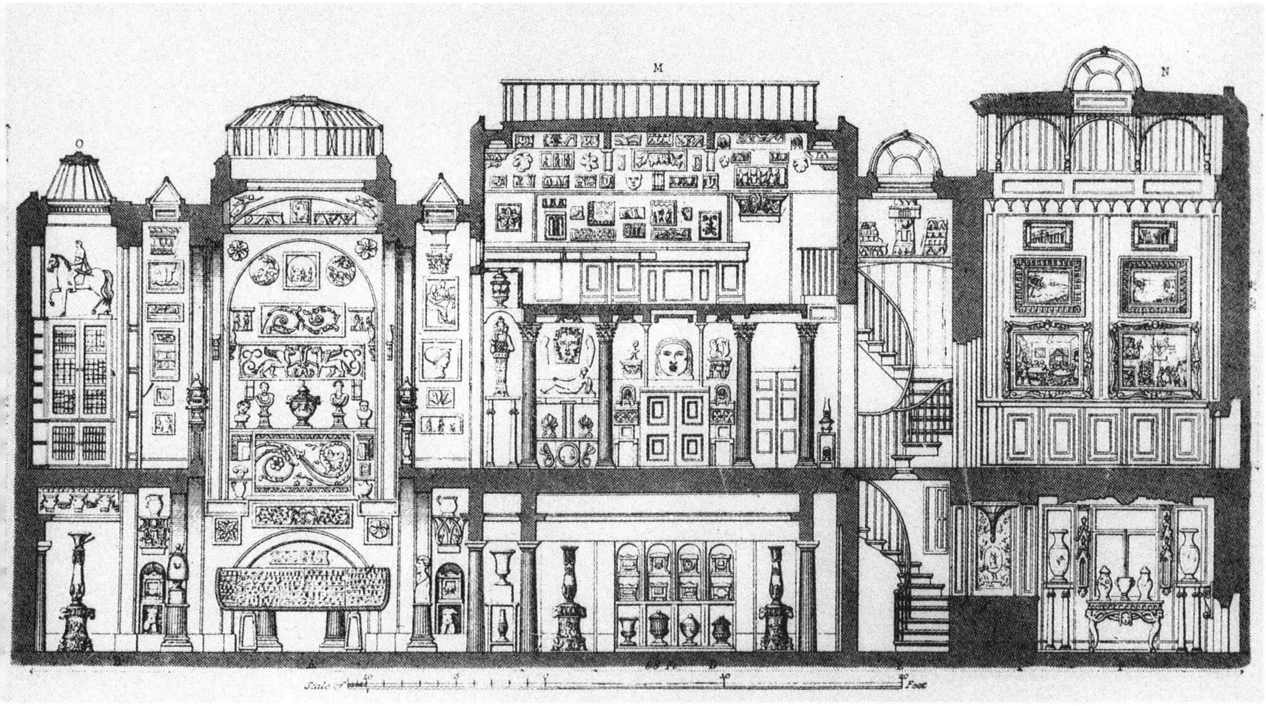

A section drawing of Sir John Soane's Museum in 1827.

The preserved dining room at Sir John Soane's Museum, Lincoln's Inn Fields, London.

Quex House, containing the Powell-Cotton Museum at Birchington, in Kent.

Part of the unique collection of Imperial Chinese porcelain in the Powell-Cotton Museum.

The four Yates & Thom twin furnace Lancashire boilers and Frank Pearn feed pumps at the British Engineerium, Hove.

missionary zeal in the way he went about it. Like a good pastor, he was not to be deflected from the path he knew to be the right one for his 'flock', the ordinary Geordies.

## *Mark O'Neill: Springburn*

Mark O'Neill has come out of the same mould as Frank Atkinson, a generation later. But his parish is Springburn in the industrial north-east corner of Glasgow, once the largest centre of locomotive manufacture in the world, now a sad maw of unemployment and deprivation.

Springburn had been a country village before the railways came, and like so much else the iron road changed its character, its size and its population. In the sixty years from 1840 it developed into an industrial suburb with some 30,000 souls, with 9,000 men working on steam engines and their carriages and wagons. Pottery, cables, rope and beer were made in Springburn in due course, and there were several iron and steelworks.

'I was much struck by the immense growth of Glasgow on its north side,' wrote Sir William Stirling Maxwell in his diary of 1875. 'The Cowlairs and Springburn I remember, the one a country house the other a squalid village, are now becoming stately suburbs.' By 1913 Springburn was squalid again, with disease stalking the population through overcrowding and bad sanitation. But Springburn was a tight-knit community and it thrived. It had its tenements and its villas, its public baths and cinemas, its library and its bandstand. In 1920 there were seven schools and sixteen churches. But it started to die when its life-blood, locomotive steam, was stopped. Tower blocks replaced 85 per cent of the pre-First World War housing, and many of the tower blocks were knocked down in the 1960s and 70s. All the cinemas and the baths have gone, ten of the churches and most of the tenements have been demolished. Like a final blow to despatch the stricken community, a motorway was driven straight through the centre of it. By the early 1980s Springburn was a depression black spot with 30 per cent unemployment and worse threatening. One brighter spot was the annual Springburn Festival which lifted folks' spirits, but in 1984 the community programme money which paid for it was stopped.

But the community itself survived, and was still determined. 'A lot of people involved in the festival wanted to go on doing something,' said Mark O'Neill, 'and they came up with the idea of a museum, and the local planning office identified a building.' It was the reading room of the local Ayr Street library, a listed building (one of two in the district) dating back to 1906 and the golden age of rail and Springburn.

Capital costs were expected to be £56,000, and running costs were estimated at a modest £40,000. 'Glasgow District Council couldn't give any money, so they applied for urban aid for inner city renewal from central government.' It meant that 25 per cent of the money they needed came from Glasgow District Council as sponsor – who would undertake to care for any collections should the museum close – and 75 per cent came from the Scottish Office.

The original museum committee represented all local interest groups, including community council, churches and tenants' associations, and relied on eight-to-ten committed individuals, local activists who worked without any formal constitution. The first chairman was a redundant steel worker, the secretary a chalky and the treasurer a grocer whose shop had been closed down.

'When I lived here,' said Mark O'Neill, 'I was the only person with a degree.' Having done two trained jobs in Irish museums after his University of Cork degree, he had studied on Britain's only museum curators' course at Leicester University. Then he answered the advertisement by the Springburn Community Museum Committee. 'No-one else from my class applied. Setting up a museum in an inner city area didn't seem attractive to most people, but the chance of setting up a new museum was irresistible to me, and all the things I've ever wanted to do with museums, to shake them out of their complacency, can be done here with virtually no money – you don't need money to do the right thing.'

Mr O'Neill found a committee with a definite idea of what they wanted in their museum, an idea which did not quite match his own:

> They had very traditional expectations – a museum about the past that would bring back memories of Springburn before it was devastated by urban recession. I've changed what they wanted quite a bit, but I think I've brought them with me all the way.
>
> I felt that they thought the museum should be for people who had an interest in the past, whereas I think that the museum should seek to represent the entire history of the community up to yesterday, which is slightly different because their idea of the past is what they remember. A lot of the exhibitions challenge the good old days approach, but I've come round to agreeing with them that there were values which have been lost.

He joined on 1 October 1985 with the knowledge from the Leicester course that it takes at least eighteen months to set up a museum. Springburn Museum opened on 20 May 1986 with no collections, just a long-term exhibitions list which would look at the demography of this industrial suburb as a microcosm of industrial Scotland.

The first exhibitions reflected the interests of the committee rather than the curator – the St Rollox Works (one of the four great locomotive works in the area, the other being Cowlairs, Hyde Park and Atlas), the Petersfield Football Club, and churches in the area (his chairman is a kirk elder). Mr O'Neil has a canny sense of timing. 'The St Rollox exhibition was about the future of the works, asking questions about unemployment, and 1600 redundancies were announced the day the exhibition opened.'

Still, he had a blank sheet of paper to draw his own shapes on, even if his drawing pencil was a mere £2,000-a-year exhibitions budget, and no permanent collection to fall back on as yet. What were his options?

> Given a lot of money you could do a Jorvik thing that would attract a lot more money.
>
> We had such a tiny budget I had to find a way of attracting people in to look at exhibitions, and the only way to do that, as far as I could see, was that everybody would

> be represented in the exhibitions – anybody could come in from any group you want to define and find something that touched their lives in a personal way, and that means bringing every exhibition up to the present, and some are exclusively about the present.

In 1988 O'Neill did an exhibition about teenagers, called 'See They Young Yins'. 'Teenagers have no interest in the past. The committee were a bit worried about that, they don't like young people much, which I thought was a good enough reason for doing it. At the opening we had a rock band and a pop quiz and kids of all ages running up and down. The committee loved it, they saw young people behaving themselves.'

'Me? I was born in 1956. I don't like young people much either.'

Out of his £2,000 he gets six exhibitions a year, which makes his the most productive museum in a city of museums. 'We get the money in January and they ask us what we do with it in December, so there's a freedom to do what you want. The money comes in a four year lump, and then there's a possible extension when you're expected to negotiate with the District Council.'

Mr O'Neill claims to have the only architectural heritage trail in Britain which includes tower blocks and maisonettes, and he believes the life of his museum is in its temporary exhibitions – the steadily growing permanent collection serves to furnish them, not as permanent fixtures on show. 'The permanent exhibition is the death of most museums,' he said. 'The longest exhibition here is eighteen months, and it comes down, ruthlesslessly, even if we're in tears when we do it.'

Two-dimensional exhibition boards are sent to local schools, and he works closely with local history teachers. Exhibitions such as the teenagers one, whose subject is as much the present as the past, rely heavily on photographic material – 'You can tell the level of interest by the number of photos that are stolen.'

Every year there is a study of a population group from the community. Following the teenagers was a 'Mother and Toddlers' project, 'too encourage a group of mothers to review their present lifestyle, celebrate positive aspects, identify needs and select appropriate solutions, involving further education or training if desired,' said the museum's statement of aim while the exhibition was being planned. 'Community Education funded a tutor to work with a group, so it's very much their view and they can decide what goes in, what's important: the day in the life of the mother of a six-month-old child, or they can interview their own mothers or grandmother and make it historical, it's up to them,' said Mark O'Neill.

There had also been 'A Place to Stay', about housing:

> The only historical survey of Scottish housing ever, and certainly the biggest exhibition on housing, from the 1790s to 1987, and it showed that housing was always a problem, it wasn't invented two years ago by the council, and we did architectural history, the housing acts, and living conditions in the past – cholera and single rooms with families of ten in them.
>
> 'Instead of having the standard reconstruction, we just chose a dozen key objects – a range a ceramic sink, a washing machine, a gramophone, a TV set. Instead of just being the local history of anywhere, it's all very personalised and that has worked very well. We're quite proud of that.'

Fond as he is of his museum – 'I don't know where to go because I can't think of any other place where I'd have the same fun,' he says, even though he had to move out of his Springburn flat because he found living in the community too depressing – he does not believe in the monolithic palace, there for all time for the instruction and entertainment of the people.

> I maintain that there should be such a thing as a temporary museum. It's worth having one for seven years, say, and then having none at all, and as long as you safeguard the collections that's reasonable. We have an agreement with Glasgow District Council that if we close they take over the collections.
>
> Some people say it's unprofessional to start up a museum whose future isn't guaranteed, but that's a very institutional way of looking at it – it's the collection that needs to be looked after, for ever, not the museum. Most social change takes place not by any major decision but by generation, and museums are bogged down with the generation who got in in the 60s when it was easy to get in, and it won't change until they die, or draw their retirement cheques.

The only major change in the museum Mark O'Neill has made has been concerned with presentation: 'There was no designer in the brief, which I think is very significant for the way whoever advised the trust to set up a museum thought about it.'

'They would think a local museum, doesn't need a designer, whereas good quality design is essential to respect the people and respect the subject. So when my administrative assistant wanted to go part-time instead of getting another one I got the brief changed so I could have a part-time designer, and we've since got her made full-time. The idea that anybody in the late eighties should set up a museum without a designer when there's no financial reason why they shouldn't have one is quite ridiculous.'

Mark O'Neill may not draw the tourist market to his library in Ayr Street, but the 800 visitors he was getting in the museum's first six months had turned into 1,600 a month thirty months later.

Springburn was famous for its steam locomotives, but it was not a train that was chosen as the community museum's logo, but a drinking fountain. The fountain had belonged to Cowlairs Co-operative Society, founded in 1881 by a group of railway workers against bitter opposition from their employers. The inscription on it reads: 'Each for all & all for each.'

# PART THREE

# 7. What makes them tick?

*Museums have taken technology and the science of industry beyond the schoolroom paper mechanics of a generation ago to create not only working recreations but hugely successful entertainment. In this chapter we trace what happened from the beginnings of the Science Museum via Ironbridge Gorge Museum, the British Engineerium at Hove, the Greater Manchester Museum of Science and Industry and Green's Mill and Science Centre near Nottingham to glimpse at the future, and Catalyst, the chemical industry's new museum at Widnes.*

## *The Science Museum*

RIGHT at the start of his South Kensington enterprise, Prince Albert had science and industry in mind. In 1853 he wrote a memorandum spelling out that Britain 'would recede as an industrial nation, unless her industrial population became much more conversant with science than they are now.'

The understanding of science, and grasping the new developments which have always been present in a discipline in which the only constant seems to be change, has been a function of museums from their earliest manifestations. The natural sciences, botany, zoology, medicine, inspired the early cabinets of curiosities as much as ethnography and art, and it is no accident that the founders of many of our key museums, or the collections around which they were made, in the eighteenth and nineteenth centuries were, as we have seen, doctors.

But the concept of technology and the science of industry was a new one to museums. Fortunately it was being presented at a time when the museum concept itself was at the very start of a sea-change, and Prince Albert's museum dynamo, Sir Henry Cole, saw nothing contradictory in art and science being side by side in the context of manufacture and design. So, in 1853, the Science and Art Department was set up to 'increase the means of industrial education and to extend the influence of science and art on productive industry', with Cole as secretary for art and Dr Lyon Playfair, Cole's friend and the self-proclaimed saviour of the Great Exhibition, his science counterpart.

Playfair had joined the exhibition committee just at the point when things appeared to have stagnated and Cole thought the whole massive project was doomed. They met, by chance, in Whitehall as Cole was on his way to resign, but Playfair – whose tact and diplomacy was to lead him to the Speaker's chair in the 1880s – talked him out of it. 'Had the accidental meeting not taken place,' he wrote in his autobiography, 'the Great Exhibition would never have been held, for its mainspring would have been broken.'

It was a perfect metaphor, and among the objects which were eventually to form the Victoria and Albert and Science Museums were models of machinery, examples of structures and building materials. Along with Cole's fine and applied art specimens, these all went under the same iron roof in what in 1857 became the South Kensington Museum.

Playfair had taken a chemistry chair in Edinburgh by 1874 when the Royal Commission on Scientific Instruction and Advancement of Science recommended the first collection of apparatus preserved for historic interest, rather than for teaching and instruction, and it opened in 1876.

In 1883 the Science Library, now the Science Museum Library, was founded, and in 1884 the Patent Museum, collated by the assistant to the Patent Commissioner, Bennet Woodcroft, who had included in his brief such national industrial treasures as Stephenson's *Rocket* and Arkwright's spinning machine, became part of it.

The gradual dividing of the art and science collections was almost organic, with the same inevitability, and it was in 1885 that the Science Museum became an entity of its own, if not in a building of its own. For by the time Queen Victoria laid the V&A's foundation stone in 1899, the Science Museum was still a part of it, and was to be for another two decades. Parts of the stucco in the V&A, opened in 1909, still have the monogram 'S&A' for Science and Art, even though the old department had ceased to exist in 1899.

But a committee, under the industrialist Sir Hugh Bell, was set up to consider what should be done about the science museum, and in 1912 it reported that there should be a new building, work on the first wing of which was begun and then interrupted by the First World War. Gradually it was finished and opened to the public after the Armistice under the aegis of the first real director Sir Henry Lyons, director from 1920 to 1933, and it was opened, with double the space it had had across the road, by King George V in 1928. Under Sir Henry there were some innovations which are eerie echoes of things to come. Exhibitions had been held since 1919, but in 1926 Lyons introduced a new sort: one which had to be sponsored, and which the sponsor took complete responsibility for. Museums would not give *carte blanche* to a sponsor these days, the temptation to make the whole thing into an advertising float being too much of a risk, but the sponsorship element, so much a part of museums now, was established.

Then there was the Children's Gallery. The working model had quickly become something of a characteristic of the Science Museum, and in 1933 the principle was extended by this gallery, described in the Science Museum's 1987 *Review* as consisting 'almost entirely of demonstrations, operated by the visitor, or scientific principles' (Lance Day). In other words, hands-on science learning. The response to all this from the museum-going public was that the 600,000 who came in 1926 had turned into million by 1929, and a million-and-a-half by 1933, making it the top national museum.

The museum was closed for most of the Second World War, reopening in 1946 when the next development began to be contemplated. For only Bell's first wing had been completed; in all these years the centre block had never been built, but work was begun in 1951. It was eventually completed in 1961.

Interim, Henry Lyons's 1926 sponsored exhibition scheme had matured. In 1954 the first permanent gallery in which industry and the museum collaborated was opened: the gas gallery had exhibits and finance contributed to it by the Gas Council.

In the 1960s display techniques were getting to be less formal, and a design department was set up; temporary exhibitions became a more frequent feature – there were 146 between 1967 and 1977.

The irony of the early crucial patronage of physicians to the museum establishment is that none of the national museums had accepted any responsibility for the history of medicine, and it was not until 1976 when the Wellcome Museum gave its collections devoted to the history of medicine to the Science Museum that this was, to use an appropriate word, remedied.

In common with most of the other national museums, the Science Museum has its branches: its National Railway Museum opened in York in 1975; in 1980 its Concorde Museum opened at Yeovilton; and in 1983 the National Museum of Film and Photography, Museum of the Year in 1988, opened in Bradford. At the time of writing there are plans for at least two new branches; a Museum of Information Technology (for computers) which will probably manifest itself in Reading in time to celebrate the 1992 bicentenary of the birth of the father of computers, our own Charles Babbage, and a National Museum of Food and Farming.

In 1987, a year after he had taken over as director of the Science Museum from Dame Margaret Weston, Dr Neil Cossons had staged a sort of reverse palace revolution by creating a new inner administration of assistant directors – covering public services, marketing, administration, the collections and research. By the following year most of his new cabinet were in place, and he was able to launch his £10 million five-year plan to reshape the museum, both in appearance and ethics. It is a transformation which is almost certain to influence thinking on how to make very large urban museums for the twenty-first century.

Not the least new component is two new museum personalities, the steward and stewardess, whose task is to advise, direct, explain and sell to a public – 'the customers' – and in their smart couturier-designed uniforms they are to be a couple of notches up from the demonstrators of places like Beamish. 'Their job is to generally present a friendly and helpful face to the public – a museum this size can be a daunting place,' said Karen Booth, the museum's new marketing executive, a Canadian who had been behind the marketing of the successful Freud Museum which opened in Hampstead in 1982.

The stewards and stewardesses manage the central information point, a gleaming steel crater in front of the redesigned East Hall opened by the Queen in 1988, which is itself now presented in a new livery of vivid green. Massive steam engines which had stood as lifeless monuments to the Industrial Revolution were cleaned, oiled and and some set periodically working.

Above the information dais on a circular series of panels a constant audio-visual light show is suspended to explain how to get the most out of this National Museum of Science and Industry – as its title has always been but by which it has never been known – and how its exhibits evolved. A glass lift takes passengers on a ride through all three floors.

'The level of understanding at the scientific base of our culture is almost non-existent,' Dr Cossons said. 'I want people studying the proper communication of science.' Part of that process was the creation of a professorship in the history of science jointly with the Imperial College of Science and Technology next door, the aim being to explore ways of 'raising the public understanding of science and its history.'

In 1986 the successor to Sir Henry Lyons's Children's Gallery opened with the name of 'Launch Pad'. There is more about the thinking behind the £7 million venture in Chapter 8, but it was immediately popular and at the same time a failure, because it was situated right next to the main entrance so that the thousands of new visitors it brought into the museum ventured no further inside. In October 1988 it moved to a larger space on the first floor. Its place has been taken by a shopping gallery dotted with specialist niches selling books, models, stationery – 'anything that is appropriate and that people will need,' said Miss Booth. They had to be situated near the main entrance so that the new turnstiles could be erected near them, a few weeks before admission charges were instituted for the first time, and shoppers had to be encouraged to use the shops, a vital revenue earner, without being obliged to pay to get in first.

These innovations were to be followed by a cafeteria/restaurant opening in the pre-turnstile section, and the British Festival of Food and Farming was to be celebrated in 1989 by the opening of the country's first gallery devoted to nutrition, with its own restaurant. Terry Suthers was brought in by Dr Cossons from running the Yorkshire Museum to be assistant director in charge of public services and the food gallery was his special project. 'We want people to understand better what they have seen by sampling the kind of thing the gallery is talking about,' he said. 'The menu will reflect the gallery. We believe people have to participate if they are going to get the full learning value out of the museum.'

The same ethic has been applied to the new Launch Pad presentation. While children could discover science with the hands-on experiments, displays had hitherto been spread around different parts of the vast museum, and these were drawn near to explain what the experiments prove while they were still fresh in the young minds.

Other new galleries in the plan included a £4-million aeronautics presentation, complete with a flight laboratory, and another medicine gallery.

The philosophy is one which is being applied steadily throughout the new technological museums, one which has evolved from the likes of Ironbridge Gorge where aspects of industry are made to speak for themselves: a static museum leaves a static expression, an active one invites interaction.

'What we desperately need is a stronger scholarly base for people who understand what the history of contemporary practice of science and technology is, but also are capable of conveying it in our galleries, because our galleries have not interpreted concepts with the veracity or vividness that we need,' Dr Cossons said. 'We have to get used to the idea of treating our visitors as valued customers who are not fools. They come here wanting to find out and to enjoy themselves doing it, and it's our duty to make sure they don't go away disappointed.'

## *Ironbridge Gorge Museum*

It is interesting that in the nineteenth-century museums boom the influences of change were the national museums of natural history and art. Industry as a subject was not celebrated, but the influence in the twentieth-century boom has been the industrial museum idea.

The British Engineerium at Hove is the creation of Jonathan Minns, an industrial archaeologist who was appalled at the complete absence of conservation for what should be the living monuments of our industrial development. The Engineerium is a cross between a conservation workshop and a museum, with education almost as important component of its structure as the restoration of the machines.

Opened in 1976 the museum gave new life to one of the great parish churches of industrial life, Brighton's pumping station. That year was the centenary of the station's own beam engine which has been restored to working order, and the coal station was turned into the main exhibition space. More importantly, Minns's museum has become a recognised centre for the conservation of ancient machinery, and the massive monuments to British engineering which go there are brought to life for fascinated youngsters in particular, but adults too who find themselves, so to say, as they watch them being restored. The Science Museum itself is a frequent customer for the skills of the museum and its chief engineer, Peter Fagg.

Neil Cossons has been seen as something of a guru for industrial and scientific museums, and of museums generally – he has worked in local authority, independent and national museums. Before entering the national orbit in 1983 with the Maritime Museum (he became director of the Science Museum in 1986), he was director of the Ironbridge Gorge Museum at Coalbrookdale near Telford in Shropshire, a phenomenon which time may show to have been as influential as South Kensington Museum was.

Coalbrookdale was where Abraham Darby, a Quaker pot founder who had rented a blast furnace, first smelted iron ore commercially in 1709 using the plentiful coke instead of the expensive and difficult charcoal, and as such the place likes to be known as the 'Birthplace of the Industrial Revolution'. Claiming that is almost like Montmartre calling itself the birthplace of Impressionist painting: it may not be untrue, but it is not the point, for the Industrial Revolution was born in men's minds. But if anywhere has the right to claim it, Coalbrookdale has. Abraham I's process was perfected by his son, Abraham II, whose development created the means to forge Britain's industrial, then military and political, world supremacy in the nineteenth century.

The iron cylinders for Newcomen's steam engines were made at Coalbrookdale and the first iron railway wheels were cast there, as were the first iron rails. In 1779 the world's first iron bridge was built across the gorge by Abraham III, and Richard Trevithick's steam locomotive, built at Coalbrookdale, was driven over it in 1802.

At the end of the eighteenth century a quarter of Britain's iron was smelted at Ironbridge, but as the the great new towns like Manchester developed and others began to overtake the comparatively humble operation at the place which was by then – the mid-nineteenth century – known as Ironbridge, attention there was switched to more dainty products: decorative castings, kitchen ranges and stoves, and china porcelain, and a 'new town' was created to make the pottery. They called it Coalport and it operated until 1926 when Coalport China moved to the Staffordshire Potteries where it is still made. A tile industry was developed which flourished until 1952.

The River Severn was the key to the whole historic complex. It provided the water vital to all the processes developed, and the transport to bring in the raw material and take out the finished product. 'From Coalport to the Iron Bridge, two miles,' wrote Charles Hulbert in his *History and Description of Salop* in 1837, 'the river passes through the most extraordinary district in the world: the banks on each side are elevated to the height of from 3 to 400 feet, studded with Iron Works, Brickworks, Boat Building Establishments, Retail Stores, Inns, and Houses, perhaps 150 vessels on the river, actively employed or waiting for cargoes; while hundreds and hundreds of busy mortals are assiduously engaged, melting with the heat of the roaring furnace, and though enveloped in thickest smoke and incessant dust are cheerful and happy.'

Assiduous industriousness ripples along those banks again, but the industry is the museum now. More accurately, *they* are museums, for the Ironbridge complex is six museums in one, grown in response to demand and ingenuity just as the original town did. The river provides another vital component today: it creates a stupendous view.

Almost always there is a single mind behind the success of a museum project, as Flower obliquely observed a century ago. Although the Ironbridge Gorge Trust was established as long ago as 1967 when industrial archaeology was just beginning to emerge as a legitimate historical study – the trust's aim being to do something worthy with the wealth of historic material relating to this historic place – the mind did not arrive until 1971, and it belonged to the same Neil Cossons, a thirty-two-year-old deputy director of the then City of Liverpool Museums. His belief was that it was not enough simply to preserve these objects, but that they must be made appealing in a presentation coherent and undemanding enough to attract a lot of people to a fairly remote part of England; and having been attracted they must be cared for and eventually leave wanting to return. It meant an extensive programme of development on different sites, because of the range of the area and the activities which needed to be represented, and it meant providing car parks, toilets, refreshments and nice people on hand to explain things, the forerunners, perhaps, of the Science Museum's stewards yet to come.

It meant creating a museum on an archaeological site rather than taking the site off to a museum, a technique pioneered in the United States with Colonial Williamsburg but an alien one in Britain.

The trust had an executive board which included nominees from the local authorities and the Telford Development Corporation, with money coming from commercial sponsorship and from local and central government grants. An educational link with Birmingham University was established early on and maintained, but the whole thing was, essentially, autonomous and free to develop as it needed in order to survive and fulfil its interpretive role.

'This concept of the integrated management of the historic sites of the Gorge by a single authority has provided both the inspiration and the challenge of the Ironbridge project every since,' Dr Cossons wrote in an article in 1980.[1] He continued:

> For the first time, a 'purpose-built' organisation, and a non-statutory one at that, has had the opportunity to plan, co-ordinate and manage the conservation and interpretation of an area which was geographically coherent and desperately in need of care and attention. The scheme, significantly and rightly conceived as a 'museum', by no means satisfied the full requirements of a 'national-park' type of approach, but it was practical and, with the beneficent ingredient of independent charitable status, it was also achievable.

The whole thing began, and begins, with what is now the Museum of Iron, with Abraham I's original leased blast furnace in the grounds of the Great Warehouse which was built in 1838 and now houses the key exhibition and items about the industry. Next to it is the Elton Gallery, based on the Elton Collection of paintings of the Industrial Revolution. The Coalport China Works are now a museum as well, with reconstructed workshops, bottle kilns and the rest.

The Severn Warehouse was built by the company in the 1840s, and it and its wharf have been restored to house an audio-visual introduction to and exhibition about Ironbridge Gorge, a few hundred yards upstream from the bridge itself which has another exhibition in its tollhouse.

But the pride of the whole complex, the perhaps slightly off-centre heart of the complex because its subject matter veers from the central theme of the Darby works but is what people love the most, is Blists Hill. This was where the blast furnaces,

[1] 'The Museum in the Valley, Vol. XXXII, No. 3, *Museum*.

brickworks, coal mines and a railway operated, but by the time the trust was formed it was derelict. Now it is a re-created town in the Beamish ethic, with cottages, a pub, a wheelwright's, a colliery pit head (with a collier there to explain life as it was a century ago), a bakery where you can buy bread, a chandler's where you can buy candles, a printer's, even a bank where you can get nineteenth-century money to spend in the town.

There had been a wrought iron puddling[2] shop at Blists Hill and in 1987 it was revived to become the only wrought iron works in the world. They not only demonstrate the almost forgotten craft there, they produce a certain amount commercially, so that they were able to provide new clappers for the bells of St Paul's Cathedral, clanking away for nearly a hundred years with inferior cast clappers.

Ironbridge Gorge Museum opened in 1973 and was a great gamble. It attracts more than 300,000 people a year, and so Dr Cossons's achieved his goal. But Ironbridge's success meant a turnaround in the thinking of what museums can and should do in this country. The need not only to present technology and its history but to demonstrate it quickly became an established part of museum theory; it also introduced the concept of the museum as theme entertainment. But, more important, it proved for the first time that an independent organisation with commercial goals, standards and strictures, could create a public museum meeting all the traditional requirements, betraying none of the principles, but employing a host of new techniques undreamt of in the traditional curator's mind.

However vital a contributor Ironbridge was to the cataclysm of the Industrial Revolution, *the* industrial city of the nineteenth century is undoubtedly Manchester, the dirty old town with the dark satanic mills. For most of this century civic efforts have been striving to somehow excuse the grimy past and present a cultural antidote, which it certainly succeeded in doing with such international achievements as the Halle Orchestra, the Royal Exchange Theatre and two of the finest art galleries in the country, the Manchester City Art Gallery and the Whitworth – the name of which is more than just ironic, it was founded a century ago in a legacy from the prince of toolmakers, Sir Joseph Whitworth, a Manchester man.

In 1830 the world's first passenger railway station was built at Castlefields in Manchester, and 150 years later its derelict buildings were designated the site of a new North West Museum of Science. Three years later it opened, as the Greater Manchester Museum of Science and Technology, and quickly became one of the largest museums in Europe. In 1988 it opened an extraordinary feature, Underground Manchester, in which a large area of the ground had been torn up to reveal the sewerage and services systems of the Victorian city; fundamental civic technology is no less valid or necessarrily less interesting.

Ironbridge and Manchester celebrate the Industrial Revolution, the phenomenon

[2] A process for converting pig iron into wrought iron by heating it with ferric oxide in a furnace to oxidize the carbon.

The National Museum of Wales in 1922 when it was informally opened to the public.

Interior of a miner's house at the St Fagan's Folk Museum, a branch of the National Museum of Wales.

The delightful Guernsey Museum and Art Gallery of 1978 in the island's Candie Gardens.

The Weald and Downland Open Air Museum at Singleton.

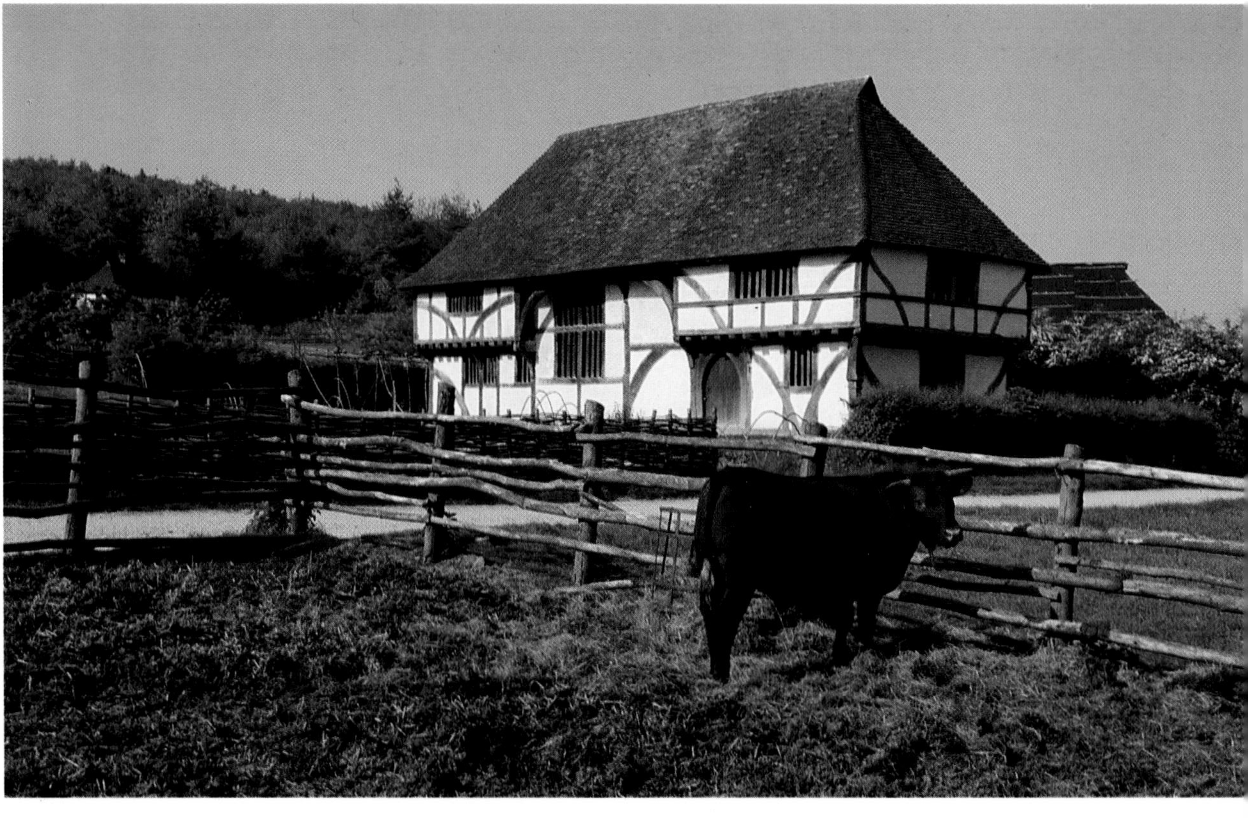

Powhatan's Mantle, one of Tradescant's prize exhibits, now at the Ashmolean.

William Hunter, founder of Glasgow University's Hunterian Museum.

Major Percy Powell-Cotton, hunter, zoologist, ethnographer, collector and museum founder, wearing the jacket in which he was almost mauled to death.

The hunter hunted: a diorama including the lion which, in life, almost killed Powell-Cotton.

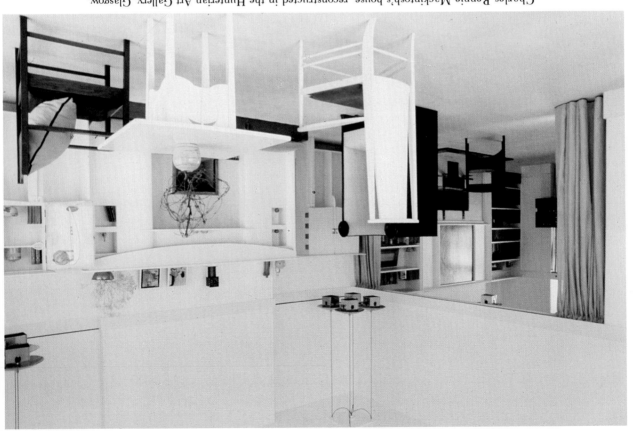

Charles Rennie Mackintosh's house, reconstructed in the Hunterian Art Gallery, Glasgow.

Robert Opie and his National Museum of Advertising and Packaging.

Bread being baked in a coal-fired oven at The North of England Open Air Museum, Beamish.

Abraham Darby's original furnace at Ironbridge Gorge Museum.

Green's Mill near Nottingham, where George Green lived and worked out the basis for much of modern science.

Dove Cottage – Wordsworth's birthplace.

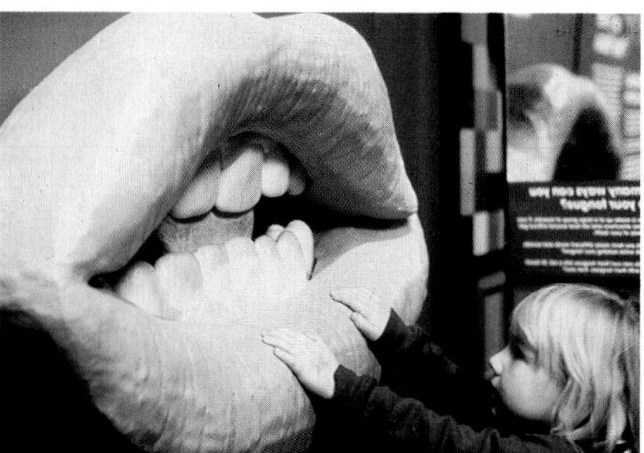

The giant mouth, part of Eureka!, the new children's discovery centre in Halifax.

A restored tug at Llanthony Warehouse, Gloucester Dock, now converted to become the National Waterways Museum.

Models being made by sculptors at York for the Canterbury Pilgrims exhibition at Canterbury, opened in 1988 by the creators of the Jorvik Viking Centre.

Inside the re-created tomb of Tutenkhamun in Dorchester.

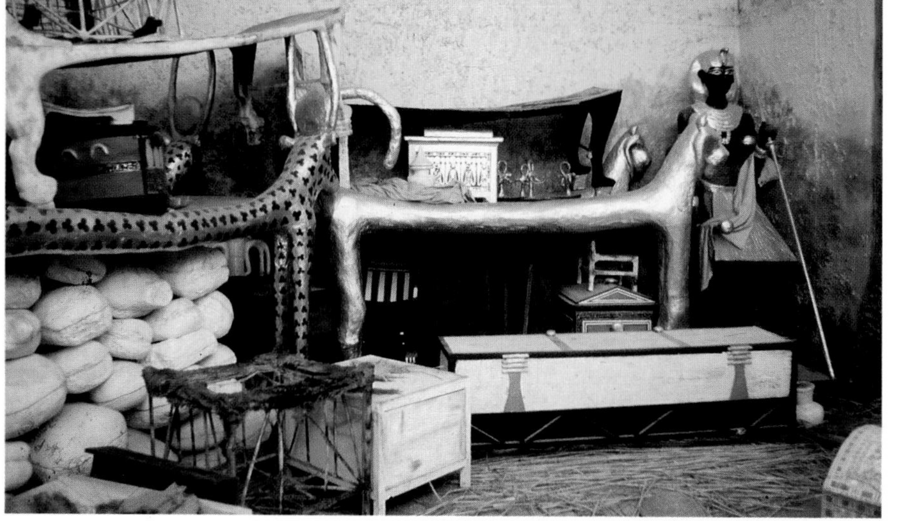

'Turtle', part of the display at the Royal Navy Submarine Museum at Gosport.

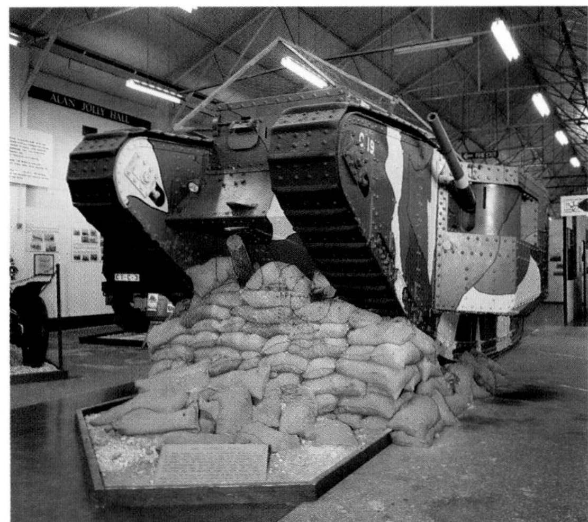

The Mark I Tank, on display at the Tank Museum at Bovington.

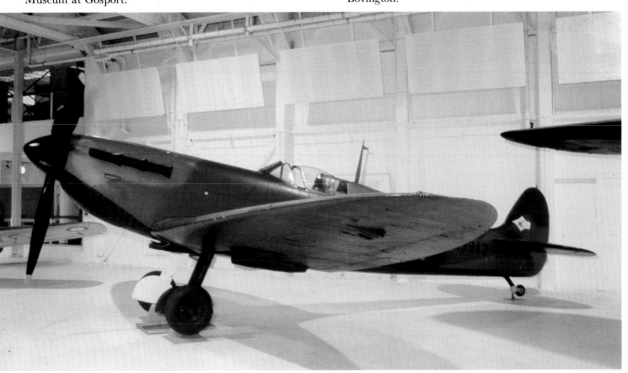

A Spitfire at the Royal Air Force Museum, Hendon.

American P51D Mustang and Focke-Wulf FW190 in the Imperial War Museum.

Jigsaw of Laurel and Hardy at the Museum of the Moving Image.

L. S. Lowry's studio, re-created at Manchester City Art Gallery in 1987.

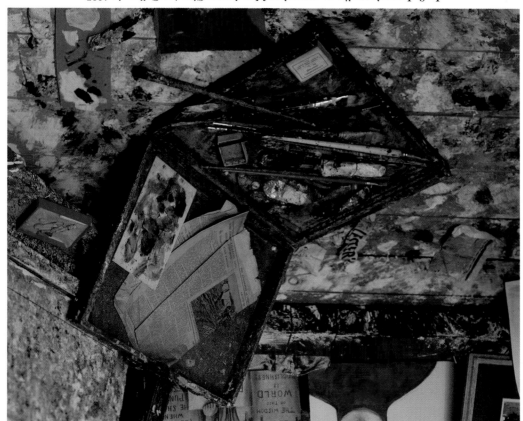

The National Gallery of Scotland.

which probably had a more cataclysmic effect than the Norman Conquest, the Black Death and the Civil War put together. Before it, heavy industry was pretty much represented by the blacksmith and the miller.

## *Green's Mill and Centre*

George Green was a miller. The name means nothing to most of us and at first sight there is no reason why it should mean anything. It belonged to a man who left school at the age of nine, had seven illegitimate children and died in his windmill in 1841 at the age of forty-seven in the obscurity in which he had lived his life. There is no picture of him, even; it had never occurred to anybody that there should be one, least of all Green himself. Yet in 1828 this man who had completed four terms at school before his father decided he was of more use to him in the mill produced a mathematical theorem which has had an influence probably at least equal to Newton's.

Professor Lawrie Challis, head of the physics department of Nottingham University, is the chairman of the George Green Memorial Fund which, with a great deal of help from the City of Nottingham, has restored Green's windmill and turned it into an integral part of a highly popular museum. He explained Green's importance to me:

> If you read Kelvin's collected works on electricity and magnetism he puts innumerable footnotes to Green's work. Clearly he had an enormous influence on Kelvin and others who were developing the theory of electro-magnetism which of course led to the whole of modern technology.
>
> That was the technique. He had a big influence on the way in which the elasticity theory developed – stresses and strains – and on how light was reflected interfacing in the first theory of internal reflection, which is the basis of the optical fibre.
>
> The thing one really realised about George Green was in the 1950s and 60s – which goes on to the present – when almost every other scientific author was writing using Green's Functions. They became applied by a chap called Schringer who won a Nobel Prize, and during the war he was working on the use of Green's Functions for designing things in radar tubes – the classical science, the sort of things Green's Functions were used for from about 1840 to 1940.
>
> After the war Schringer went back to his academic research and he realised that these techniques could be used in describing nuclear particles, and a tremendous range of modern physics, and it was then that we almost became a Green's Function generation of physicists.

George Green was the child of a prosperous Nottingham baker who sent his only son, born in 1793, to Goodacre's Academy at the age of seven. After less then eighteen months he had left, to work in the family firm. In 1807 his father had become quite wealthy and expanded the business by building a windmill outside the city near the village of Sneinton, and the family moved into the house he built alongside the mill, Belvoir Mount. The running of the mill became the responsibility of young George and a manager.

The mill manager's daughter, whom he never married, was to bear him seven children, and a year before the first one was born, George Green joined the Nottingham Subscription Library to continue his education. Study, it seemed, had not stopped when he left the Goodacre Academy, but had continued as he sat alone on the dingy first floor of his mill with books, pencils and paper.

The library in Bromley House was the intellectual hub of Nottingham, and here he read about French mathematics. If he had a mentor during this time his name has not come down to us, but perhaps it was John Toplis, headmaster of Nottingham Free Grammar School, who had also studied the new approach to mathematics preferred on the Continent. Whatever the learning process, Green's 'Essay on the application of Mathematical Analysis to the Theories of Electricity and Magnetism' was published in 1828 when he was thirty-four. It effectively introduced the concept of electrical potential, a key to the electromagnetic theory, and the essay has been described as 'the beginning of mathematical physics in England'.[3] It presented mathematical ploys for solving physical problems, processes which became known as Green's Functions and Green's Theorem. He published it at his own expense, not daring to send it to 'one of the learned societies' because 'coming from an unknown individual it might not be deemed worthy of notice', his brother-in-law was to write.

The following year his father died, his common-law wife had their third child, and he took sole responsibility for the milling business. The essay was forgotten. Then, in 1830, a Lincolnshire gentleman mathematician, Sir Edward Bromhead, took Green up and they became friends, the baronet encouraging the miller to expand and write more on his mathematical considerations, and these were published by 'learned societies', and Bromhead made sure the Cambridge mathematicians saw them. 'It is in the hands of such men that I should wish it to fall,' he wrote in gratitude.

Bromhead had been at Cambridge with some of the greatest scientific brains of the era: Charles Babbage; John Herschell, the astronomer; George Peacock, the polymath who was to become Dean of Ely. They had adopted the French, or analytical, style of maths, and had formed themselves into the Analytical Society. He wanted Green to visit Cambridge with him, and the miller replied in 1833:

> You were kind enough to mention a journey to Cambridge on June 24th to see your friends Herschell, Babbage and others who constitute the Chivalry of British Science. Being as yet only a beginner I think I have not right to go there and must defer that pleasure until I shall have become tolerably respectable as a man of science, should that day ever arrive.

But the idea of studying at Cambridge had been discussed by them. 'Unfortunately I possess little Latin, less Greek, have seen too many winters, and am thus held in a state of suspense by counteracting motives,' Green wrote, asking, 'which college would be most suitable for a person of my age and *imperfect Classical Attainments.*' In October 1833 George Green, aged thirty-nine, was admitted an undergraduate at Caius College.

[3] D. M. Cannell, *George Green, Miller and Mathematician*, 1988.

What happened to Jane Smith, mother of the now four Green children, and her family at this time is not known, but Green would have had to keep quiet about them as a potential Fellow: Fellows had to be celibate.

He got his BA, with first class honours, and was awarded a Fellowship in 1839 – from freshman to don in six years. He published more work, on hydrodynamics, reflection and refraction, and sound. 'He stood head and shoulders above all his contemporaries inside and outside the University,' wrote an undergraduate at the time, Harvey Goodwin, who later became a bishop.

But six months after getting his Fellowship George Green's brother-in-law recorded: 'He returned, indisposed after enjoying many years of excellent health in Sneinton, Alas! With the opinion that he should never recover from his illness and which became verified in little more than a year's time by his decease on 31st May 1841.'

A few weeks before Green died William Thompson came to Cambridge from Scotland to continue his studies. He is better known as Lord Kelvin, a pioneer with Michael Faraday in the development of electrical theories. Both men were to use Green's Theorem, and the unknown miller was celebrated in history as the father of technological science.

But George Green remained in obscurity, despite the efforts of mathematicians throughout the twentieth century to unearth the story of this extraordinary man. Six of his children died without issue, and the one surviving line of descendants were virtually ignorant of who their brilliant progenitor was, apart from being the miller of Sneinton. None of his papers survived, and only the letters he sent to others had been kept. Bits and pieces were put together, however, enough for Nottingham Castle Museum to mount an exhibition in 1974 with the help of Professor Challis. A year later a bypass plan threatened to demolish the mill, by then a ruin with its queer conical roof gone and the brickwork stained black by a 1947 fire. The plan was abandoned just as Professor Challis formed the George Green Memorial Fund, and he approached the city council with a rescue plan. In 1979 the mill and millyard were acquired and restoration began.

It took eight years and a succession of Youth Opportunities trainees and local volunteers. A new cap was placed on top in 1981, new sails were fitted in 1986, and by the end of that year the millstones began to grind flour once again. The project was finally completed in 1987.

The windmill remains a monument to George Green the miller, once again run by a miller who must be one of very few with a Bachelor of Science degree, but in the outbuildings in the millyard is the museum of George Green the mathematician. There is a science area with a dozen or so exhibits which attempt to tell the enormously complex story coherently. Professor Challis described the museum and its aims to me:

> What we have tried to do is to identify the areas of science in which he worked. For example there are displays of internal reflection, so you have a radio and a curved rod with a light going up the rod taking the signal from the radio, and then you have another

> plastic rod and when you line the two up the light beam hops over and the loudspeaker plays the radio – internal reflection.
>
> There's no way in which you can explain Green's mathematics to an average visitor, including a relatively young child. All you can do is say these are the physical phenomena which fired him, and this is what came out of his work.

In the millyard is a fountain sculpture, the result of a national competition, which illustrates Green's Theorem 'which had to do with flow from surfaces, illustrating the ways he was thinking mathematically.'

What the museum has done is to make full use of a romantic story which could easily have come from a Brontë or a Hardy novel, with a few adjustments, to introduce something schoolteachers have been trying and failing to convey for generation upon generation: the romance of mathematics.

In 1988 the English Tourist Board revealed that Green's Mill and Centre had received the biggest increase of visitors after Westminster Abbey's Undercroft Museum – 79 per cent, to 60,000.

If the engineers of the nineteenth century have their counterpart in twentieth-century Britain, it is probably the chemists who have shifted a gear for our technology if not changed direction so profoundly as the likes of Green did. That has not been recognised in a dedicated museum, but will be in Catalyst, which was due to open its first phase in 1989. An 1860s chemical laboratory complex has been restored and adapted for the museum which is the result of zealous backing from the industry and a successful £4 million appeal of which the managing director of British Petroleum was chairman.

It will be a controversial project in this part of the country where both the blessings and the curses of chemicals have coloured regional life, but it will be even more valid for that addressing the controversies as well as the developments. The technological museum of the future, Catalyst looks likely to show, will be a live wire.

# 8. Discovery

*Science has taken museums by storm, both in application and as a subject. It has demanded a new kind of museum presentation, such as at the Exploratory in Bristol, the Science Museum's Launch Pad, Jodrell Bank in Cheshire, Eureka! in Halifax and Techniquest in Cardiff.*

THE local museums of 100 years ago were mostly about science, nearly always natural history, their object being to bring visitors, who would as often as possible be children in to as close contact with specimens as the confines of a glass case would allow. Sometimes they would go further, but 'hands-on science' then meant botany, a ramble across the local woodland which would have more to do with feet than hands. 'Hands on' now is purer science, physics and often even chemistry. It is the oldest learning process, and the newest technique for museums.

## *Exploratory*

For Richard Gregory, professor of neuropsychology at Bristol University, hands-on science began as a way of keeping his two children amused. With his wife stricken by debilitating illness while they were young, Professor Gregory found himself being both father and mother for large parts of their growing up. 'We'd throw eggs over the house to see if they'd break, which of course they didn't. Eggs are designed so that they can fall out of nests without breaking, as we discovered,' he said. One of those children, Mark, became the BBC's labour correspondent.

Professor Gregory is the son of an astronomy professor, but his interest has always been in the physical activities closer to home. He wrote *The Oxford Companion of the Mind* which was published in 1987, three months after his 'Exploratory' opened in temporary rooms in Bristol.

'Learning by doing', he believes, is not confined to the nursery school. It has its place in the university too. 'When you interact you get yourself into the situation of the experiment, you're part of it – no way can you learn music without being a performer.'

He caused a stir at Cambridge when he went to teach philosophy there and created practical classes, unheard of in that cerebral academe. 'Philosophers lose out by not looking at actual experiments, so we tried some: we would have a bright light, a dim light, another light between and have to work out where it was in the middle – a lovely philosophical problem.' In fact he made his students do experiments almost exactly the same as his present Exploratory ones.

In the 1930s Jean Piaget, the French educational psychologist pronounced, 'I do therefore I know', borrowing from Descartes, and that theory of perception is very much at the heart of Professor Gregory's pioneering kind of museum.

To call Bristol's Exploratory his 'brain child' is peculiarly apt. He is director of Bristol University's brain and perception laboratory, and his other enthusiasm is akin to but more concerned with everyday people and their joy in finding out.

The Exploratory, or 'hands-on science centre' as it is subtitled, is a physics playground. The professor has invented a word, 'plore', to describe the experiments which have names like the Plasma Globe, Chladni Plates, the Puck Table and Ruben's Tube. They all have to do with mathematics, perception, mechanics, chemistry and so on, but those ghastly textbook words never rear their ugly heads, and there are 'pilots' on hand to guide explorers to the experiment. Nor is the Exploratory reserved for children. 'I like the idea of families being involved, in which generations can communicate,' said Professor Gregory. 'The interactive approach is trying to reverse the trend towards mysterious black boxes and stop people dismissing whole concepts by exclaiming 'Augh, computers!' We're trying to shed the scales from people's eyes which form whenever they are confronted by science.' In 1988 it was the winner of the Automobile Association's 1988 Museums of the Future Award.

By the summer of 1989 the Exporatory was due to have three times as much space at Temple Meads as it had in the Victoria Rooms, but Professor Gregory found that space was not such an urgent requirement as had been expected when they originally opened in 1987:

> We have an equal number of adults and children. The kids switch the adults on and the adults keep the kids in order – all without talking, through a kind of body language,' said the professor. 'It's like a party, and the fact that we're all crowded up together in a fairly small space actually makes it work, and funnily enough you don't get resentment. People don't mind it because they're doing things. It's enormously exciting.
>
> What is good is that all sorts of people with real enthusiasm have popped in; the public response to it has been really extraordinary. It's important to have events, and we had a bubble party, for instance, where people put bubbles inside other bubbles and so on: it's good for the staff and it makes people think of things in a different way.

Professor Gregory discovered that hands-on techniques could be applied in a museum setting in the mid-1970s. Lecturing in San Francisco, he met Frank Oppenheimer, brother of the atomic physicist Robert Oppenheimer, who had started something called the Exploratorium where adults and children were encouraged to lay hands on things and so learn about them. Professor Gregory was delighted: 'The object was simply to show how science works.'

He brought the concept back with him, scribbling ideas on the backs of envelopes in the aeroplane, but it was to be ten years before the opportunity to develop the project in Britain came, and even as he was struggling to raise the £350,000 he needed in 1986 he was envisaging a network of hands-on science centres across the country.

Some of the plores were invented by the professor and his team, some were brought back from San Francisco, like the gyroscope chair which rotates as you sit in it, tilting a spinning bicycle wheel. 'People like the gyroscope chair, which is surprising because it involves a certain amount of skill and the experience is an odd one, and then if you're intellectual about it you wonder why it happens. The glowing gases which you look at with a spectroscope are very popular: you look at the coloured lights, and you suddenly realise that's what the stars are made of.'

He was right about the network. It is happening. Jodrell Bank has one now, presided over by none other than the Astronomer Royal himself, where the infinite science of astronomy at one of its most famous centres is available in the context of other hands-on experiments, in a natural process of explanation. Liverpool museums have established one; so have Tyne and Wear Museums at Newcastle; Nottingham's Green's Mill and Science Centre is one; and the professor's collaborator on many plores, Professor John Beetlestone, opened his Techniquest in Cardiff Bay in 1988. Eureka!, with £5 million of Clore Foundation money, was due to open in Discovery Road, Halifax, in 1989.

## *Launch Pad*

Perhaps Professor Gregory was the pioneer who was just beaten to the public arena by the Science Museum, perhaps the Science Museum had been ahead all along, perhaps some kind of osmosis which so often occurs when revolutions are forming made the two come to the same conclusion independently but almost simultaneously.

Launch Pad opened in August 1986, but it was not its first manifestation at the Science Museum. As long ago as 1932 there had been the Children's Gallery in the basement, a technological amusement arcade which was hands-on only to the extent of thumbs pushing buttons. Launch Pad was what Dr Anthony Wilson, the museum's education head, described as 'a quantum leap forward in the idea of visitor participation.'[1] The whole thing began in 1983. 'It was felt that the museum should be doing more for its young visitors, and that an interactive exhibition would also fulfil the wider function of showing that science and technology could be made accessible and can provide exciting and rewarding activities,' he wrote.

Two research and development groups were set up to work out the exhibits, and there was laboratory testing before they had a trial run for a month during the 1984 Christmas holidays when 20,000 people went, including the prime minister. They

[1] *Science Museum Review*, 1987.

called it Test Bed, because the thirty experiments were on trial, and some of them failed the test.

The successful ones tended to be larger and simpler: robotics, for instance, broke down a lot and the grainpit, designed to help children understand flow and the mechanics of keeping the flow going, was always getting clogged up with beads of grain, beads which had a way of getting into other experiments as well. But this was far more valuable than lab testing, and the research and development people were able to go back and come up with the real experiments which would comprise Launch Pad.

Launch Pad opened, having cost over £1,000,000, and was an overwhelming success – an extra 20,000 visitors crammed themselves in on the first day. Overalled monitors were on hand, like the pilots of the Exploratory, and that first day was a test bed for them. Project officer Mike Williams, a former science teacher embarking on a new career, was trying to explain what was going on to a non-English-speaking adult: 'Launch pad. It's where you launch things from, we're launching children.'

It was being seen as an experiment which would extend to other parts of the museum, and the new Nutrition Gallery is a case in point where the exhibits or their close relations are on sale in the adjacent restaurant. Dr Wilson wrote in his 1987 report:

> The experiments extend their meaning. 'It [Launch Pad] does this less through its actual exhibits than through the attitudes it embodies: the idea of an exhibition where things happen and where museum people interact informally with visitors; the emphasis on trying to provide a particular sort of experience, directed towards explicit objectives and targeted to a specific sub-group of museum visitors; the idea that visitors should be 'managed' and that an exhibition is something that can develop and evolve through its life, rather than something set up and then forgotten; the need for flexible resourcing, to allow it to respond to changing patterns of visitor demand; above all, as an exhibition which is broadly 'interpretive' to the whole Museum, it raises questions about just what the museum should be trying to do through its public galleries.

Just so. Subsequently the museum's director, Neil Cossons, announced a complete rethink of the whole place in a five-year, £10 million programme (see Chapter 7), which included as a priority the correcting of one Launch Pad blunder: it was put in the only space available in 1986, 3,000 square metres next to the main entrance, so that 250,000 people were coming in for the hands-on games and going straight out again, missing all the rest of the museum, including the shop. Launch Pad has now been shifted to twice as much space at the rear of the first floor.

## *Eureka!*

The money for Launch Pad came from a three-way split between the museum's own funds, the Department of Technology and the Leverhulme Trust. Most of the money for Eureka! which was scheduled to open in Halifax in 1989 has come in the shape of a £5,000,000 grant from the Clore Foundation, the charity which provided the money for the Tate Gallery's new Turner extension.

The whole project began in 1979 when Mrs Rosemary Goldsmith, the wife of a Trusthouse Forte executive, took her own children to the children's museum in Los Angeles where they were encouraged to play with the exhibits, something I'd never seen before.' She came back home determined to establish something similar here, consulted experts, founded a charity called Children's Discovery Centre, got a £50,000 government research grant, and, with supreme optimism that the museum would be established, hired as director Stephen Feber, an ex-polytechnic teacher who had been, literally, toying with the idea himself. By 1985 they were ready to produce a brochure to try and attract sponsorship money, sent them out on a mailing list of thousands, and waited.

Just then Sir Charles Clore's daughter, Mrs Vivien Duffield, took her children to the Boston Children's Museum, inspiration of the Los Angeles one Mrs Goldsmith had seen. 'Here was this fantastic place for kids to "learn by doing",' she said, 'and nothing in Britain remotely like it. I came back wondering why not and Stephen's brochure came through the post, quite by chance. As I'd just seen these things I knew what it was about.'

For three years the project was called The Children's Museum, but by the time the Halifax site, 12 acres next to Halifax station, was found in 1987 it was called Eureka! The principle was broadly the same as the Exploratory's, although it prefers to borrow its epithets from the Americans rather than the French. Mrs Goldsmith quoting Dr Spock: 'I hear and I forget; I see and I remember; I do and I understand.'

But Eureka! goes beyond pure and applied science, aiming, like Launch Pad, at children in the sub-eleven age group. It has four themes: town and work life – which will have whole buildings cut away to show the workings of a house, a factory, a supermarket and a bank; the children themselves, exploring the human body and tackling the tricky matter of physical handicap; aesthetics and culture in which children will walk into a giant 'cello and be able to mix tapes in a recording studio; and design and technology computers and computer-based design.

Mr Feber was a convert to hands-on museums before he knew it. 'I had not liked the formal education system very much,' he said. 'I prefer informal situations which are either concrete or contextual. Each exhibit must allow the learner to experiment, so it has to be a variable situation. The definition of an attractive exhibit would be that it allowed play and experiment to take place for the learner.'

It is interesting how the preferred noun for a museum-goer is changing with the diversifying nature of museums: for Stephen Feber it is 'learner'; for Professor Gregory it is 'plorist'; for Dr Cossons of the Science Museum it is 'customer'. But Eureka! has experiments such as a pedal car which will only work if the four occupants pedal in harmony: 'Clearly it's as much a social event as a learning one.'

Stephen Feber wants children to be prepared for the business of living; Anthony Wilson hopes to encourage children to take up technological careers in due course; Professor Gregory has grander ambitions. He sees the natural progression of his

Exploratory to be 'inventories', where the dying breed of amateur scientists can be revived to the benefit of science and industry. 'I want to get industry interested in bright young people with ideas, and I want to help people invent things. It'll make the whole movement more positive. 'I'd like to have some real science in it, and we could have some on-going experiments maybe with socially interesting problems – pollution and so on – to get the public involved. That's the vital next step. And we need a research group on validating "hands-on", what works and what doesn't. So far we're just at the theology stage.'

## *TECHNIQUEST*

John Beetlestone is another professor, this time of science education at Cardiff University, who has been captivated by interactive learning, to the extent that in September 1988 he opened the biggest hands-on science centre in the country so far, TECHNIQUEST. It stands in what was Cardiff's notorious Tiger Bay district, now being nurtured to a renaissance by the Cardiff Bay Development Corporation who are Professor Beetlestone's landlords. He knows Professor Gregory well and the teams from TECHNIQUEST and the Exploratory have worked closely together on developing their projects, but they do not always see eye to eye; Professor Beetlestone stresses that the differences concern emphasis rather than fundamentals:

> Richard Gregory's team appear to work in the tradition set by the Exploratorium in San Francisco: the exhibit developer starts with a particular concept in mind and devises a clever 'plore' to illustrate it. Exhibits like this have a great appeal to visitors with some scientific background. Our approach starts with the visitor: what exhibits will have a wide appeal, how will the exhibit and its design contribute to the overall 'visitor friendly' ambience of TECHNIQUEST? Frequently, this approach involves 'seat of the pants' judgement – 'that appeals to us, and it will appeal to a range of people' – and what you end up with may be something based on more than one concept. Visitors choose how far they wish to go in understanding the science.

TECHNIQUEST has burst onto the Cardiff scene like a tidal wave, announcing its presence in November 1986 in a former city centre gas showroom on a six months' trial and getting 45,000 people in in that time, making it suddenly the third largest draw in the city after the Castle and the National Museum of Wales.

For John Beetlestone hands-on science started thousands of miles away, not this time in the United States but in Africa:

> My interest in science education was not what went on in schools but, in the jargon, non-formal science education outside schools. I'd seen the possibility of doing something of this sort when I was teaching chemistry in Nigeria. I was in a fairly well equipped chemistry department, perhaps the best in the third world, with forty or fifty highly sophisticated research students, but you'd walk out of the gate and suddenly you were in a traditional society. I was struck with the contrast between those people where science had become part of their culture and the rest of their society where it had no part at all.

He came back to Britain and found that the phenomenon was pretty much the same:

> For most of the population, science was something which was awful at school, boring, it was crazy people in white coats, it was about nuclear power, it was bad and people were alienated from it. I don't think this alienation from science is inevitable and it could be economically disabling: you cannot have modern production systems or even modern services where the people operating them are alienated from the whole basis of what they're making. It just won't work.

In June 1985 TECHNIQUEST was one sheet of paper in his filing cabinet, and a year later he had gathered a small group of enthusiasts who were turning the drawings they had on paper into actual exhibits. The opportunity of filling the space in the old gas showrooms, while British Gas planned the building's future, was their introduction not only to the public but to the development funders and the sponsors who were eventually to contribute over £1 million to the next phase of the project – the major sum from a Sainsbury Family Charitable Trust.

Almost a matter of days before they were due to leave their first site the Cardiff Bay Development Corporation was created and immediately adopted the TECHNIQUEST idea. That was April 1987, and they were promised their present Bute Street home for up to five years. The final plan was on the table in June 1988, and in September TECHNIQUEST opened again.

'We find that teachers bring the kids because it's a good stimulus, the children bring their parents and the parents get hooked. Wherever they live when they become parents themselves, they'll be saying "Where's the science centre in this town?" '

Centres like these, the Exploratory and Eureka! are examples of how the independent sector can bring a wanted extra dimension to the museum ethic, and the probability is that if the projects had been publicly funded they would have taken four or five years to develop before opening: the Science Museum's Launch Pad was three years in gestation, and local efforts in the north-east, north-west and Hampshire which began more or less simultaneously with TECHNIQUEST were still experimental when TECHNIQUEST opened for the second time with its eighty exhibits which range from a metal dragon that all but flies if you work out its principles, to an infra-red camera.

The first visit, as for all museums, is an important one, but the second is the one which shows that it works. 'We've got to provide a menu of educational dishes,' said Professor Beetlestone. 'Some people want fish and chips, some want caviar, some want to go on a diet. Hands-on science centres, if they're going to retain their educational integrity, have got to do more than just have the exhibits; they've got to begin to put in place those various dishes on the educational menu.'

But, to leave Professor Gregory with the last word, one of the smaller entries in the massive million-word *Oxford Companion of the Mind* – Oxford University Press's best seller in 1988 – says: 'Mind may depend as much upon the hands as it depends on the senses for gaining knowledge and so developing.'

# 9. The Water Margin

*Whether it was Britain which ruled the waves or vice versa, water courses through our veins more than any other nation's. It is an increasingly popular motif for heritage developments, and here we see the National Maritime Museum, the National Waterways Museum at Gloucester, the Ellesmere Port Boat Museum, and Dundee's development around Scott's ship, Discovery.*

IT was 1934 before we got a National Maritime Museum, and that was established at the nation's centre rather than a maritime one. Half a century later it went through a dramatic change to celebrate, said its director Richard Ormond, more than the expected Drake, Cook, Nelson face of history, but the nation's maritime life. The whole museum was recast, not only in its galleries but in its management because it was not only historical demands which had to be met, but those of a public increasingly aware of the charms and influence exerted on us by water.

One boat museum curator, Tony Hirst of Ellesmere Port, talks about the 'water explosion' in museums in the 1970s and 1980s, because it seems that every puddle gets a heritage centre set up beside it. It has been a symptom of the visitor emphasis to use not only historical motifs, but attractive ones as well, and in Britain it is hard to travel far without finding an appealing waterside.

Albert Dock in Liverpool has revitalised the city, and at the heart of it is a maritime museum, joined by the Tate Gallery's satrapy which opened in 1988, and a whole industry which brought over a million tourists to the water's side beneath the Liver Birds' patrician gaze. On the same coast, Maryport and Whitehaven have their maritime museums.

When Chatham Naval Dockyard was closed by the Ministry of Defence in 1984, it was almost immediately reopened as Chatham Historic Dockyard, pledged to re-create the history of the port where Drake learned his craft and the *Victory* was built. The Rope House never ceased production, 'cables' and 'sheets', to use the naval words, being spun through the length of the 800-yard building to the delight of increasing numbers of tourists each year. Robert Opie set up part of his collection in the Dockyard as an extra attraction, the sloop *Gannet* was brought in to be restored in full and open view, and Chatham was gradually becoming a working pageant of maritime history.

Thomas Sheppard, father of Hull's museums.

Thomas Sheppard's early Albion Street Museum in Hull.

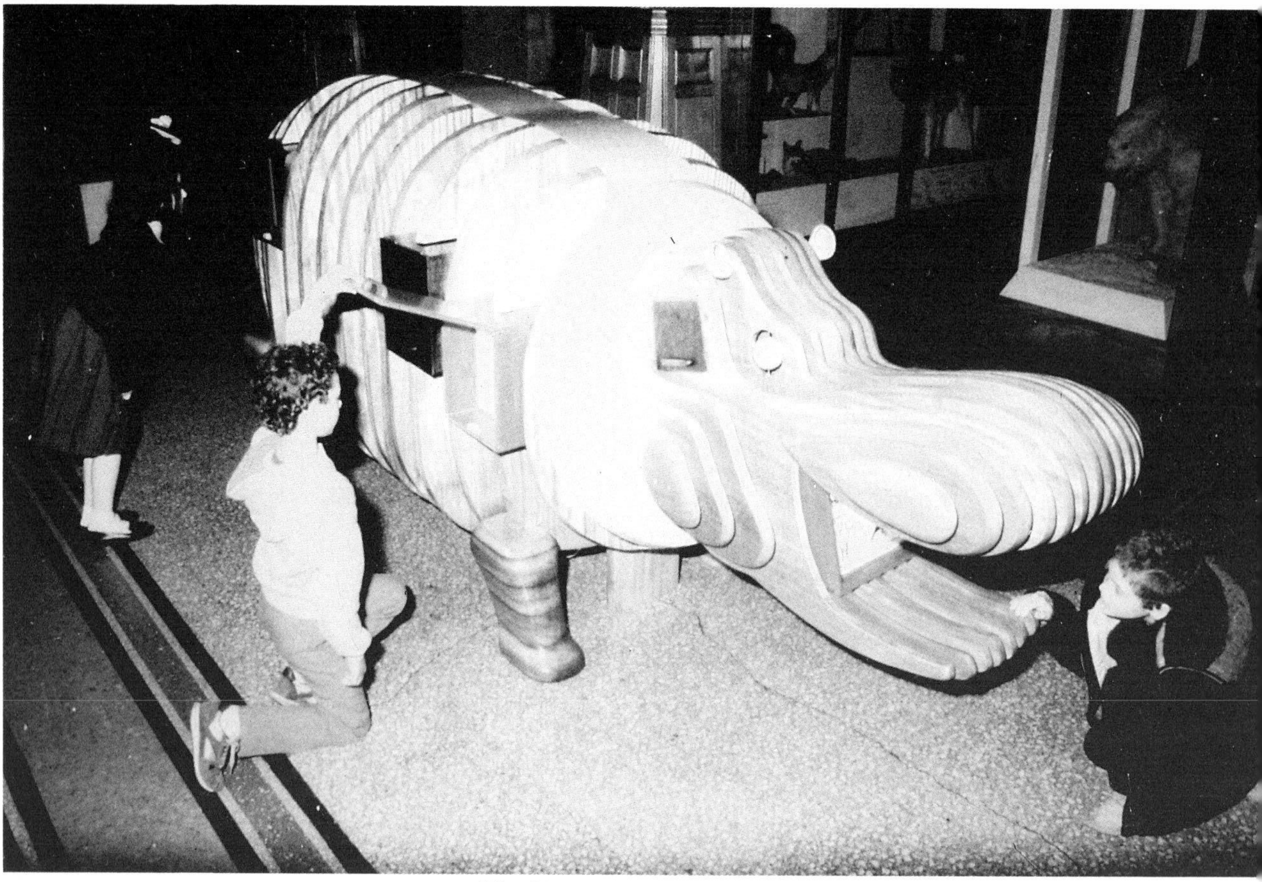

The Manchester Museum.

Actors perform social history at Wigan Pier Heritage Centre.

The Sun Inn, reconstructed at Beamish Open Air Museum.

Pit cottages, removed from the original site and rebuilt at Beamish with their interiors faithfully copied.

The 1890s library which was to become the Springburn Museum, Glasgow.

The Teenagers Exhibition at Springburn Museum in 1988.

In Portsmouth, England's naval navel, the Royal Dockyard, was being turned into Portsmouth Historic Naval Dockyard, with the Royal Naval Museum and a heroic fleet of exhibits: HMS *Warrior*, the ironclad which was the biggest, fastest and most fearfully armed warship of the 1860s; the *Mary Rose*, Henry VIII's warship which famously sank in 1545 during a Royal Review and just as famously was brought to the surface in 1982; and the most famous of all ships, HMS *Victory*, Nelson's warhorse and the oldest surviving ship of the line.

A massive £30 million project by British Ferries (which operate across the English Channel from Portsmouth) was under way to combine these attractions by creating a consensus community with shops, catering, additional attractions, which would attract three million visitors a year, said the head of the company, James Sherwood, by the time of it completion in 1993.

And Bristol Docks is fairly bristling with museums and galleries, from SS *Great Britain* to the National Lifeboat Museum, and at Exeter the Maritime Museum, opened in 1969 and run by the International Sailing Craft Association, has a new lease of life as well as new director and is drawing 80,000 visitors year to its restored warehouses in the Exeter Canal basin.

## *The National Waterways Museum, Gloucester*

In the second half of the industrial revolution, England's motorways were the canals which ribboned the country, the container lorries were the barges, narrow boats and assorted rivercraft which plied up, down and across.

'The fascination is seeing how they go through the landscape in a way that now appears to be natural, and knowing that they were all man-made and the motorways of their age, the commercial heart of the country,' said Tony Conder, curator of the National Waterways Museum at Gloucester Dock which the Prince of Wales formally opened in 1988.

It comes as a surprise to some to know that Gloucester, Cotswold capital and county town of one of our most agricultural shires, was an important port – for them there are more surprises to come, such as Lancaster which has a long-standing but newly enlarged and recast maritime museum celebrating its seafaring history, Wigan whose pier used to be a music hall joke and is now a phenomenal museum success, and Portland Basin at Ashton-under-Lyne against the Pennines where, at the junction of Peak Forest, Ashton and Huddersfield Narrow Canals opened a museum in 1988 in a canal warehouse.

Gloucester's Llanthony Warehouse is an imposing Victorian dockside sentinel for a long waterborne trading history for the city which elsewhere has developed out of recognition. Its cathedral is 900 years old, its maritime trade in corn and wine goes back beyond the reign of Richard I, and the chartered port of Gloucester dates from 1580. The River Severn gave it an inland highway too, so that the industries of iron, tanning, bell-founding, cloth and coal had no shortage of outlets within the kingdom.

In the spilling of canals on to the British countryside of two centuries ago, Gloucester was one of the first cities to establish its place at a central junction in the network of canals which criss-crossed the country. Dickens described Gloucester as 'an extraordinary inland port', and the seven-storey Llanthony of 1873 is only the most imposing of the most complete collection of early nineteenth-century buildings in an British inland port, with twenty listed buildings in 23 acres. So it is not so surprising that British Waterways decided to establish their National Waterways Museum here.

In their heyday there were 5,000 miles of canals through Britain, and most of them are still meandering, aimlessly now, through the countryside. Some are still carrying goods, some supply water, others have simply become part of the land drainage system. And more and more, like the Bridgewater and Leeds-Liverpool, are being restored.

But the new museum is concerned with history, 'The impact of canals as the major transport network around 1800,' said Tony Conder, who had been recruited from the Waterways Museum at Stoke Bruerne in Northamptonshire, also belonging to British Waterways and founded in 1963. 'That is a museum which displays objects in the traditional manner, whereas Gloucester tells a story and we tackle the subject in a different way.'

Llanthony was refurbished in a two-year £500,000 programme beginning in 1986, with its cast-iron columns, its large rectangular windows and its oaken floors. A replica canal maintenance yard was built alongside it which reused parts of old cannibalised canal buildings, including the roof and columns of an abandoned pump house. There is a smithy and a carpenter's workshop, both working. On the other side of the museum, in the Barge Arm where once goods were transferred from the ocean-going ships to the canal vessels for their inland journey, is a collection of historic canal craft.

The museum ventures to tell the canal story on three floors, so far, of the warehouse. It is a complex, and largely forgotten, tale: of the navvies who dug them; of the 'canal mania' when dozens of individual Acts of Parliament were rushed through, sometimes after construction had actually begun; how the distinctive canal boats themselves evolved; and of the people that worked the canals, their language, dress and folklore.

But the canal story is not one of just pastoral water-ratting, messing about in delightful roses-and-castles-decorated narrowboats gliding silently behind plodding horses. The steam age existed as much on the waterways as in the dark, satanic towns.

The little 20-foot tug *Walsall* worked on the Birmingham canals as a kind of industrial litter warden, siding away mud hoppers loaded with rubbish and bringing back the 'empties'. Now, with cut-away sections displaying its entrails, *Walsall* the bantam tug is the centrepiece of the section on propulsion. There is the 1890 steam engine which drove a narrowboat on the Basingstoke Canal; there is *Bluebird*, the 1924 river launch from the Worcester-Avon Canal; the *Oak*, a 1934 narrowboat designed to bring more comfort to those who worked her for the Severn & Canal Carrying Company.

Helping to tell the story is the heaviest, youngest and most unusual museum guide in the business: Peter, a five-year-old shire horse weighing a ton which lives permanently on the site and pulls the carriage which provides guided tours around the site. His ancestors pulled ocean-going boats up and down the canals, now he guides ocean-crossing tourists around the canals' history.

For there is as much outside the warehouse as within, and the star exhibit is an 82-foot-long steam dredger which worked the Gloucester & Sharpness Canal until as recently as 1982, and is fully restored as a floating, working exhibit.

The canal maintenance yard demonstrates how one would repair a lock gate, or any of the other thousands of fixtures or fittings which kept the canals and their passengers working through two centuries. The last section of the museum's current development programme opened in the winter of 1988 on the third floor, and is devoted to how canals work. Here visitors are able to steer electronically their own boats, open their own locks and 'get to grips with the technology of canals,' said Mr Conder. 'People are beginning to realise just what a valuable asset canals are. Some like to be actively involved, some like just to wander along the towpath, but we are introducing a lot more people to the magic of canals.'

By the end of its first summer season, in 1988, the National Waterways Museum at Gloucester had attracted 80,000 visitors through its galleries, well on target for the 250,000 predicted by 1991.

## *Ellesmere Port Boat Museum*

But Gloucester leaves boat repairs as such to the other national waterways museum. 'There was a bit of a farce over the name,' said Tony Hirst. 'We're both registered as the National Waterways Museum, so we've made a pact: everything that comes from there says "National Waterways Museum at Gloucester", ours says "The Boat Museum, Britain's Premier Canal and National Waterways Museum".' Mr Hirst's 'national' museum is at Ellesmere Port, a name created by the canals, and the museum predates the Gloucester one by twelve years. There is a friendly rivalry now, and an increasing degree of co-operation. 'We know Gloucester well, we get on with them and we have a fair amount of correspondence, and we swap bits,' said Mr Hirst, the museum's director. 'We've had discussions about having a much closer relationship, even to the extent of swapping trustees or board of management members. It makes sense.'

'Canals in the early 1970s were being regenerated,' said Mr Hirst. 'Old ones were being reopened, the hire boat industry was booming, you had lots of pleasure boat owners, so the canals as such were safe. But the traditional use of the canals was disappearing rapidly. Particularly the wooden boats, and the way people lived on them, operated them and maintained them, were very quickly going to vanish.'

Before the canal mania, Ellesmere Port was called Netherpool, a quiet little fishing port 20 miles up the Mersey from Liverpool. Businessmen at Ellesmere another 30 miles south in Cheshire caught the bug: they wanted to connect with the booming Merseyside, with the Dee and Severn rivers and also provide an artery to industrial North Wales, so they created their own canal system via the Shropshire Union.

But it was not the first choice site for the museum when a group of canal enthusiasts – including the then director of The Manchester Museum, the late Dr David Owen – began to realise a dream of bringing together old boats, restoring them, sailing them and creating a small museum around them and the life and techniques of the canals.

At first the museum to preserve all this was to be at Preston Brook near Runcorn, close to the junction of the Trent and Mersey and the Bridgewater Canals, a trans-shipment point where barges would come off the Mersey, up the locks at Runcorn, and off to Manchester. Instead the site became a housing estate.

'Ellesmere Port was a very big site, derelict mostly, and was at the end of a canal line, so it wasn't seen to be a particularly practical place to go, and the money didn't seem to be around,' Tony Hirst recalled. They went away again and looked at more alternatives, but returned in 1974 – just after local government reorganisation which was to bring major changes to the museum scene in Britain – and talked to the council. 'A number of councillors thought it would be a good idea to reclaim their derelict dockland and open an industrial museum or something, so the idea of having a boat museum was welcomed. We were told that the money wouldn't be available to do it properly, but we decided the best bet was to set off in a small way restoring one small building with collections, restoring more boats, and opening to the public in the summer 1976.' It opened every summer for the next few years, and gradually grew.

A job-creation scheme was invented for the project, and the local authority got a derelict land grant too, the first time it had been done for a museum: 'Normally under that system buildings are cleared and the land is left to nature until a developer comes along,' said Mr Hirst. 'Instead, because it was a conservation area, the local authority went to the Department of the Environment and said it would cost much the same to restore the buildings as to clear the land, and the DoE went out on a limb and agreed to it. That's now policy so all your Albert Docks and your Castlefields (site of a railway station which now has the Manchester Museum of Science and Industry on it) and your Wigan Piers have all been done on the same principle.'

But it might yet have remained a rather precious little enthusiasts' centre, despite a visit by the Queen and Prince Philip in 1979 which gave it national publicity, and an English Tourist Board grant, if it had not been for the Toxteth Riots of 1981. Tony Hirst had become director of the museum in 1980, and he related to me the next chapter in its story:

> Michael Heseltine came round with his cheque book and his Mr Merseyside hat on, looking for initiatives. We did a development plan, expanding the museum into the

> derelict areas – we were only occupying about 20 per cent of the site then – using other buildings around, clearing up the dereliction, and very quickly several million pounds arrived to do this work, through the Merseyside Task Force.
>
> This money and job creation is one of the most interesting things in modern museum development because it's generated a whole stack of money which would never have been there otherwise.
>
> Unless you have the riots and the initiatives to do inner cities and the rest, the capital money for most of the major industrial museums would not be there. They all happened because somebody decided they wanted to clear up the inner cities.

Many waterside museums were being generated out of docklands sites in the late 1980s by developers who chiefly wanted a commercial estate with housing and leisure facilities, and who saw the museum as a useful way to keep heritage watchdogs happy and provide an extra dimension.

Other developments are growing around the Ellesmere Port museum now, but the regeneration here happened the other way round. 'The museum came first, but the pay-back to the government for investing £8 million in that part of the land must go for some other commercial development, so the museum is being surrounded by houses,' said Tony Hirst.

The Boat Museum Trust was formed in 1981, and all seven remaining buildings have now been restored and fitted out. There are some sixty boats, some in the water, some on dry land, some inside; there are shops, a cafe and boat trips. The museum's brochure sets the scene for its visitors:

> Forget the world of computers and imagine that you drive a long-distance lorry and live in it with your family. You have no other home and you may or may not own the lorry. To eke out a living your family must assist with the driving, loading and unloading. You may make long journeys right across the country or short ones, within a confined area.
>
> Now, instead of a lorry, imagine that you all live in a small cabin about six feet by eight feet at the end of a boat which you have to navigate with its cargo along the canals and that each one of you must work from dawn to dusk. The family must be dressed and fed, the horse or engine has to be fuelled and watered, cajoled and led; you have to manipulate the docks, swing-bridges, sluices, and cranes. The cargo must be delivered as soon as possible, whatever the weather.

The main exhibition deals generally with the canals, their history and how they developed, how they declined, and the effect on the populations in the areas around them. There are also exhibitions about carrying goods on the waterways, the Manchester Ship Canal, horses and the 'cut', the town of Ellesmere Port and its history.

The public like the boats best, it is what they return for, according to the museum's marketing research. There are also four restored cottages. 'We show the social history of the people who lived on the coast, and we also show how they lived on the shore. There used to be twelve 1830s cottages, and eight were demolished to make way for a garage. We kept four, restored them and they're set out as they would have been in the 1840s, 1900s, 1930s and 1950s.' Even, like Beamish's houses, with roaring fires, for the museum is now open all year round.

Visitors have probably reached their optimum numbers at 100,000 a year, 'As high as it can get without significant changes in the local environment and the local authority wishing to promote itself and put some money into tourism.'

It had been a traumatic time for an area which in the late 1970s and early 1980s had been badly hit by recession, the Vauxhall motor factory cutting its labour force dramatically, the paper mills closing down and the oil refineries reducing operations. Now it has become a centre of out-of-town shopping in the resurgant Wirral.

The Boat Museum has become something of a community centre, as the Victorian inner city museums were, with a conference centre which the county council uses for training, concerts, events and community days when the museum is opened cheaply, and there are craft fairs.

But, like most of new museums in the late twentieth century boom, certainly the industrial ones – Ellesmere Port Boat Museum is a working museum, and the chief work is restoration. 'We restore out in front of the public. Part of the attraction is to see people working, and sometimes participating in some of the work,' Mr Hirst said. 'We also let the people go on the boats, so we try and use all the senses.

'When we restore the boats we sail them. One of them has just been down to the Black Country Museum in the Midlands and it's come back with 16 tonnes of gravel on board. We restored an ice-breaker, the *Marbury*, the first wooden ice-breaker we've attempted, and we're hoping for a short, sharp cold winter to try it out.'

## *The* Discovery *Centre*

The ship builders of Dundee, Scotland's fourth city, know all there is to know about seafaring in Arctic conditions, and at the turn of this century were internationally pre-eminent. 'Dundee played a fundamental part in Arctic and Antarctic exploration,' said Jonathan Bryant, chief executive of Dundee Industrial Heritage. 'The reason we were building those ships here was that it was Dundee fishermen who went up to the Arctic and hunted whales there, in fact Amundsen came to Dundee for advice while he was preparing for his South Pole expedition. In 1904 Scott was relieved from the ice in the North Sea by a Dundee whaling captain.'

It was Commander, later Captain, Scott who, on behalf of the National Antarctic Expedition Committee which was sponsored by the Royal Society, the Royal Geographical Society and the government, commissioned Dundee Shipbuilders Limited to build him a research ship for his 1901 Antarctic expedition. She was the Royal Research Ship *Discovery*, now back home after a life of Odyssean adventure, to be the focal point for a £5,000,000 waterside heritage development.

*Discovery* took Scott and his party to the southern ice and brought them home again three years later, but it was not this ship which carried the explorer on his fatal race with Amundsen for the South Pole in 1912, for *Discovery* had been pensioned off.

'At that time she was working for the Hudson Bay Company, plying across the Atlantic,' said Mr Bryant, whose company is the commercial arm of the project, the charity, formed by the local authority, being the Dundee Heritage Trust. It was the *Terra Nova*, another Dundee-built ship, which took Scott on the journey south from which he did not return, and which was eventually sunk by German torpedoes during the Second World War in the North Sea.

'*Discovery* did all kinds of things after the first Scott voyage,' said Mr Bryant. 'After 1904 she went to the Hudson Bay Company, and she was running guns for the French in the First World War. Then she was a general cargo and trading ship for a while.' In the 1920s she was refitted at Portsmouth and was back on Antarctic duties as a research ship investigating the whaling grounds around South Georgia, and then came possibly the truly high point of her career. 'In the early 30s she went on an Antarctic expedition again, for the British, Australian and New Zealand Antarctic Research Expedition led by Mawson. *Discovery* really did a tremendous amount of work at that time, and in many people's view did a more useful scientific research job then than she did carting Scott off with all the hullabaloo in 1901–04.'

Then, when *Discovery II* took over her role, the thirty-year-old withdrew to the East India Docks for five years, in reluctant retirement and rather a sorry state. But in 1936 she was found a new job to do, moored at the Victoria Embankment, a role that several generations of schoolboys came to know her in: she became a training ship for sea scouts and sea cadets, and then was commissioned by the Admiralty as a drill ship for the Royal Naval Volunteer Reserve. 'She was training all the way through until the Admiralty got fed up with her running costs in the late Seventies,' said Jonathan Bryant. 'In 1979 the Maritime Trust convinced the Admiralty that they shouldn't just tow her out to be torpedoed or set fire to, but that she was worthy of preserving. The maritime Trust set her up on St Katharine's dock as part of an historic ship collection, and she became a public visitor vessel then from about 1980 to 1985.'

But, although *Discovery* had been saved from becoming target practice for the Royal Navy, her time in St Katharine's Dock was not a success. There was no parking for visitors, berth rental was high, and the arrangement meant that tourists were able to see the ships without contributing to her upkeep.

'When we came along and said we could restore the vessel well in Dundee and safeguard its future, the authorities were keen to listen.' She left St Katharine's Dock on the high tide of 27 March 1986, piggy-back on the support vessel *Happy Mariner*, and thousands of Dundonians were on the quay to welcome her home six days later.

'What we have now,' said Mr Bryant, 'is a project based on local pride and enthusiasm for a tremendous symbol of Dundee's industrial trading past, and a new property development in Dundee in which *Discovery* has a prominent part, while at the same time the development helps support the maintenance costs of the ship in the longer term.

Because she was much altered in the refit of 1923–24 – including the removal of a mast – she was being restored to her appearance in the late 20s and early 30s. Restoration proved to be an even greater task than expected because the structure of the ship itself was found to need immediate and urgent attention, a lengthy restructuring which had to be completed before the interior of the vessel could be tackled. But she was nevertheless opened for a short twenty-week season in 1988 and attracted 50,000 visitors. Actors were recreating scenes on board, and slipping into role-play with visitors, to bring the atmosphere of the old ship to life.

'The shore-based facilities, the *Discovery* Centre which is part of the new waterfront development, will include all of the interpretation, displays and exhibitions,' said Mr Bryant, 'so that when we restore *Discovery* we're not creating a museum but re-creating the ship of the 1925 period.' Restoration was costing £500,000, with the support facilities costing some £5,000,000, three-fifths of which was being generated out of the property development. More money was coming from the Scottish Development Agency.

'We have been looking at models in Baltimore, Boston, and South Street in New York,' Jonathan Bryant said. 'What we've done is to take the best practice elsewhere and tailor it for the particular circumstances in Dundee. We've turned to theatre in advance of restoring the interior of *Discovery*, with role-play which goes back to the 1901 building and expedition, and takes the story right through.'

The *Discovery* Centre, due to be finished in 1991, sets the ship's history in the context of the industrial story of Dundee. 'What we'll do is take people through the story of 'jute, jam and journalism' to the shipbuilding and the *Discovery* herself, taking them through the atmosphere of the Antarctic via the *Discovery* Dome. So we'll set the scene for the building of the ship, the voyage to the Antarctic and the Antarctic itself.'

All this has been conceived by a veteran exhibition and museum designer who was born only seven years after *Discovery*, James Gardner, former Cartier jeweller, advertising artist and wartime camouflage expert who had been awarded the CBE in 1958 for designing and organising the British exhibit in the Brussels World Fair. Among his later triumphs is the Commonwealth Institute in London, and up to 250,000 people are expected to visit his Dundee creation.

But, like the Ellesmere Port Boat Museum, the *Discovery* Centre is being geared to two markets: the tourists of the summer, and the local visitors who will come again and again. 'Local people haven't had that kind of facility before,' said Mr Bryant. 'We're using flexible spaces so we can look at all kinds of innovative programmes. This *Discovery* Dome, for example, is collapsible in winter to make theatre spaces to do other things in.

'A new museum is opening every eighteen days in Scotland, and what we're going to have to do is look at developing facilities which attract repeat use by local people far more than we've been used to doing in the past. There'll be meeting space for local societies overlooking the ship, so that people can come and be at home with us, so we're not alien and a separate organisation.'

# 10. It's real, but is it true?

*Making history live has its obvious appeal, and is one of the elements responsible for drawing such huge numbers into our museums. To see if and how it works this chapter examines Jorvik Viking Centre and the other developments of its creators in Canterbury, Oxford and Edinburgh, the Tutenkhamun Exhibition in Dorchester, Arbeia Roman Fort in South Shields and, once again, Beamish Open Air Museum.*

WHAT is a museum? The definition in the Introduction seems pretty straightforward, the translation of a Greek word to mean a tranquil place of enlightenment and inspiration, a definition which might have been enough 200 and 100 years ago.

But it will not do any longer. The Museums and Galleries Commission launched a museums registration scheme in 1988 designed to weed out the museums which fall below a minimum standard, but they launched themselves into a dilemma which would not have existed 100, 50 or even 20 years before.

The key factor is a collection of specimens, objects or artefacts, their curation and cataloguing. But while the major phenomenon of the 1880s was the recognition of the needs of the non-expert visitor, in the 1980s it was the emergence of the museum designed to teach through entertainment, appealing to visitors to invest their leisure time rather than their learning time in visits.

Does Madame Tussaud's count? It attracts something like three million people a year who come to see history, as they have done for a century and a half, and leave content that they have. The tableauxe have mostly been created in accordance with precise historical research, but it would not qualify under the MGC guidelines; nor would the new Tussaud creation at Windsor, where, on the famous station, Queen Victoria and her entourage are seen arriving.

While the Jorvik Viking Centre will be recognised under the MGC's definition, it is not because of its main display, the re-created Viking village of the tenth century with authentic sounds and smells as well as sights; it is a museum because of the small archaeological collection it has. But Jorvik has been the pioneer for a new breed of museum with no collections, but scholarship, entertainment and consummate commercial acumen as their basis.

Kicking his heels in York in 1977 after being demobbed from the Army, ex-Major Anthony Gaynor decided to join the tourists and have a look at the archaeological dig going on at Coppergate. The result was a multi-million pound operation which many regard as the most significant advance in museum thinking so far. A gregarious sort, Mr Gaynor got chatting to York Archaeological Trust's Peter Addyman about costs. 'It struck us that here we had a super story: York is a tourist destination, let's let people in to show them what the excavation's all about.' Dr Addyman admits that neither of them knew where the adventure was going to take them, but for him there was nothing to lose and the financing of his excavations to gain. For Anthony Gaynor there was a complete recasting of the ideas for his future, the eschewing of a possibly lucrative career in the Far East as a Chinese interpreter.

'At the start it was my wife sitting by a tatty old table taking donations and selling postcards, and we gradually increased the sophistication until we had a couple of Portakabins, a slide-tape show and we started making money, all of which went to finance the dig,' he said.

The York Archaeological Trust was founded in 1972, and three years later a sweet shop and a pub on the medieval Coppergate site in the city were demolished to make way for a new shopping complex. The trust had six months to investigate it, but the developers ran into difficulties, so that six months turned into six years. In the end the development had to be built around the dig, not in its place. 'As the archaeologists got further into the ground they saw the greater richness in the deposits and deduced more from it because techniques were progressing almost as they worked,' said Mr Gaynor. 'So this marvellous story unfurled.'

As they dug deeper into the ground they dug further into history, and the site became a major curiosity. It was at this point that the Gaynors arrived, and before long more sophisticated means of testing public reaction were being tried. 'We started taking visitor surveys. The thing that was for ever coming up was, "Isn't it a pity that it's all going to be destroyed".' Gaynor and Addyman started to think of ways of saving it, and began talking to businessmen, including garage magnate Ian Skipper. 'What he brought was not only a certain amount of money, he also imposed disciplines upon us, and gave us tremendous help in allowing us to expand along the correct lines later on. He gave us the confidence to do it.'

But still, what they had was a big hole and no precedent to work on, only a forest of by-laws and regulations to peer through at their goal.

They went to the drawing board many times with different approaches: walk-rounds, lifts that went up and down, a four-storey building where visitors started at the top and worked down through a corkscrew to the floor. They were all discarded, and memories of Disneyland – almost an obscenity in the museum world of 1977 – where people were conveyed round in carts began to influence matters.

The big problem was the hole factor. 'We decided to make a disadvantage into an advantage. One of the important conceptual aspects is that the Viking Centre is physically in the ground where the Vikings were. You had somehow to disorientate people from the twentieth century and take them back to the tenth.' And that is literally what they did: visitors enter trollies like roller-coaster carts and are whisked back through the centuries to the village of AD 940, Jorvik, the word which became York.

'One of the benefits was that we were not hampered by a conventional museum upbringing. We were not looking at this through the disciplines which the museum profession normally look at these things,' said Mr Gaynor, adding: 'I have no qualifications apart from the ability to make other people work.'

But they still had the disciplines of scholarship, which demanded unrelenting accuracy. The archaeologists were able to provide enough evidence to pinpoint the layout of the Viking settlement, and to this was added not the tailor's dummies and wax fruit of some displays, but sculptured figures drawn from life. Sounds were added, research at Nottingham University having shown that the Viking language was uncannily similar to modern Icelandic; smells were provided, too, of smoke, wood, leather, fruit, even the odour of a privy.

What they thought was going to be a handicap, assuring fire authorities that they would not overload the basement, was turned into an asset because the limiting of numbers to 100 on the basement floor at any time meant they could regulate accurately and be more sophisticated in the effects – they suffer virtually no vandalism. There are twenty-one cars carrying four passengers on the twelve-minute trip, and each one has an explanatory commentary coming through a speaker in the seat-back, spoken by a genuine Icelander, television personality, Magnus Magnusson, but in English.

The financing of the whole enterprise was critical, and as this has been an object lesson to many other heritage enterprises it is worth looking at how they did it. First Gaynor, Addyman and Skipper formed a company, Heritage Projects Limited (HPL). Then they persuaded the English Tourist Board to start the bandwagon rolling in the quest for £2,650,000; they chipped in £250,000, persuaded by Skipper's own investment of another quarter-of-a-million. He then went to bankers NM Rothschild who created a syndicate of seven banks to provide £1.4 million; £200,000 lease-purchasing of equipment and £550,000 from agreed deferred contract payments with the builder, Wimpey, provided the rest. The centre was £2.2 million in the red when the Prince of Wales opened it in 1984, but within two years £325,000 had gone to the York Archaeological Trust. 'Priority one is to educate the public in archaeology; priority two is to make money for the Trust' – and by the summer of 1988 the whole debt was cleared.

After a year they were getting 600,000 visitors, after two they had reached their optimum, 890,000. Success was not so much a surprise, but the extent and speed of it was. Perhaps it should not have been. 'It was a totally new type of project, our marketing was extremely good, our location in a major tourist centre was right, and I think the close support of both Magnus Magnusson and the Prince of Wales helped greatly.'

But by that time they had new projects running, others being planned. From Jorvik's turnover HPL bought a redundant church in Canterbury, St Margaret's, to become The Canterbury Pilgrims' Way at a cost of £1.3 million, £1 million coming from HPL's own resources this time, £120,000 from an ETB grant and the rest from another Rothschild consortium. The scholarly link is the Canterbury Archaeological Trust.

The Canterbury project would have difficulty meeting the MGC's criteria for a museum; conventional museum curators have condemned it as not being historical, merely a superficial representation of a piece of medieval literature for mass consumption. But the project has been researched by scholars, and provides an enjoyable insight into medieval life and the Canterbury Tales quite probably by modern people who would never come into contact with Chaucer or his writing in any other way.

Scholarship had to be beyond doubt for The Oxford Story because the university itself was picking up 20 per cent of the £1.75 million bill; the rest was again HPL cash bolstered by another ETB grant, this time for £150,000. It tells the story of Oxford, its university and its personalities – on three storeys of a former book warehouse right in the centre of the dreaming spires.

The Edinburgh Tolbooth was the next HPL enterprise, opening in 1989 in the former Church of Scotland's General Assembly church at the end of the Royal Mile and in the shadow of Edinburgh Castle.

Heritage Projects have also diversified, offering a consultancy to the likes of the Scottish Whisky Distillers for their new display in Edinburgh which opened in 1988. They offer marketing advice, and ran the visitors' centre at Winchester's The Brooks archaeological dig, providing information, leaflets, lecturers and, in effect, a temporary museum for the duration of the dig in the summer of 1988. They run the Museum Association's own shop in London. They have also gone into partnership with a development company to provide heritage aspects for inner city developments. They have been criticised for distracting the public's attention from more worthy museums with their brand of heritage entertainment, but this meets with a shrug from Anthony Gaynor.

> People expect to have information imparted to them in a digestible format now without being made to feel inferior because they don't understand the subject. I think quite a lot of museums have been somewhat patronising in the way they have treated their visitors. A lot of it is to do with the mental approach adopted by the museum professional, which is changing dramatically now. Our historic heritage is that part that tourists come to see.

'What we have established beyond doubt is that there is a volume market for correctly interpreted, fairly complex academic subjects. To say that any subject is far too complex for the average visitor to comprehend is damning and elitist,' said Anthony Gaynor.

The danger for Heritage Projects may be that they grow too fast and become too ambitious to sustain their own growth, often the fate for successful new enterprises. Mr Gaynor,has devised a strict programme for projects over the next ten years to ensure that they do not overreach themselves: measured progress, the basic training of an infantry company commander.

But whatever their future, what they have done with our past is to revolutionise the way of looking at it, so that any member of the public who can afford the admission price can enjoy history. It is not so different from Sir William Flower's New Museum Idea of a century ago.

'Heritage Projects,' says Ian Skipper in their glossy brochure, 'is a new breed of company, formed with the prime objective of presenting our worldwide cultural heritage to the broadest public in a manner which combines entertainment and educational values whilst maintaining the essential integrity of the subject matter displayed.'

## *Tutenkhamun Exhibition*

The practice of bringing archaeological digs to life has become almost commonplace, with major digs at least having viewing platforms if not visitor centres, as the need for funds to finance excavations became more acute and the public were being seen as a source. But for Michael Ridley the archaeology of a particular site, and not a British one, obsessed him for many years before he found the right outlet for what he believed was a crowd-puller.

Dr Ridley is an egyptologist who had been involved with the British Museum's great Tutenkhamun exhibition of 1972, contributing to the catalogue. It was perhaps the first blockbuster exhibition since the Second World War, and astonished organisers with the way it caught the public imagination.

He maintained contacts with the Egyptian authorities, and dreamt of re-creating at least the essence of that exhibition as a permanent display: the tomb of the boy king. He had been curator of Weymouth and Portland Museums (so that his professional grounding was quite different from Anthony Gaynor's), and he gave up his job in order to travel the world researching his project.

What he wanted to do was bring the tomb of Tutenkhamun, as it were, to life. He needed to study all the major archives in Egypt and New York, not just for the political story and the social history, but also for the details of how the objects found in the tomb in 1922 by Howard Carter were made, and from what materials.

'We wanted everything made by living craftsmen because that way you inject a degree of life into an object. Casts would be cold and lifeless,' he said. He wanted to recreate precisely the appearance of the tomb, with the exact objects and works of art in replica, all of which, once he had researched them – and Howard Carter had kept detailed notes on everything – he had made within 100 miles of his site, a redundant monastic church in Dorchester. 'Carter even noted the smells as he entered the tomb, a very valuable description because it gave us a base to work on. We were able to use the original oils and similar ointments to re-create them.'

The choice of Dorchester for the site was not by chance. Dorset is museum-rich but property was relatively cheap compared with London, and the county town is close to motor and rail routes.

Tutenkhamun's Tomb relies greatly on Dr Ridley's scholarship to make it work. It's first section explains the Egypt of 1300 years ago, introducing the young king and 'the whole process of life and death as they saw it. Then come the burial chambers themselves, with the curious life of their own which catacombs often seem to have. In the third area are facsimiles of some of the most famous works of art from the ancient world, celebrated in the 1972 show and re-created here, the main piece being the mask of the king, solid gold inlaid with enamel, along with a statuette of Tutenkhamun as a harpooner, a figure of the jackal-headed god of embalming, Anubis, and the lotus head of the boy king being born out of a flower.

With much moral support from his Egyptian friends but no money, Dr Ridley raised all the finance – 'hundreds of thousands of pounds' – from local businesses. The Tutenkhamun Exhibition opened in 1987, and is an example of what can be done by a museum-trained curator with a scholarship burning to get out, no money but an idea which appeals to those who have money to help him create the objects. It stands almost opposite a famous old municipal museum, Dorset County Museum, and they complement each other in one of England's more delightful towns.

## *Arbeia Roman Fort*

South Shields has kept its delights to itself. A town of the nineteenth century, it was an uncompromising seaside resort of industrial Tyneside, one where nobody made jokes about the landladies. But in the second century it was very important indeed, as archaeologists in the 1970s gradually discovered. It had a fort: Arbeia; that much they knew from their history books, and excavations had been going on for more than a century. What they began to realise was that it was *the* fort, as far as the north of Britain was concerned, which has been the heart of Roman activity, and was archaeologically unique. 'What makes the fort very important is that South Shields is the only permanent stone-built supply base that has ever been excavated in the whole of the Roman Empire,' said Paul Bidwell, the excavation director.

Arbeia was built in AD 163 and was the supply centre for the Emperor Septimius Severus in his three-year campaign to subjugate the Scots (he died at York in AD 211), and it continued to be the larder for the garrisons along Hadrian's Wall through the third and fourth centuries.

'At first it was a fairly conventional fort, but about forty years later it was enlarged and completely replanned. It became a supply base and the interior of the fort was filled with stone-built granaries – twenty-four of them with a capacity of about 3,500 tons of grain,' said Bidwell. 'It's an urban area with no landscape value, such as other Roman sites like Halstead and Chester,' said Mr Bidwell. 'We came up with a project which is a very radical departure from the way ancient monuments are usually treated and we thought it was the appropriate thing to do.'

What they came up with was, in archaeological terms, a very daring plan indeed: to reconstruct the fort's gateway in the centre of the town exactly on the foundations of the original second-century building, the first time it has ever been allowed in this country. The Tyne and Wear Museums Service, the local authority's parent unit for the scheme, had to fight English Heritage all the way to a public inquiry to win final approval.

'Up to then,' said Mr Bidwell, 'the policy had been to conserve as found, and this had been adhered to quite rigidly since the later nineteenth century. We felt that the principle in general was sound but that we had special circumstances – the remains are much more poorly preserved than many others, and the setting of the fort is quite different.'

So they built their 35-foot gateway, towering above the town, to summon a ghost of an existence reaching back further than Jorvik to a civilisation which succeeded Tutenkhamun's. Arbeia has a collection and a museum, Mr Bidwell being its curator now, and is acceptable in the MGC's definition.

The gate tower itself has become a museum, with a typical quartermaster's store of the late second century reconstructed within it and replicas of the kind of foodstuffs, utensils, pottery, glass, tools, weapons, which would have been issued from Arbeia. Roman armour and weaponry are displayed in another room. 'What we've tried to do is point up the differences between the life of a modern soldier and that of a Roman,' said Paul Bidwell. 'They had to carry out a lot of tasks which were not military at all: they had a wide range of skills as craftsmen – building, surveying, metalworking, and semi-private things like working jet into objects, and we've also tried to convey a bit about the religious aspects and leisure activities such as hunting and gambling. There were also similarities. Even for a Roman soldier, the Army was a profession that offered job security, welfare was well organised, they served for a set term, twenty-five years, and there were compulsory savings that went towards a retirement grant.'

In the summer schools are invited to act out a day in the life of a Roman soldier, and ordinary members of the public can take part in making pottery, weaving, even preparing Roman food.

Much of this has become conventional museum activity. What they did with Arbeia was to challenge accepted thinking in order to bring their subject matter to life, to recreate something which had passed out of existence less than two centuries after Christ's death. That dominating tower is an attempt to bring people in touch with a distant life, and 50,000 people a year go to this unprepossessing corner of the country to make contact.

## *Beamish Open Air Museum*

Bringing people into closer contact with their own lineal past was Frank Atkinson's dream, related in Chapter 6, in creating Beamish Open Air Museum a couple of dozen miles to the south-west of South Shields. He wanted to celebrate 'Geordie life' in the fifty years which straddle the turn of this century as best he could, and his success can be seen in the 450,000 people who celebrate with him every year and the awards he has won.

But where is the trades union struggle? Where is the appalling mortality rate? Where is the daily struggle to survive, for mothers and wives to make ends meet? Where, ask the critics, is reality?

Mr Atkinson was succeeded in 1987 by Peter Lewis, a one-time department store manager, theatre marketing man and founder of Wigan Pier, who in respect of museums ethics has carried on where the founder had left off. 'Beamish has been accused of being rosy and cosy, and I think there is a selective kind of criticism going on. What Frank was actually saying when he first did this was, "I'm going to collect buildings, artefacts, things that relate to what life was like during the appropriate timespan, and I'm going to exhibit them without anything coming between them and the visitor". It's a very purist approach.'

That purism was, of course, diluted by discreet didactic here and there, and the fact that there has always been someone to ask. Whatever the Lewis formula, in eighteen months he had increased attendances by nearly 50 per cent and launched a £3,500,000 development programme partly to fulfil more of Frank's dream, partly to realise some of his own, by the early 1990s.

'Critics say you must be showing how awful the world was and how dreadful it all was, and I don't think that was necessarily true. I think it's an arrogant presumption; it's like the Monty Python sketch about the old men who compete with anecdotes of the poverty of their childhood which ends with one of them saying, "I was born in a hole in the road." It's nonsense. They – the critics – will come along and say the miner's cottages are wrong, the size of the rooms is wrong, the furniture is wrong, but that is the furniture which was in those rooms, those are the actual miners' cottages. Our taste may have changed, but not history.

'We are extending the farms; we will farm and plough, we'll have reaping days, but I think it very unlikely that we'll castrate sheep in front of the public, though in a purely professional sense I suppose we should.'

If it is the British way to Romanticise the past in trying to present a revived reality in a way a modern audience will appreciate, a curious fact is that it is not the local visitors who are swelling the visitor numbers at Beamish – up 50 per cent, says Mr Lewis, in the first eighteen months of his tenure. The new visitors are the discerning foreigner, Australians, Canadians, South Africans, New Zealanders, and there are school trips from Scandinavia, West Germany and Holland across the North Sea.

Open-air museums allow space – in this case 300 acres – to paint on a broad canvas, which gives infinite scope for re-creation, re-enactment and, it may be true, revision. They are undeniably popular, whatever their accuracy, which is of an increasingly high order.

The new realism which Jorvik, Ironbridge, Beamish and perhaps the Science Museum is ushering in, along with scores of other museums in Britain, in their presentations is a response to the demands of a public thirsty for entertainment in their education, and these demands are being monitored as never before. The museological finger is more and more on the public pulse, but not on behalf of all museums or all museum watchers.

Peter Lewis summed-up his own personal museum *credo*:

> If I was the kind of business marketing man which I am often conveyed as being, the first thing I would crop would be the archive, I'd sell some of the collections, and the last thing I would try to do is develop the educational provision because it costs money. I could have Nissan on the side of that bus because they have just created 2,000 jobs in this region and they would pay handsomely; while we might well accept Nissan's sponsorship for education purposes, there's no way I could put their advertisement on the side of a period vehicle for whatever the money, but I can think of a few curators who might.'

# 11. Sticky fingers

*It is not only the project work of the new GCSE exams which have made museums suddenly even more important for children than they were, it has been the quest for entertainment in the increasing sterility of other forms, and even the realisation that childhood itself and its chattels are of museological interest. Here we visit the Bethnal Green Museum of Childhood, the Toy and Model Museum and Haggs Castle.*

VICTORIAN museums were primarily educational, but their market was the adult who wanted to improve himself. Children were tolerated in the big museums, but it was only the enlightened curator or the local museum who would organise anything specifically for children, and when he did it was mostly in the form of natural history rambles or Saturday morning lectures. On the whole museums were places where youngsters were seldom seen and never heard.

When Arthur Sabin took up the children's banner in 1923 he was pioneering something which only became an established part of museum management fifty years later. Now museum displays are specifically aimed at children as a discerning section of the public which works as a useful barometer for the rest of the museum-going population.

Sabin joined the Victoria and Albert Museum in the year it opened, 1909. In its previous existence, as the South Kensington Museum, its first home had been a prefabricated iron and glass building designed by the Royal Engineers architect, Francis Fowke, and known with little affection as 'the Brompton Boilers'. In 1872 the building had been superseded, and because of its built-in transportabilility it seemed the perfect answer to the current cry from the East End philanthropists for a trade museum to cheer the place up. The idea was that it should be the East Enders' own museum, to be stocked however they wanted, but it never worked liked that. It became an out-station of South Kensington, filled with the collections no longer wanted in the main building: the food museum and the animal products collection. By the end of the First World War the registers had notes against exhibits such as 'thrown away, perished' or 'removed, much affected by moth'.

There was also art on display, and if the green and brown decor did little to uplift the Cockneys, they poured in in their thousands to see Queen Victoria's Jubilee presents in 1888.[1]

[1] Lecture to the Association of Art Historians, by Anthony Burton, 1985.

## *The Bethnal Green Museum of Childhood*

The First World War brought children to the attention of the V&A's director, as the present keeper of Bethnal Green, Anthony Burton, told the assembled art historians. 'As a result of the war there were many children at a loose end in the holidays, and the then director of the V&A, Sir Cecil Smith, arranged activities for them, and set up a special room in the V&A which contained dolls' houses, dolls and other things from the V&A collections, which might be expected to appeal to children.'

It was a success, and the idea stayed with Arthur Sabin when, in 1922, he was sent to Bethnal Green Museum as officer-in-charge. He repainted the place, finding dust 18 inches deep behind some cases, and made a temporary exhibition space where, that same year, he put on a children's exhibition.

'In a district like this,' he was reported as saying in the *Hackney and Kingsland Gazette* in 1925, 'children have no background in their own homes which will help to create a love of beauty in their minds. They have to come into a building like this, where there is space around them and pleasant things, in order to be taught why it is desirable to have pleasant things about them. We hope that when they come to choose their homes these ideas will have an influence on them.

'This is a poor neighbourhood with very little colour in the children's lives, he recalled in the *Weekly Telegraph* in 1935, 'and I found they used to come in here and wander round unseeing, bored and sometimes noisy,' and his temporary exhibition became a permanent children's section.

His children's gallery caught on and he won supporters who wrote in the newspapers advocating a children's museum: the historian C. H. B. Quennell, author with his wife of the famous *History of Everyday Things in England* which introduced millions of children to history for the first time, wrote in the *Daily Herald* in 1929 calling for 'a place where the past can be brought to life for the young'; it was taken up in other papers, the *Manchester Guardian* claiming that in its city there was already a *de facto* children's museum, the Horsfall Art Museum, which traced the history of painting, sculpture and architecture in such a way that they 'become matters of real interest to children'.

In 1932 the *Museums Bulletin* revealed the successes of the Brooklyn Children's Museum in New York, and called for something similar in Britain. The following year plans for a children's gallery at the Science Museum were revealed (see Chapter 8).

But the instructional institution which was by now being talked about was not what Arthur Sabin had in mind. He simply wanted a place to satisfy 'the children hungry for beautiful things to look at', as one of his greatest supporters and contributors, Mrs Mary Greg, quoted him as saying.

Mrs Greg, a great amateur collector of dolls who travelled the world in search of them, had already contributed generously to the Manchester City Art Gallery, and she joined Mr Sabin's crusade almost from the start, using her considerable wealth to buy dolls, dolls' houses, miniature shops and other exquisite toys, and she was to be his most lavish benefactor until he retired in 1940.[2] He also won the support of an even more distinguished lady, Queen Mary. She met Mr Sabin at the museum in 1923: 'I explained my purpose to arrange a Children's Exhibition in the Autumn,' he wrote in his official diary, 'and Her Majesty generously undertook to furnish a dolls' house, and supply other things; which she did.'

Queen Mary was already keen to brighten up the lives of unfortunate children, and at the time of that first visit, *Pearson's Magazine* reported, 'no fewer than fifty dolls' houses were despatched from the Palace to the children's wards of various hospitals and other institutions. Some of them having been finally got ready by the Queen in person, who makes the work a hobby of ever-increasing interest.'

She came again in 1929 and the curator recorded: 'The Queen, after spending an hour and a half in the galleries, paused as she approached the exit and said in a clear outspoken voice, "I must congratulate you, Mr Sabin, on the great change you have made in the Museum. It is wonderful what you have done here." And she shook hands and smiled in a most friendly manner.'

Queen Mary's interest had been revived, for she sent on two dolls, one German and dating from 1825 which wears a ball gown and bears a curiously striking resemblance to the present Queen Mother (then Duchess of York) as she looked at that time. More royal gifts came, a model butcher's shop, then five dolls which had distinct personalities – including the 'Albert Edward', a model of the future Edward VII.

In 1934 the *Glasgow Evening Citizen* reported:

> The Queen sent a mysterious parcel today down to the East End of London. It arrived at Dolls' House City, in Bethnal Green Museum. When Mr A. K. Sabin, curator of the museum and unofficial Lord Mayor of Dolls' House City, opened the parcel, he found that the Queen had sent a miniature bazaar stall to be added to the street of little shops where all the dolls in the city do their shopping. . . . The children of Bethnal Green have a fairyland of dolls 'just round the corner'. And the fairy godmother who has done more than anyone to create this fairyland is the Queen.

By the mid 1930s Arthur Sabin was a leading sage in the field of children and museums. The London County Council sought his advice on how schools could use museums, and as a result developed its Horniman in south London and Geffrye in the east to be educational – although not children's museums in the way Bethnal Green was to become.

Arthur Sabin retired in 1940, and the museum became a wartime restaurant. It reopened eventually in 1950, but Mr Sabin's vision seemed to have been written out of its future. In fact, its future was very uncertain. At first the plan was to turn it into a museum of English costume, transferring the V&A's collections there. Then a new director, Sir John Pope-Hennessey, decided it should house the main museum's

[2] Anthony Burton and Caroline Goodfellow, *V&A Album*, 1985.

nineteenth-century continental art, and the incomparable collection of Rodin's sculpture was a central feature. It was not until another new director arrived in 1974 that the idea of a children's museum was revived, and one of Sir Roy Strong's first acts was to rename the place the Bethnal Green Museum of Childhood.

'He was confirming a development that had begun in 1915,' said Anthony Burton, whom Sir Roy appointed to take charge in 1981. Gradually the Austrian furniture, the Rodins, the other sculpture, the bits and pieces that had had no place in the main museum and had been shunted off to the out-station, were removed. The unrivalled dolls and dolls' houses, particularly, were re-cased, puppets were given space, temporary exhibitions relating to such things as schoolgirls' literature, German automota, Punch and Judy went on. An annual institution crystalised around the one time of the year which children are allowed to lay claim to when Mr Burton introduced 'Spirit of Christmas' exhibitions, each year with a different theme – the tree, Father Christmas, the cards, the carols, for instance.

The galleries were gradually, and at considerable cost, refurbished in a three-year programme which began in the spring of 1982. 'The nation's toy cupboard has been completely overhauled,' Anthony Burton announced when it was complete, ignoring for a moment the sensibilities of some of his curators which he had very much in mind when he had said earlier: 'When visitors refer to the Bethnal Green Museum of Childhood as 'the Toy Museum' or 'the Doll Museum' in the hearing of curators, you might notice these otherwise bright and cheerful people showing signs of despondency. For the fact is, we are called a 'Museum of Childhood' and think of ourselves as such.'

But the refurbishment was barely under way when the museum was threatened with closure. The government, in a round of management and efficiency investigations, had asked for a report on how the V&A could best save money. The answer was a simple one: close Bethnal Green Museum. There was an immediate outcry, with the Arts Minister receiving thousands of letters of protest from public figures and ordinary members of the public. A House of Commons Select Committee considered the whole thing, and recommended that not only should the museum be saved, it should be better financed. It was saved, at least.

There are a growing number of small toy collections in Britain, either in general museums such as the Museum of London, Tunbridge Wells Museum or the Castle Museum in York, or forming small museums of their own, as at the Pollock Toy Museum in Covent Garden, London, the Burrows Toy Museum in Bath or the Museum of Childhood at Beaumaris in Anglesey. Only Edinburgh's Museum of Childhood approaches Anthony Burton's inherited theme of a museum not only for children, but as much about the social phenomenon of childhood – the clothing, the furniture, the literature of childhood. But Bethnal Green has the extra dimension of Arthur Sabin's early vision, the strong emphasis on the dolls and miniature houses thanks to a great extent to Mrs Greg and Queen Mary.

The colours are bold and appealing, almost a reaction to the dreariness of the 1950s and 60s. Visitors are now guided around the exhibits instead of directed straight through, so that they are obliged to look around them in order to see where they are going. There is a shop now, an orientation point, and special exhibitions space in the centre of the hall. There is a puppet gallery, dominated by a large Italian marionette theatre, a gallery of games, another of ethnic dolls. The upper galleries are devoted to the more serious social study of childhood.

'A later generation could easily take it all away and start again, bringing about yet another transformation in this institution which stands in London, but it is, I hope, of more than local interest. I hope that my picture of it as a junction of various paths of study and enquiry is not too naive or self-indulgent,' said Mr Burton. 'But for the moment I cling to Baudelaire's dictum: "The toy is the child's first initiation in art; or rather, it is the first appearance of art to the child." I hope that the bright miniature sculpture of the toy galleries will awake children's sensitivity to form and colour.'

## *The London Toy and Model Museum*

'There's a whole world which the Bethnal Green Museum doesn't deal with because it wasn't given those things,' said Allen Levy. 'All those mechanical things from the industrial revolution were popular and real, and they've been ignored.'

He does not ignore the mechanics of children's play in his own museum, which won an award in 1985, three years after it opened, for being 'largely responsible for the recognition of toys and models as an intrinsic part of the national heritage.' It is the London Toy and Model Museum, a private venture of Mr Levy's and his former wife which occupies two Victorian houses in Bayswater's Craven Hill.

In 1979 Allen Levy was a successful chartered accountant who had diversified into publishing, who lived in a villa a few yards from where the museum now is and whose boyhood hobby of collecting train sets had followed him into adulthood. In fact it had extended, to other working models, and it was becoming unwieldy. He offered it to a national museum but they could not guarantee it would go on display, so he withdrew his offer. It gradually dawned that he had the makings of a highly individual and unusual attraction which could stand alone, and a child's enthusiasm started to become a museum.

'It began when we published a book in 1974, *A Century of Model Trains*, which I'd written. I'd been collecting railway artefacts for many years; all my smart friends were collecting Georgian silver and so on, but I saw the trains as very honest reflections of the times in which they were made, honest reflections of commercial history. I had no intention of forming a museum at all.'

But strolling around the area of their Porchester Terrace flat, he and his then wife Narisa Chakrabon saw a house for sale. 'It was under offer, but we thought it would make a marvellous museum because it had this great garden in the back. We thought about this inside-outside idea which didn't seem to be prevalent,' said Mr Levy. The other offer collapsed and they bought it in 1980 for £200,000 to turn it into a museum which opened two years later.

'I can't make any claim that this was an inspired culmination of something I'd wanted to do over the last 20 years, because it's not that sort of story, but it's one of coincidence and opportunity. I didn't see a state museum addressing itself to the sort of things a toy museum ought to – mainly the interaction between adults and children.'

But they very quickly found themselves cramped in the one building, unable to do the displays justice by providing a proper flow for visitors, or to provide the kind of facilities which are now essential – refreshments and toilets. 'Luck plays a great part in this business because two years later the house next door came up for sale,' Allen Levy said. It was in appalling condition, and financing the purchase – this one was £215,000 – and refitting the new extension was costly. An English Tourist Board grant helped and then they got planning permission to make three flats at the top of the house which were sold off.

The museum is on three levels of the two houses, basement, ground and first floor. The objects range from cuddly to kitsch, with intervening examples of sheer genius in the engineering and craftsmanship of some of the models. The 1888 demonstration model of a fire engine, with all its pieces detachable even to the tool kit, must rank as one of the finest examples of Victorian miniaturism to be seen anywhere.

There are penny toys, tin toys, animals in various stages of anthropomorphy, dolls and their houses, Dinky toys, Matchbox toys and the most wonderful collection of trains and train sets. 'Coming here as an adult you're coming face to face with a bit of your own past,' said Mr Levy, making the point that not all children's museums are exclusively for children. 'In London it's not that easy to find somewhere that's accessible to the whole family, and the garden element was the one thing that made me think it could be done.' For the garden has a train set which kids can actually ride over and round a pond; even better, there is a steam train running on a Sunday. There is a a café, too, which doubles as a gallery dedicated to the model trains and cars collected by Narisa's father, Prince Chula Chakrabongse of Thailand and his cousin Prince Bira, once a racing driver.

It is a small museum, and its smallness is one essence of its delight. It manages to encompass the sense of a toy shop – very few of the vast collections are in traditional cases, but arrayed behind glass panels which stretch from floor to ceiling like a shop window – and an attic in which forgotten treasures pop out from unlikely places.

The core of the display is the collection of Allen and Narisa Levy, but there are loan collections too, like the Paddington Bear Corner (appropriate with the station itself being no more than a rocking horse ride away).

'My attitude is that if one small museum like this, with the cost base it has, can collect 100,000 objects, I'd rather have ten of these than one that gets a million.'

He is critical of the national museum system which places large buildings in central urban areas, and then offers highly academic presentations which only the academically minded could appreciate. 'Academe attached themselves to those sort of museums which could only deal in their own subjects. If I wanted a graduate who specialised in toys I couldn't find one because the system can't train them, so in fact this has become a minuscule British Museum, a first-generation enthusiasts museum.'

In truth, the national museums have not fitted that description for some time, and they would protest bitterly that they are only too well aware of the importance of the child's-eye view – the average object label is aimed at an intelligent fourteen-year-old, not because all their visitors are fourteen or because the average adult has the intelligence of an adolescent but because the average visitor is not academic and will only be prepared to commit a certain finite degree of concentration to an exhibit. Their very largeness, believes Allen Levy, is their downfall, because it intimidates younger visitors, who may never again be won over to museums.

> Some of them are just vast parking lots for material – how can you look at 150 tractors lined up in a row? The reason this seethes is because it's on a scale children can relate to. People's attention span is 40 minutes, half an hour for a cup of coffee, maybe another look, ride on a train, and after an hour it's beginning to become marginal whether it's keeping their attention; if that hour is spent going round a building where the nearest loo is a ten-minute walk, then it's a stressful experience. These big museums are like the *Encyclopaedia Britannica*: everybody buys it and nobody reads it.

The collections are overgrown, he believes, and consequently their conservation requirements cannot be met by the in-house staff and objects are stored unseen. Exhibits which may make an important contribution to a display in, say, his museum if on loan, are not seen in such a context and therefore – not seen at all.

Allen Levy's belief is that 'Conservation should become separated from the showing of objects, and I think the funding of it should go to a new body with proper facilities and staff and based in areas which need the employment. Then I would loan the objects out, send them on circulation, make them travel round the country or even lend them to commercial companies who can actually do something with them.'

But the Levys created a movement which has been noted and acted upon at large and small museums; a family atmosphere which is as much to do with the surroundings as the subject matter. And they have learned from the larger ones to the extent, for instance, that their own version of Launch Pad, the Science Museum's hands-on gallery, has been built in the basement. The guiding principles of their museum were clear from the start:

> We intended to have artefacts and objects which were of interest because of people's pastimes, particularly as this country is such a great one for hobbies. We took the view that everybody's had a toy but nobody's ever had a Rembrandt, everybody's crowding in to see paintings that have no relevance to their life at all, so why wouldn't they come to see things which they would get pleasure from being reunited with?
>
> This is probably one of the best cross-sections available of toys and artefacts made over the last 150 years because of its balance. When we had our survey we found that most young children said it was the train ride and the bus in which they can turn the wheel that they liked the best. It's turned into a place where young children come to their first museum, it's activity-related for them, with the nostalgia-related to the adults who are able to explain their past to their children – they've all had toys.

The East Hall of the Science Museum in June 1988 shortly after its reopening by the Queen.

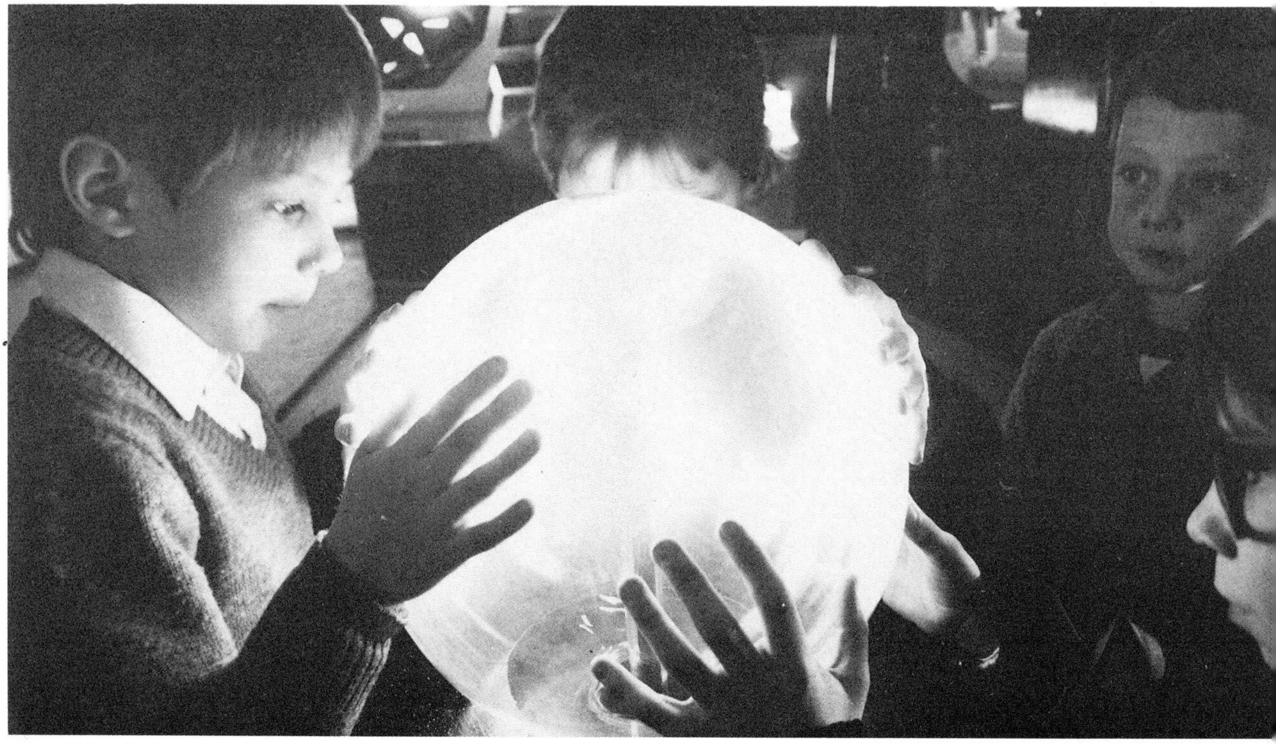

As well as an observatory, the Astronomer Royal now presides over a science museum at Jodrell Bank, Cheshire.

King George V opens the Science Museum in South Kensington in 1928. Sir Henry Lyons, first director of the Science Museum.

Boys at the Science Museum's Children's Gallery in the 1930s.

National Railway Museum, York.

The TV studio, one of the most popular of TECHNIQUEST'S exhibits.

So it's become a multi-generation place, like a niche restaurant: the menus here are such that nobody feels they're being intimidated. It's centrally located, it's a place of entertainment. We would rather be like a great restaurant that people know about and support up to a level, museum gourmets.

## *Haggs Castle*

There is an enduring image of a very regal throne on which lay a thoroughly regal velvet cushion on which should have rested an ultimately regal crown. Instead there was a half-eaten apple, the crown now adorning an eight-year-old head. It was at Haggs Castle, Glasgow's accidental kids' paradise.

It is a rather irreverent image of a rather grand house, built in the murky days of Mary Queen of Scots on a rangy bank of moss by an equally rangy chieftain, Sir John Maxwell (one of several John Maxwells in this ancient line), and after a turbulent first decade following its building in 1585, the house settled into a peaceful grandeur until the 1660s when it became a meeting place for the fiery Presbyterian factions. It settled to another century of passive domesticity, then was allowed to decline almost into dereliction – at one point the ground floor was used as a smithy serving the horses of a local coal mine – until it was restored and enlarged by another Sir John Maxwell in the 1860s. In the 1940s the family converted it into flats, and in 1972 the council bought it.

The accident is in the fact that it was not at first intended to be the unique centre for playing with history which it has become, but a base for a new department of the Glasgow Museums and Galleries, the largest local museum service in Britain with nine museums in its orbit.

A brief of 1975, the year before Haggs Castle opened to the public, explained that the new branch was to be called Extension Services, and Haggs Castle was to be a sort of vivid educational aid, to these specifications:

Principal activities will take place after school, in the evenings and at weekends or in the holidays. There will be a permanent display which will explore the development of landscape around Haggs Castle, examine a kitchen *c.*1600, and the life and times of John Maxwell (1648–1732). Contact with the castle is then broken; there will be a small room for hanging a few specially selected pictures; a room looking at Victorian toys and dolls, and a room which explores such subjects as age, technological development and so on.

It could easily have been the manifesto of a Victorian local authority intent on improving the education of the deprived, but before the year was out the municipal mind was changing; a later brief had a different tone:

For the last 100 years most museums have been more concerned with the inanimate objects which they collect and preserve than with the people for whom they are preserving them. There is no point in preserving them unless people are helped to appreciate them.

Extension Services aims to make the museum more meaningful, more approachable and more enjoyable for the public, not a place for those sufficiently 'cultured' to go to the museum, but a place for everybody.

By 1976 when the place was nearly ready to open, the advertising leaflet was saying: 'Haggs Castle represents a new adventure in the museum world. . . . The museum is being planned with children in mind. It is not a 'Children's Museum' in the traditional sense of a museum about children . . . it is simply a museum with a limited theme, brief and often interrogative labels and a high percentage of practical activities which will be based on a theme, enabling greater understanding by children.'

What precisely the 'traditional sense of a museum about children' was would have been very interesting to know, but what emerged was a bit of each of the intended museums, but the whole of none of them. The period rooms – sixteenth-century kitchen, seventeenth-century bedroom, nineteenth-century nursery – are all there but of the stern 'permanent display which will explore the development of landscape' there is no sign.

'We were intended to go out into the community and set up exhibitions in other branch museums within the Glasgow community,' said the curator, Rosalind Shipsides, 'but finances got cut back and we never got properly set up as an Extension Services Department. Rather than that, we've developed more as an education department, but with the advantage of having a museum of our own which we can work in and do displays, whereas otherwise you tend to have to work with just a collection of objects without the backdrop of exhibitions and a whole museum.'

Miss Shipsides came from the archaeology department at the main Kelvingrove Museum in the summer of 1987 to become the assistant keeper in charge of Haggs. 'It's a funny sort of role, you're a bit of everything: an education officer, publicity officer, curator, but the main thing is co-ordinating and organising activities and the changing exhibitions three times a year.'

Rather than be too coldly instructive, the exhibitions are intended to be an extension of what goes on in the classroom, which combines with activities to make a kind of three-dimensional, breathing, illustrated textbook with very few printed words.

'The permanent collection is the toys, basically, which was built up slightly *ad hoc*,' said Miss Shipsides. 'What we do is to draw on collections from the other museums in Glasgow for our activities – each of the exhibitions is drawn from the other collections.' The exhibitions for 1988, for instance, were 'Get the Message?' which was about communications, 'the whole range, post office, telephone, semaphore, sending a letter, cards, satellites, even smoke signals – using things taken from the other museums, the Burrell, Kelvingrove, the People's Palace, we tapped everybody.'

Then came 'Digging for History', which took a successful exhibition from

Kelvingrove designed for adults about the Scottish Archaeological Trust and turned it round to make it for children. 'It looked at what archaeology was and introduced children to the methods of archaeology, with practical handling tables. We made up record sheets which they had to fill in themselves as if they were recording an object. The original exhibition would have been too highly set, it wouldn't have caught the children's interest, and it was quite a success,' Miss Shipsides said. Then came 'Desperate Journey', based on a children's book which was being read in Scottish schools at the time, about a family of crofters from Sutherland who are evicted and who go to Glasgow, eventually emigrating to Canada.

'One of the more remarkable things about Haggs Castle is that you will seldom hear the words "Don't Touch",' wrote Miss Shipsides in a short article. 'Children are actually encouraged to touch objects and to investigate displays and for those who want to do more than just look there is a large range of quiz sheets and Treasure Hunt cards to be tried.'

So Haggs Castle goes beyond being a mere extended education department: it is a a museum in its own right, if a slightly parasitic one. 'We're very fortunate in having all these collections to draw on, and our main plus factor is that we can have access. And we don't seem to have an exhibition budget.' Wear and tear is not inconsiderable, money is going to have to be found to refurbish the rooms, which in only twelve years are showing chipped corners, worn floorboards and carpets.

Before we choose anything from any of the departments it has to be fairly solid and also fairly large so that it's not pocketable, but the departments don't tend to lend us things that either very fragile or very valuable, because children are a risk,' said Miss Shipsides.

'But it certainly brings the period to life for them. The Friends Association of Glasgow Museums made a complete range of costumes for six-year-olds up to thirteen-year-olds, both boys and girls, from the Mary Queen of Scots period; those have been very successful and much worn, and now we've started a project of Victorian costumes which is another area in which the schools are very interested now.'

The little boy with the crown had forgotten his apple, but was fed up with being king. 'I want to be the one with the bells now,' he said, looking wistfully at the jester's cap on his friend's head.

## *Dewsbury Museum*

Beaumaris is almost a fairy-tale town, with its dominating castle up on the Gwynedd peninsula of North Wales, so Robert Brown's little trip to the nursery in his Museum of Childhood at Castle Street seems perfectly appropriate. It has been there since 1973 and its 2,000 items, he says, are the artefacts of 'the more pleasurable aspects of family life', and there are demonstrations of some of them to prove it.

Dewsbury Museum used to be the Dewsbury Galleries, but the mostly nineteenth-century building in Crows Nest Park was reopened in 1985 devoted to childhood themes – but not only the 'pleasurable aspects' so much as the Dewsbury Museum used to be the Dewsbury Galleries, but the mostly nineteenth-century building in Crows Nest Park was reopened in 1985 devoted to childhood themes – but not only the 'pleasurable aspects' so much as the harsh working life Industrial Revolution children had to lead in this part of West Yorkshire, and Edinburgh's Museum of Childhood, probably the world's first to study the social history of childhood when it opened in 1955, has been extended and attracts a staggering 300,000 visitors to itself each year; Sudbury Hall in Derbyshire chooses to look at the seventeenth-century house and the history of childhood together through period settings, and the exploitation of children as cheap labour is not passed over here either. Other general museums have either childhood or children's sections in them, as at the Judges' Lodgings in Lancaster and the Strangers Hall Museum at Norwich.

But the draw is the essential ingredients of childhood, play, and the things that go with it; no matter how harrowing infancy could be through the ages, there have always been toys, games and dolls to enliven and amuse children's minds. To go back to Arthur Sabin and his vision for Bethnal Green, it is worth quoting from his preface to *Catalogue of the Greg Collection of Dolls & Dolls' Houses* of 1923 as a finishing note:

> Man cannot live by bread alone; and from the beginning of civilisation, when he made his first domed hut as a needed shelter for his wife and child, he has been moved in all his best labour by devotion to others. And in particular those things that have been done for children, the payment of which has been in no earthly coin, embody the noblest qualities of men's labour, because of the innocence of their motive and the love that inspired them. So in their turn these children's things become an inspiration.'

# 12. The whizz-bang dimension

*Fifty years after the last European war military matters are more fascinating to museum goers than ever. Regimental collections are being combined and presented in new ways, new and lively museums are emerging from stagnant stockpiles of militaria. The pinpoints in this section of the museum map are the Royal Navy Submarine Museum at Gosport, the Tank Museum at Bovington, the Guards Museum, the Imperial War Museum, the Royal Air Force Museum, and the Museum of the Manchesters at Ashton under Lyme.*

NOBODY knows how many museums there are because they open, close, combine and acquire branches at a rate the watchers are finding it impossible to keep up with, but by 1989 the figure was reckoned to be about 2,700. No-one knows precisely the number of military museums either, but at least one estimate, taking in all sorts of martial collections, is about 1,000 – 25 per cent more than all museums twenty-five years before.

Terence Wise runs the country's biggest military bookshop, Athena Books of Doncaster. He used to be an author, specialising in medieval soldiery, but demand for the books he sells has elbowed out any time for the books he was writing. He also publishes a two-yearly *Guide to Military Museums*, and the 1988 edition was his fourth (there had been two in the previous ten years under another publisher).

'We don't know how many military museums there are, we can never keep up with them, but we have to publish every two years to try to be as up-to-date as possible,' said Mr Wise. 'We think there are about 274 regimental and purely military museums, but there are all sorts of others on the fringes. Originally the guide was just for regimental museums, then we included naval and aviation collections, but in the last few years there's been an increase in privately owned museums, particularly military vehicles and aircraft. People seem to have established their own collections and then, manning them on a volunteer basis, opened them to the public.'

As just one example of this entrepreneurial spirit, at Retford a collector has established a very valuable collection of armoured fighting vehicles which, since 1987, he has been opening to the public on one day a year. 'This chap imported something like twenty Russian T34 tanks complete with the ammunition in the racks – how he got them nobody seems to know. You go past on the train to London and you think you've had a dream.'

Military museums had been expanding at the rate of about 20 per cent a year when Mr Wise first began publishing his guide, but in the mid-80s there was a dramatic contraction of regimental museums. 'A lot of them have been disappearing – Shrewsbury used to have three regimental military museums, now it's got Shrewsbury Castle (the Shropshire Regimental Museum opened there in 1985 and represents the King's Shropshire Light Infantry, the Shropshire Yeomanry and the Shropshire Royal Horse Artillery). York is just the York Military Collection, and for instance the East Yorks who were at Beverley lost their regimental museum; the people of Beverley who served in the regiment and had their own museum resent losing it to York. The old regimental museums were more family, but they didn't have the modern facilities museums have now.'

What has happened is that the collections have been absorbed and combined to make larger museums, and probably more sense for the public. 'The collections are still there,' said Mr Wise 'but they're not on view in the way they used to be.

'One of the rifle regiments at Shrewsbury had stuff all over the place in an old guardroom, absolutely jam-packed with old weaponry and bits and pieces. They weren't fenced off, and they were immaculately bulled by the recruits, and very intimate with all the stuff clearly visible and touchable if anyone dared. Next to it was the Light Infantry Museum, which is very modern, and everything is tucked away in cases, very sparsely displayed. You only see a fraction of the collection, and there's so much that you don't see.'

But the family regimental museums were largely the privately accumulated collections of what were, in essence, extended families, the regiments themselves. So they were seen by few people other than those who knew the regiment's history well enough already, and the objects on show were trophies, the visual reminders which are the essence of regimental pride.

Now there is a museum-going public which is interested, but for which the history has to be spelled out; and they do not need to see a pile of immaculately bulled Lee Enfields, one will do nicely. Mr Wise has a circulation of 5,000 readers he calculates to be museum buffs, not military experts. 'There is a big interest now and I presume it's because we haven't had any big wars. The interest is not so much in the heroic, gung-ho yarns as the technology, and as everybody knows, the greatest progress in technology is in wartime.'

## *The Royal Navy Submarine Museum*

'The technology of fighting in inner space, as the seas and oceans are sometimes called,' may seem an odd introduction to the nearest the Royal Navy may have to a regimental museum, but that is how Commander Richard Compton-Hall, director of the Royal Navy Submarine Museum, describes his subject matter.

The similarities of under-sea and outer space have not escaped the conceivers of the vessels designed to cope with the unfriendly elements of either atmosphere, and

Commander Compton-Hall's display shows that man is barely any nearer conquering the former than the latter.

HMS *Dolphin* is the Gosport headquarters of the Royal Navy's submarine service, just across the harbour from the Royal Naval Dockyard which has its own clutch of new museums in what is becoming known as the Portsmouth Historic Dockyard.

But the submariners established their own museum in 1963, a small branch collection formed in a room above the submarine base chapel, out of public bounds. In 1975 it started to expand under Richard Compton-Hall and in 1978 it acquired, on permanent loan from the Ministry of Defence, a retired submarine, HMS *Alliance*, whose design is vintage Second World War.

Between 1979 and 1980 £410,000 was raised by public subscription to lift *Alliance* 'high-and-dry', outside the base's security fence, to be the main exhibit of what would be a new museum – it would have to be a new one to go outside the perimeter as well and allow public admission, and it was purpose-built and paid for out of the public appeal funds. It was opened in 1982.

'Since then we've gone from strength to strength,' said Commander Compton-Hall. 'We're the only comprehensive submarine museum in the world, though there's plenty of competition crowding on our heels, and we do deal internationally, although we're focused, obviously on the British submarine service.

'And we are most certainly the only museum that's a true charity in the sense that since 1982 we have actually given £57,500 to submariners and their dependants who've fallen on hard times.'

The seaward tip of Gosport was cleverly picked as the submarine nest because it is the end of a a peninsula, but it is a rotten place for a museum. The fact that in 1987 it attracted 88,500 paying members of the public, as well as 6,500 non-paying servicemen, says much for its magnetism. By comparison the local Gosport Museum can boast 23,000 visitors a year.

Although *Alliance*, with her crew's quarters set as they would have been in the austere days of the 1940s and 1950s, but with the rest of it streamlined and adapted to more modern armament fifteen years or so after the war, is the centrepiece of the display, she is no longer the star of the show. 'Our most prized exhibit,' said the director, 'is our very first submarine, *Holland I*.'

In the dying years of the nineteenth century a brilliant if somewhat erratic Irish-American called John Philip Holland caught the American imagination with what seemed his crazy notion that you could go to war underwater with complete safety (unless, of course, the enemy decided to do the same thing) and even threaten the mighty British fleet. He went underwater with his invention himself, resurfaced and did not seem so crazy.

Despite legitimate fears by the admirals that underwater warfare would spell the end of battleships, the British bought Holland's plans. In great secrecy the first was built at Vickers in Barrow-in-Furness (still the birthplace of many of the Royal Navy's submarines), and on 2 October 1901 *Holland I* was launched.

By 1913, however, the first submarines had been superseded many times over, and the original five were towed away to be scrapped. The first, *Holland I*, did not have her hatch properly shut and, while under tow, sank near the Eddystone Lighthouse where she remained until 1982.

She was salvaged under Commander Compton-Hall's supervision, and he was the first on board. 'The boat looked marvellous, even then, with the water still draining out of the hull,' he said. 'The torpedo rear door swung open with only a slight pull. I couldn't believe it.' For some reason, which scientists have been unable to explain, the interior of *Holland I* was in a miraculous state of preservation, although much of its innards had been removed before heading for the breaker's yard. 'But Vickers had kept the original drawings so that, thanks to the inexplicable state of the interior, we had a fairly straightforward job.'

'Now she's completely restored to her in-service condition,' said the Commander. 'She's absolutely as she was, even with the talking figure of the coxswain, Petty Officer Waller, explaining the boat to us. And it's cost the museum itself not one penny.' The restoration of *Holland I* was completed in September 1988 with a great deal of voluntary help, generous donations by Vickers and the National Heritage Memorial Fund, the expertise of retired naval engineers under Captain Alec Wale and the former Manpower Services Commission who adopted the project.

There was a good deal of luck about the *Holland I* story, as Richard Compton-Hall is the first to admit, but the zeal with which it was salvaged, conserved and restored to bring the very roots of the service to light shows what can be done.

Commander Compton-Hall is not a trained curator. He was a submariner until he left the Navy in 1969 to become director of services for a department store chain, then to write books about submarines. He took over the museum under tragic circumstances, when the director had suddenly died at the point when a small collection was being transformed into a big museum.

'I was determined to make it a commercial success, and I think we can confidently say we've now done that. If we can give away £57,500 . . .' His visitors come for the romance which always adheres to the submarine service, but also for the manifestation of the science of the impossible, the 'technology of inner space'.

## *The Bovington Tank Museum*

Submarines first saw active service in the First World War, and perhaps it is because of the ultimate land-war technology it represented in the same conflict that the Bovington Tank Museum at Wareham in Dorset has flourished without having to join any other corps collection. It has been an object lesson in how a subject which can be, frankly, distasteful to many people can be made hugely entertaining, under the direction of another of the stamp of Commander Compton-Hall: Lieutenant-Colonel George Forty.

It may seem new but the Tank Museum, one of the finalists in the 1988 Museum of the Year competition, owes itself to a chance remark made as long ago as 1923 by none other than Rudyard Kipling. He had seen the rusting old tanks as they were being broken up for scrap metal at Bovington, and casually mentioned that they should be kept to form a museum. But to call it a museum would have been extending the definition, even then, because little more was done than put a rope around the pile Kipling had seen, and jabb a sign into the ground in front which read 'Royal Tank Museum'. Later they were found a shed to go into on the Royal Armoured Corps ranges in Dorset, and kept for the instruction of tank commanders and other interested specialists.

The collection had gradually grown over the years to be a fairly random selection of about 100 armoured fighting vehicles by 1982, the year Colonel Forty retired from the Royal Tank Regiment and became the museum's curator. There are now over 200 which constitute the biggest and most varied collection in the world weighing, in a statistic only the military would have handy, 3,500 tons. They range all the way from Little Willie, which grew out of the 1909 Hornsby Tractor, to the modern Scorpion light tank.

'Frankly it was a bit of an embarrassment to the Army,' said Major Neville Anderson, the museum's assistant curator. 'It had terrific potential but didn't have the resources to use that potential. The public were tolerated and they might come here on a wet afternoon. It's still an army museum, but the difference now is that the public are encouraged to come.' They are encouraged to the extent of 250,000 visitors a year.

Colonel Forty exercised the same kind of zeal Commander Compton-Hall used to bring the Navy's first submarine back to life, but his patient was not just a single object but the whole museum. For its sixtieth birthday in 1983 he instituted the Diamond Jubilee Appeal which brought, not more tanks, but a cinema, a restaurant, a new entrance block and a library, and a new roof was put on the old buildings.

In 1986 the World War One exhibits were given their special home, the new George Forty Hall, and in 1987 a permanent exhibition about the inter-war years was completed, all from sponsorship. In 1988 the Duke of Kent opened the British Steel Hall which tells the story of the development of armoured fighting vehicles since the Korean War, up to the Chieftain tank of the 1970s and 80s, and in 1989 two more buildings were scheduled to bring the entire collection under cover.

Very little in the way of new objects is purchased, however. Exchanges are made with other armies, but the cost of items of the military heritage is so great now that even the successful Bovington Tank Museum can seldom afford them.

And great care has to be taken with exactly whom the exchange is being made, said Major Anderson. Even a World War Two Russian tank, which ought to be obsolete, could still fetch a price on the illegal arms market. 'So we have to steer a very fine line: we do exchanges only with *bona fide* collectors and foreign government museums.' The acquisitions of Terence Wise's Retford collector were, it seems, to say the least rare.

Plans to make the museum more 'inter-active', as more and more museums are striving to be, are problematical. 'Children and heavy metal don't mix; it always ends up in blood and tears,' said Major Anderson. 'But outside we've got an adventure playground with tank turrets made safe for them to play on. Inside we've got a couple of vehicles made safe which they can go into. We've got a guided missile turret, and if they look through the sights and they can guide a dot of light. It brings it all to life. I'd love to have a tank turret they could traverse, but with a barrel sticking out the front they'd be bound to knock someone's block off.'

There are plans for a 400-yard test track on which tanks and armoured vehicles could be put through their paces before an appreciating audience. 'So you can see, we're alive.'

## *The Guards Museum*

The smallest boy's image of a soldier, even today, is of a tall man with a very tall furry hat and a red tunic: the guardsman, the man millions of tourists flock to London to see each summer, representative of the oldest and most senior regiments of foot in the British Army.

But in the Guards Museum, which opened in 1988 in Wellington Barracks by St James's Park, just a sergeant-major's shout from Buckingham Palace itself, the ceremonial guardsman has no place. 'We want to put over that we are not just ceremonial soldiers but have a fine fighting record,' said Lieutenant-Colonel Paul Adair, the museum's curator and retired Coldstreamer who has been associated with the mission to create the museum for twenty-five years. Contrary to the popular image, the Guards have always been at the forefront of technical innovation, so the emphasis is on the five Regiments of Foot and their role as fighting soldiers.

The Guards began abroad, as the Royal Regiment of Guards, raised by Thomas Lord Wentworth in 1652 to be Charles II's Praetorians in exile, eventually returning after the restoration. General Monck, once Royalist, then Parliamentarian, then Royalist again and created the first Duke of Albemarle to help him not to change his mind again, added his battalion, so that Charles II decreed: 'The Regiment of Guards should take precedence of all other regiments, with the General's Regiment to take next place.'

After a campaign in Scotland for which the regiment recruited heavily around Coldstream in Northumberland, the General's became the Coldstream Guards, and the Royals became the Grenadiers at Waterloo. The Scots Guards were added with the Act of Union in 1707, the Irish Guards after the Boer War and the baby of the family, the Welsh Guards, in the First World War.

'The five regiments have always worked as a composite,' said Colonel Adair. 'The composite guards battalion was companies of each of the three older regiments way back in the seventeenth century, so it's no new thing for us to act as a composite force like this.'

For no regiment takes precedence in the museum, they are all represented as part of a whole. There had been a Guards Museum of sorts at the Guards Depot in

Caterham, Surrey, from the early 1930s, and it is still there in a vestigial form. 'Before then any regimental treasures that came up went either to the Guards Club or to the five regimental headquarters, or else they were bought by individual regiments for the officers' mess,' said Colonel Adair.

'We started trying to form a Guards Museum in London the in the 60s and opened up a pilot scheme in the East Guardroom in the old Wellington Barracks which lasted for ten years, and now there is this one which was about ten years in gestation.'

They were anxious to get the public in to shake off some of the ceremonial image, 'to keep the record straight'. They raised money with the Guards Museum Appeal Fund, which still provides revenue along with admission charges and a decreasing amount of public funding – 'we're moving to a position where we will eventually be entirely independent.'

It is an easy museum to look at, which many military museums are not. There are no desk-cases to peer down onto, squinting through the reflection from the ceiling strip lights. All the cases are shop windows, and the first one is a dramatic life-size diorama based on Lady Butler's painting of the winning of the Army's first VCs at the Battle of Alma, by an officer and an NCO of the Guards.

The exhibits follow the Guards all the way to Tumbledown, and you cannot get further from Horseguards Parade than that. Even so, it is very much a military regiment, run by the military with their own story 'presented in a positive way'.

Warfare in the twentieth century is the particular remit of the museum in what was Bedlam, the Bethlem Royal Hospital in Lambeth, south London, and is now the Imperial War Museum. Opened just before the end of the First World War, it is the national war archive and its collections have grown many times to cover every martial involvement for Britain.

In 1989 the first phase of a massive rebuild was completed at a cost of £17 million which doubled the size of the exhibition space in the main building, and £2 million of the money was raised from a highly successful public appeal. Two more phases, to be completed when funds are available, will establish permanent education and conference centres and a new restaurant. The IWM also has its branches, as do most national museums now, with the Cabinet War Rooms in Whitehall, the underground emergency offices restored to their appearance for the Cabinet meeting at 5pm on fifteenth October, 1940, and opened in 1984. HMS *Belfast*, the Second World War cruiser moored by Tower Bridge, and the former RAF station at Duxford in Cambridge are also part of the Imperial family of museums.

The north of England is rich in military memory with many recently rationalised museums to record it. Lancashire's regiments are now brought together in the County and Regimental Museum at Preston, the most recent addition be in the 14th/20th King's Hussars in their own gallery opened in 1987. Humberside is a particularly thriving area for museums, and the Museum of Army Transport, opened in 1983 at Beverley, represents more than a century of military vehicles. It would be tempting for it to be an enthusiasts' car park, with rank on rank-armoured personnel carriers lined up on parade for the Royal Corps of Transport buffs, but director Lieutenant-Colonel Teddy Penn has resisted that. Instead they are shown in tableaux, such as a workshop, and in the summer they are put through their paces for an annual audience of 120,000. Montgomery's Second World War Rolls Royce and Lord Roberts's Boer War wagon are stars.

## *The Royal Air Force Museum*

At first glance Michael Fopp seems an unlikely director of a military museum: he has no service background, unless you count the police force, and he came from the London Transport Museum. But then, he does not really count the Royal Air Force Museum as a military museum despite its title. It is as much to do with with social and political history as martial, and technology and science more than any of them.

'When you think of it,' he said, 'the history of the museum is surrounded by the history of the empire, the Great Exhibition, the wish of the Victorians to educate the plebs, so they had their private collections which became the great institutions of today. In Michael Fopp's view, 'It's no wonder there are so many military museums because that's all tied up in the same thing: the empire, the strength of the empire, the way the empire spread throughout the world, and how did it spread? Through military might and trading, and one obviously came before the other. So we have a legacy of the national museum from that time – but also a hell of a lot of regimental museums, I think it's about 1,000.'

The Royal Air Force was formed on 1 April 1918, four months before the war to end wars ended, combining the Royal Naval Air Service and the Royal Flying Corps. In 1919 a group of senior members of the Aircraft Board, including newspaper baron Lord Rothermere and the 'father of the RAF' Lord Trenchard, pronounced that each of the RAF's aircraft should be preserved.

In 1925 there was an exhibition at the Royal Agricultural Hall in London of the first collection of RAF equipment and aircraft. 'It was an incredible exhibition; it had every sort of aircraft from the Great War period which the RAF operated. It was very popular, people came miles to see it, and not a single one of those aircraft survived. They were all scrapped, and the idea died,' Michael Fopp told me.

The history of the Royal Air Force was almost the same, with the Army and Navy anxious to wrest back control of the air, and Lord Trenchard digging his heels in: 'He fought a rearguard action by using the RAF to police the protected states of Trans-Jordan – Palestine, Mesopatamia, the Middle East states that had been split up after the First World War and given to the empire to administer. 'The tribes were warring constantly and we sent the Army out, literally thousands of infantrymen trying to keep these tribesmen apart, and Trenchard said, "I can do it with a couple squadrons of the RAF." They operated a carrot and stick principle: first of all they dropped leaflets saying "Carry on fighting and we'll bomb you", they carried on fighting so they dropped more leaflets saying 'You'd better get out of your village because you're going to be bombed", and at two o'clock the next day they bombed them. It quietened everything down.'

So the RAF survived, albeit at a low level, until the advent of the big bombers, and the rearming of Italy and Germany. 'But it wasn't until the Battle of Britain that people realised the RAF was so important, its position as a separate service was established and it's never been threatened again,' said Mr Fopp.

But there was no equipment until the very late 1930s, a period when civil airliners were flying faster than RAF front-line fighters. 'It was a completely ridiculous situation, and the thought of a museum was completely forgotten. After the Second World War the main thought on everybody's mind was to try to forget about it, particularly in terms of equipment. The development of machinery in war is so fast that anything that doesn't perform as well as it did yesterday is thrown out, so the scrapping process started.'

Although Michael Fopp was never in the service, his father was, flying air-sea rescue helicopters. In the 1950s they were living on an RAF station in Lincolnshire. 'All around the perimeter track of the airfield were the front nose sections of Halifax bombers waiting to be scrapped, being stripped of all their instruments. 'There is no Halifax bomber complete now. We have one but we had to get it from a Norwegian fjord. 11,300 Wellingtons were built and we've got the last one.'

Trenchard's museum idea stayed moribund until the mid-1960s when the librarian and tutor at the RAF's college at Cranwell, Dr John Tanner, revived it. 'Whilst we didn't have a museum,' said Mr Fopp, Dr Tanner's successor, 'each unit had their own little museum in their crew rooms, and they always had 'gate guardians' – historic aeroplanes sitting at the gates of stations, so the RAF was aware of its history but they hadn't organised it.

'John Tanner had to arrange a display when the Queen visited Cranwell for a review; he cobbled together all sorts of material, and then saw that here was something quite special. He started to lobby the Air Force Board for support to build a museum associated to the RAF, and he was fortunate that the Chief of the Air Staff at the time was Sir Dermot Boyle, now Marshal of the RAF, who'd been in the service since the First World War. He became the first chairman of the trustees, and John started to gather the collection together, first at Henlow in some old buildings.'

But they needed a proper, permanent, site, and many alternatives were discussed – including a place on The Mall, near Buckingham Palace, where they could not have got an aeroplane in. Eventually Hendon was chosen. The government decided to make it a national museum, taking on the operating costs, provided Dr Tanner could raise £1,000,000 to build it. He did and the Queen opened the RAF Museum in 1972. 'It was mentioned in the MGC (Museums and Galleries Commission) report of that year as a place showing the way in that it was one of the new scientific and technical museums that had opened with totally unexpected visitor numbers. It's one of the first aviation museums, and it's grown and grown since then,' said Michael Fopp.

His connection with the museum began in 1979 after he had been invalided out of the police force, having broken his back in a fall from his horse during a riot. An aviation enthusiast since boyhood, he came in to try and raise £2,000,000 for a Battle of Britain Museum to complement the main museum, succeeded and stayed on as keeper of the collection. He left in 1985 to run the London Transport Museum, which he remodelled before leaving in 1988 to succeed Dr Tanner who had retired.

Michael Fopp is keen to dispel the view that the museum is only about the heroic achievements of the wartime RAF. 'We don't just hold RAF aircraft. There's the world's first jet, the ME262; the German rocket plane, the ME163; the Japanese Kawasaki; a Japanese kamikaze aircraft; the research and development aircraft which as boys we heard about, The Fairey Delta II that broke the world speed record; the TSR2.'

The RAF's role had been far beyond a simply military one. 'Because the RAF's the oldest air force with its antecedents, it did all the proving flights for all the air routes we now take for granted, and all the testing for things like supersonic flight – the Americans broke the sound barrier but a heck of a lot of research was done on this side of the Atlantic – and all the Royal Mail flights were done by the RAF to start with.'

There are Army and Navy aircraft as well, and the modern Fleet Air Arm and Army Air Corps were set up with RAF pilot training.

But within a few months of taking charge there were changes to the museum, crucially the introduction of charges for admission to the whole site, but also a new shop with a wider range and the beginnings of a new-look staff.

'All the staff, including myself,' said Mr Fopp, 'have been on customer care courses. We now know that our visitors are customers who pay for a service and deserve to get it. We've had changes in our exhibitions, in that the original design concept was absolutely brilliant in 1972 but is slightly out of date now. So we're bringing in operational aircraft as they come out of service and showing them with their equipment which we believe the public are interested in – seeing the nuts and bolts of an aeroplane that has been flown operationally rather than a pristine prototype, sparkling clean on a white floor – so we have a Lightning just out of service, we're getting the public closer to the aeroplanes. We can't allow the public into the exhibits as they are because of the damage that would be caused, so we're having cockpit sections cut off real aeroplanes and made safe for access.'

There are other enhancements coming – talking heads, audio-visual programmes augmenting scenic recreations: 'We want the public to realise what it was like for an eighteen-year-old rear gunner or flight engineer to fly in absolutely appalling weather conditions in the dark night over Germany, being fired at by anti-aircraft weapons and nightfighters. It wasn't like going for a week in the sun to Benidorm in a pressurised airliner with your dinner served up on a plastic tray. It was bloody frightening, bloody uncomfortable, and there was a damn good chance of not coming back. It's very difficult to convey that by sitting in a Lancaster or a Wellington or a B17 on the ground in brilliant lighting and showing how marvellous a piece of machinery it is.'

So the social history of aviation, most of the development of which was the direct result of war effort of one sort or another, is to be a new influence on the planning of the museum's future. 'I think we've been a little impersonal in the past, showing the equipment but not the people,' said Mr Fopp.

It is still chiefly about military weapons, aeroplanes and their loads, and the military people that worked in and on them, but not a military museum: 'It never occurred to me that we are a military museum in the sense that I think of regimental museums as showing lots of rifles, lots of uniforms, lots of medals. We're all worried that we could be accused of glorifying war – not just worried, we don't do it any more. We try to show not just the social history but the developments of the technology that we take for granted now – the fact that the engine that powered the Spitfire, the Merlin, was such an advance in turbo-charging, is reflected when we drive a Metro with a turbo engine. But at the time when Sir Stanley Hooker actually worked that out it was unknown.

'The Whittle jet is another example, and we have his jet on display; Frank Whittle was an RAF squadron leader when he first had the idea, working at Cranwell. He was given the run-around and as an RAF officer had to form his own company to produce this power jet, and now we've gone to the moon and back thanks to it. The Mosquito was a private venture, the Spitfire was a private venture, those are the stories we need to convey to the public,' said Michael Fopp.

'So we want to get down to the social history aspects of the RAF, and the individual person's experience in it.'

## *The Museum of the Manchesters*

One new military museum, the Museum of the Manchesters at Ashton-under-Lyne, decided to approach its regimental story directly from the social history aspect, not to universal acclaim at first. This anonymous letter appeared in a local paper shortly after the museum opened in 1987:

> Sir – On balance the ratepayers of Tameside should congratulate their local council on providing Ashton with a long-overdue Military Museum. But at what an unfortunate price! Included in the Museum are Labour Party posters from the early 1920s, material about the Spanish Civil War, constant stress on bad social conditions for both civilians and 'other ranks', the rise of the Chartists, women at work, conscientious objectors and a CND poster. I don't think the name of Winston Churchill is mentioned once.

The museum was not making political points, however. 'We want to show how, through the history of the regiment and its predecessors, it has had a devastating effect on lives in the economic community where it recruited,' said Geoff Preece, Tameside's museums officer.

The Manchester Regiment was created in 1881 as an amalgamation of the 63rd and 96th regiments, with its headquarters in Ashton barracks. It was always known locally as 'The Manchesters' until it disappeared in 1958. The regiment's collection had been in Manchester City Art Gallery's Queen's Park Gallery until it was closed in 1985 to become conservation studios, and Tameside local authority negotiated to bring the Manchester's home, and the new museum opened in Ashton Town Hall in April 1987.

The military story is told faithfully, detailing battle honours from the Boer War to the Malayan Emergency as any other regimental collection. But surrounding the martial aspects is the social history, which begins with the political unrest at the end of the Napoleonic wars, the Peterloo Massacre of 1819 and the Chartists' revolt of the 1840s which was the direct cause of the building of the barracks. 'The social history of soldiering in the nineteenth century is examined in some detail,' Mr Preece explained in a *Museums Journal* article of 1987, 'and this takes the story up to the First World War. Here we have a reconstructed trench (complete with sound, light and smell effects) and we look at women's experiences on the home front, especially the Ashton munitions explosion of 1917.'

In another article, this time for the *Manchester Region History Review* in 1988, Geoff Preece enlarged on the new military museum look:

> Nearly all regimental museums began as exhibitions in barracks (and some remain there) and were used more to foster *esprit de corps* than to state anything meaningful about the past. Medals, captured enemy trophies and the regimental colours became reverential icons, arousing the same loyalties and emotions as, for example, trade union banners do in quite a different context.
>
> From the 1930s onwards many regimental museums began to be integrated into local municipal museums, but even so the strictly regimental approach was always maintained, being displayed as a specialist collection in an isolated context.
>
> Social history curators have similarly shown a marked reluctance to interpret and display effectively these often very rich collections. They are after all not as fashionably desirable as pre-war Bakelite nor as popularly nostalgic as the 1920s chemist's shop in the local heritage centre.
>
> But treated effectively they have a far more vivid, relevant and personal message than any amount of wooden mangles or clog irons.

# 13. Dead arts

*Art came first in Victorian museum thinking, the fine arts being the first touch of the muses in the mission for mass education and improvement. This chapter considers Dulwich Picture Gallery, Manchester City Art Gallery and the National Galleries of Scotland, and then whether art museums really are as backward as they have been accused of being.*

JENNIE Lee, the first Arts Minister, produced a white paper called *A Policy for the Arts*, in 1964. 'It talked about the "live arts" and the Arts Council got a lot of extra money,' said Peter Longman, secretary of the Museums and Galleries Commission. 'By implication "dead arts" were in museums and galleries, and it was admitted that they had been left out.'

Politicians have lumped museums in with the arts ever since, and in the first attempts by the authorities to bring culture to the lives of urban communities it is true that it was first to the fine arts of painting and sculpture they turned, creating art galleries around benefactions and art museums around the galleries.

But the first public art gallery was not a municipal creation, and its purpose was not particularly the general uplift so much as aesthetic instruction of those already pursuing the arts. It sprang from the benefaction of an actor, a friend of Shakespeare's, Edward Alleyn. He was the son of a London innkeeper, a good grounding for a career in show business in the sixteenth century. But he made more than a career of it, he left a legacy in education and art which is still with us among the horse-chestnuts of Dulwich in the gentlest of South London's suburbs.

Alleyn was the finest actor of the age, admired by Jonson, described by Heywood as 'inimitable', and 'the best of actors'. Late in life he married John Donne's daughter. He was a theatre manager as well, and 'master of the king's games of bears, bulls and dogs', and baited a lion before James I at the Tower.

He inherited a small fortune and married into a larger one, so that in 1605 he was able to buy a huge estate which today would span the valley between Crystal Palace and Denmark Hill. In 1614 he was approaching fifty and was still childless, and became anxious as to what would happen to the estate after his life. He decided to create a school, and called it Alleyn's College of God's Gift, where, from its opening in 1619 until he died in 1626, he taught the boys acting. The school is now known as

Dulwich College, a public school with a splendid pedigree and a reputation for producing brilliant pupils of a less than usual sort – from P. G. Wodehouse to Raymond Chandler to William Pratt, who was to take up the profession of the school's founder with the name of Boris Karloff, to Bob Monkhouse.

## *Dulwich Picture Gallery*

Dulwich school also has an international reputation for a more recent development: Dulwich Picture Gallery, Britain's first public art museum, is part of the charitable endowment of the College.

For many years in the early and mid-nineteenth century the gallery had the most important collection of old masters readily available to the public in London. In Charles Kingsley's *Alton Locke*, set in the 1830s, when the eponymous hero feels the need to cultivate himself and proposes a visit to he National Gallery to study the great paintings there, his wiser cousin leads him instead to Dulwich, explaining that there are 'much better ones at Dulwich – that's the place to go.'

The Dulwich collection remains probably the finest still in private hands – until 1979 it was still known as the Dulwich College Picture Gallery – and it was founded by two scions of the Regency art establishment, one French the other Swiss by origin: Noel Desanfans and Francis Bourgeois.

Desanfans was born in Douai in 1744, and his parents are unknown. He attended the ancient university in his home town and there met the great British actor John Philip Kemble and Charles-Auguste Calonne, later to be France's first minister and a great collector of paintings.

After a glittering academic career, Desanfans went to Paris to write and won the admiration of Rousseau, but at the age of twenty-five he decided to pursue his fortune in London. He made his living by teaching languages, and married the aunt of two of his young lady pupils: he was thirty-one, she was forty-five and had a considerable private fortune.

At about this time Desanfans became a picture dealer, and a highly successful one even though he knew little enough about art – Sir Joshua Reynolds delighted to bamboozle him into buying copies of old masters. His lack of knowledge was not a hindrance: picture collecting was a craze in the 1780s and 90s, when famous names were more important than great pictures.

But he was close friends with a number of very knowledgeable connoisseurs, both in London and Paris, who supplied him with important paintings (they included Calonne).

Desanfans' closest associate was Francis Bourgeois, born in London in 1756 as the son of a Swiss emigré who had abandoned him as a child and who was later adopted by Desanfans. His mentor turned young Bourgeois into a painter by sending him to study with a celebrated French artist working in London, de Loutherbourg, and sending him on the grand tour in the late 1770s.

On his return Desanfans engineered his protégé's name into the press. In 1791 *The World* carried the comment: 'From the crowds which daily encircle the celebrated picture of "The Convicts" by Sir F. Bourgeois at the Exhibition at the Royal Academy, you are continually hearing the observation, "And is it possible that this Painter can have been excluded from the Royal Academy?" ' He had already become painter to the King of Poland, who had knighted him.

Two years later he was elected a full member, and in 1794 was appointed Landscape Painter to George III.

But in fact he was not a very good painter. Dulwich Picture Gallery has twenty-one of his paintings, and only one is hanging in the gallery, but he was popular, with paintings bought by the royal families of Britain, Poland and Russia, and by the likes of Reynolds and Sir John Soane.

Between them Desanfans and Bourgeois became even more successful dealers, and they accumulated a matchless private collection – or more likely Bourgeois accumulated the collection with Desanfans' money, and the younger man's fanatical buying almost led to them parting company in about 1803. In 1807 Desanfans died, leaving his paintings to Bourgeois.

Bourgeois had also inherited a mission from his mentor: to create a collection 'conducive to the advancement of a Science to which his anxious views and unremitting labours had been invariably directed'. He wrote to his landlord, the Duke of Portland, asking if he could turn his Charlotte Street house into a museum which 'may be gratuitously open . . . to Artists as well as to the Publick.' The Duke turned him down.

Having rejected the idea of leaving the collection to the British Museum, instead he decided to leave them to Dulwich College. Late in 1810 he was injured in a fall from a horse, and almost the last thing he did was to write his will accordingly, the pictures going to Mrs Desanfans on condition that on her death they went to the school. He died a fortnight later.

Dulwich was just right for the collection. Giles Waterfield, the director of the gallery, writes in his introduction to *Collection for a King: Old Master Paintings from the Dulwich Picture Gallery* – the catalogue of a highly successful exhibition from Dulwich which toured the United States in 1985 and 1986 – quoting an 1808 visitor: 'The estate for its entirety, the beauty and variety of its views . . . is scarcely to be equalled. . . . It is embosomed in a rich and fertile vale, whose surface is varied by detached eminences and is thus secluded . . . from the bustle and activity of trade and commerce, from the noisome air of manufacturies and the busy "hum of men".'

'The choice of Dulwich was given further plausibility by the fact that the college already possessed a picture gallery, containing the collections of Edward Alleyn and of William Cartwright,' adds Mr Waterfield – for a gallery of sorts had existed since 1661, containing a group Alleyn had bought from a painter called Gibkin, added to later in the seventeenth century by eighty or so paintings left by Cartwright, an actor and bookseller.

But the greatness of the collection lies in the bequest of masters from Desanfans and Bourgeois. By 1811 there were about 350 paintings, reflecting the artists most admired at that time: Van Dyck, Watteau, Reynolds, Murillo, de Loutherbourg, of course, Poussin, Tiepolo and the gallery's famous two Rembrandts – one of which was stolen three times and each time recovered.

The College was also left an endowment of £10,000 by Bourgeois and £2,000 to build a new gallery, and before he died he had named the architect of the new gallery: it should be Sir John Soane, his close friend and ally. Soane made his first site visit the day after Bourgeois' death in 1810, and in July submitted the last of several designs which was accepted. This was dickered about with until November, when work began. The gallery was more or less complete by 1813, and the following year the pictures were installed. The gallery had cost £9,778, and was open to the public from 1817.

There was a close tie with the Royal Academy, which advises on the gallery's paintings as a stipulation of the wills of Bourgeois and Mrs Desanfans, and in return the RA was loaned paintings for students to copy, bringing about the foundation of the Academy's first school of painting.

In its first century the gallery was run by a keeper, a practising artist whose job was to repair paintings and supervise loans, to check 'impropriety or irregularity' in visitors, and 'to have a general care of the pictures', especially 'to clean and varnish them as his own expense'.

It was a popular place to visit – the National Gallery, which opened in 1824 in Pall Mall, did not have such a big collection. Giles Waterfield records that literary and academic figures such as Hazlitt, Dickens, Carlyle, Tennyson and George Eliot came often, and artists like Canova, Samuel Palmer, David Cox and William Etty.

The hero of Kingsley's *Alton Locke* describes what he found: 'The rich sombre light of the rooms, the rich heavy warmth of the stove-heated air, the brilliant and varied colouring and gilded frames which embroidered the walls, the hushed earnestness of a few visitors, who were lounging from picture to picture, struck me at once with mysterious awe.'

In 1869 Henry James found a 'pale English light from the rainy day – a cold half-musty atmosphere & solitude complete save for a red-nosed spinster at the end of the vista copying a Gainsborough – the scene had quite a flavour of its own.'

Robert Browning wrote of 'that Gallery I so love and am so grateful to'; Holman Hunt was a copying student, John Ruskin revived himself by railing at the old masters he abhorred: 'Walked down to Dulwich Gallery,' he wrote in 1844, 'and thought the pictures worse than ever; came away encouragingly disgusted.'

It was also close to the Crystal Palace, which stood on top of Sydenham Hill, a brisk walk away for eighty years until it was burned down in 1937. Legions of copyists came, to such an extent that numbers had to be limited. Records were kept of the work done, and the most popular subjects for copying were Murillo's *Flower Girl* and Rembrandt's *Girl at a Window*.

There were two important gifts of paintings: the first was the Linley Bequest in 1835, which was the family pictures of the extraordinary Linley family, the precociously talented children of the composer Thomas Linley, the eldest of whom, Elizabeth, married the playwright Sheridan. This collection included several important Gainsboroughs. Then, over a period of eight years from 1911, there came the gift of the artist, dealer and connoisseur Charles Fairfax Murray, which included works by Hogarth, Lely and Gainsborough.

The building was badly bomb-damaged in the Second World War (the paintings having been taken to Wales in 1939), and at one point consideration was given to building an entirely new gallery in its place. Instead, it was restored to Soane's original design.

The system of keepers continued until one chairman of the gallery's committee, Henry Yates Thompson, who brought the Fairfax Murray gift to the gallery, took on the job himself. In 1980 the Dulwich Picture Gallery's first director was appointed, and he is Giles Waterfield.

'It's changed a good deal in my time,' he said. 'In the 1950s and 60s it offered a gallery of pictures for the delectation of the public and that was it – no services or exhibitions or teaching. . . . There's no doubt that Bourgeois saw it in terms of a teaching institution as everybody did at that time, not so much along the lines that we think of now – indeed, children were not encouraged – but for young art students, and it seemed to fulfil that function. It had rather withered after the war since that sort of approach was so much out of fashion.'

Over the years the decoration of the galleries has changed, and the arrangement of the pictures evolved from the excited massing which the Victorian liked to a single ribbon line along the walls. The rooms have now been restored to the look they had in a painting at Sir John Soane's Museum, with the wall colouring as near as possible to the shade recommended by the then president of the Royal Academy, Benjamin West.

'Tourism didn't have quite the same momentum, but certainly they intended to preserve the pictures and exhibit to interested visitors,' said Mr Waterfield, 'and to provide them as a source for copyists. I think those aims were realised and continue to be, but amplified.'

There had been a curious lapse in interest in the place in the middle of the twentieth century, despite the international importance of the collection.

'There was the professional keeper in the nineteenth century, usually a painter who among other things restored pictures and that sort of thing,' explained Mr Waterfield. 'Then there was the very powerful chairman, Yates Thompson, who said the he didn't need a keeper when the old one died, and he took on his duties as well. Then there was nobody in the 1920s and 30s, and after the War they appointed someone who'd been a carpenter on the estate to be keeper, which was a very curious appointment, but the idea was just to keep the place bubbling along. It was a very old fashioned notion.'

It was as if there had been a switch of values: the Victorian management ethic of having a caretaker rather than curator coupled with a modern picture presentation in which the paintings presented in a single row instead of are emblazoned over a wall. This has been replaced by a more up-to-date management system and a return to the Victorian casting of the galleries.

'One shouldn't underestimate the Victorian energy in approaching the museum, which was very considerable, but it was an old-fashioned approach – you just opened doors and closed them,' said Giles Waterfield.

'The original intention was to be more private, you could only get into the gallery if you had a ticket before you came. It was equivalent to a university museum, a part or an appendage of the educational foundation from which we still get the bulk of our income.'

But what of the future? In 1988 tentative plans for a new building in the grounds which would house a restaurant and temporary exhibition space had to be shelved *sine die* when it was discovered that a new air conditioning system would be needed at a cost of £120,000. And is there an appreciative audience making its way to this rather sleepy village atmosphere, four miles from Westminster? In 1987 there were 30,000 visitors.

'It is an international collection in a local setting, and that is a problem in a way,' the director said. 'We've done surveys of visitors and we find that about 70 per cent are either local or staying with local people. I think the steady process of making the gallery better known locally, in South London, is the way and that if we batter away at people it will work.'

## *Manchester City Art Gallery*

Dulwich Picture Gallery is where it is almost by accident – had Bourgeois chosen another school it might have been in Winchester, Rugby or Sherborne. The great municipal galleries mostly exist *because* of the city they adorn, and the Manchester City Art Gallery is a perfect example.

A century and a half ago, Manchester was a small Lancashire cotton town, much like Lancaster has more or less remained, and the Bridgewater Canal in the middle of the eighteenth century brought its fortune. It brought new textile machines and took away the fabric they produced, so that £46,000 in exports which were made in 1751 had become £5,500,000 fifty years later. And in that time the population rose four-fold, from 17,000 to 70,000.

By the 1820s it was a boom town, the capital city of 'King Cotton', and by Queen Victoria's accession its many Greek Revival buildings, the badge of municipal wealth, was making Manchester a rival of Edinburgh for the title of the 'Athens of the North'. It became a city in 1853, and the centre of the cotton towns which popped up around it – Rochdale, Bolton, Bury and Oldham.

In 1823 the Manchester Institution for the Promotion of Literature, Science and the Arts was created, and a year later it had achieved the royal patronage of George IV and raised £23,000 by public subscription for a building. The motto the society chose for itself reflected the philosophic Mancunian approach: *nihil pulchrum nisi utile* – nothing beautiful unless useful. It was also the motto of the architect, Charles Barry, who later built the House of Commons, and the building was eventually completed in 1834.

Many important works of art came to the Institution, at first by British artists then by foreign ones. There was a lecture theatre in which Ruskin expounded his theories. In 1853 a wing was given over to the School of Design, later the Manchester School of Art, and in 1857 it masterminded one of the great exhibitions which *the* Great Exhibition had inspired, 'Art Treasures of the United Kingdom', in a temporary crystal palace which was opened by Prince Albert and visited by 1,300,000 people, including the Queen.

But by the time it was approaching its fiftieth anniversary, the Institution was clearly under-financed. The corporation agreed to take it on, temporarily: it had in mind its own city art gallery which would take its place.

It was with the Manchester Corporation Act of 1882 that Manchester City Art Gallery formally came into being, and in the ensuing years surrounding buildings were bought and incorporated so that a century after the city acquired its art gallery it is the only major city in Britain without a custom-built art gallery in its centre.

Timothy Clifford was director of the gallery when it celebrated its centenary by publishing *A Century of Collecting 1882-1982*, and in its introduction he wrote: 'Had Manchester been able to build its own new art gallery speedily it might well have been possible to accommodate a superb collection of oils, drawings and prints, numbering 1,156 items and including oils by Botticelli, Rembrandt, Le Nain, Delacroix, Millet and Dégas.

'As it is, these were given to the Victoria and Albert Museum in 1900 by Constantine Alexander Ionides, a Greek textile merchant who was born in Cheetham Hill, Manchester. Other private collections were also promised but lost through no buildings being provided for them.'

Instead of a single, large, multi-departmental art museum in the centre of the city, what developed was a series of satellites around the city and its outskirts, providing a cultural armature as Manchester sprawled inexorably outwards. It makes for tedious logistics for the curators and gallery staff, but the effect is of the gallery's departments being spread among seven different out-stations. Most of them were originally residences of varying degrees of grandness before coming into the care of the Corporation, but Queen's Park Art Gallery at Harpurhey, four miles from the main gallery, was purpose-built for the city in 1884 to be a general museum. Ironically, it is the one branch which is no longer an art gallery. Its stout, brick-vaulted cellars have made it an ideal storage centre for the collection, and the Victorian and Edwardian oil paintings, and the militaria of local regiments, have been dispersed to make Queen's Park the City Art Gallery's conservation studios.

Prestwich may be in Cheshire, but it is as much a suburb of Manchester as Dulwich is of London. Heaton Hall there claims to be the finest eighteenth-century country house in the north-west, and it was built and refurbished between 1772 and 1824 by the Wyatt family of architects – brothers James and Samuel and their nephew Lewis, for the Earl of Wilton. The house and its splendid grounds were bought by the Corporation in 1901, with responsibility for the central rooms being given to the Art Gallery Committee, which had become the Cultural Committee by 1981 when it was given control of the whole house and began a programme of restoration. Gradually every part, from state room to servants' quarters, was being returned to the look reported by account books of two centuries ago.

Lewis Wyatt also remodelled the originally sixteenth-century Wythenshawe Hall, seat of the Tatton family, which was bought from them by Lord and Lady Simon and given to the Corporation in 1926. It stands now as a branch of the city museum but also as a typical residence of the 1840s – the home of a family with considerable antiquarian tastes, because it contains sixteenth- and seventeenth-century English furniture, portraits and a Flemish tapestry.

Alderman Fletcher Moss was an antiquarian city elder at the turn of this century whose passion was the conservation of old Manchester. He bought the Old Parsonage, Didsbury, which had been the home of one of Manchester's old families, the Mosleys, and in 1923 he left it to Manchester. It has now been restored to as much of its Victorian appearance as possible – some features, such as the stained glass and fireplaces, had been removed – but it contains paintings, drawings, prints and maps which relate to Manchester's developing past from the seventeenth to the nineteenth centuries, with important artists such as Arthur Devis and L. S. Lowry represented. Manchester contributed a lot to the Arts and Crafts Movement of the turn of the century, and one room has been decorated to celebrate the fact with wallpaper designed by Walter Crane.

A mile or so nearer the city centre, at Rusholme, is a far grander Palladian house with a joyously rococo interior which, along with the Platt Fields it stands in, was left to the Corporation in 1954. It is now the Gallery of English Costume, one of the largest collections in the country, which also houses a comprehensive archive on the subject. The art gallery's collection of dolls are here, seen as part of a textile heritage rather than of childhood sociology.

The Athenaeum, immediately behind the City Art Gallery, designed by Sir Charles Barry, first opened in 1839 as the Manchester Athenaeum Club, providing, among other things, lectures, language classes and a circulating library. It was bought by the Corporation a century later to become an extension of the art gallery, and now houses the twentieth-century collections, with technicians' studios in the basement and administrative and education departments on the first floor.

The seventh branch no longer exists, but its notion survives in many of the gallery's current activities and in museums such as the Bethnal Green Museum of Childhood in London. It is the Horsfall Museum at Ancoats, begun as an educational museum in 1877 by a wealthy citizen, T. C. Horsfall, and Timothy Clifford described it:

> His idea, inspired by Ruskin, was to provide a museum in the slums of Manchester for poor children, whose eyes could thus be opened to natural and man-made beauty.
>
> His collections were moved to Ancoats Hall in 1886 . . . [where] Horsfall gathered

Rope-making at Chatham Historic Dockyard.

H.M.S. *Gannet*, a Victorian sloop under restoration at Chatham Historic Dockyard.

Restored barge at the Boat Museum, Ellesmere Port.

National Waterways Museum, Gloucester Dock.

Royal Research Ship *Discovery* moored in Victoria Dock, Dundee.

The Dundee waterfront as envisaged by planners of the Discovery Heritage Centre, with Captain Scott's old survey ship—right, as its motif.

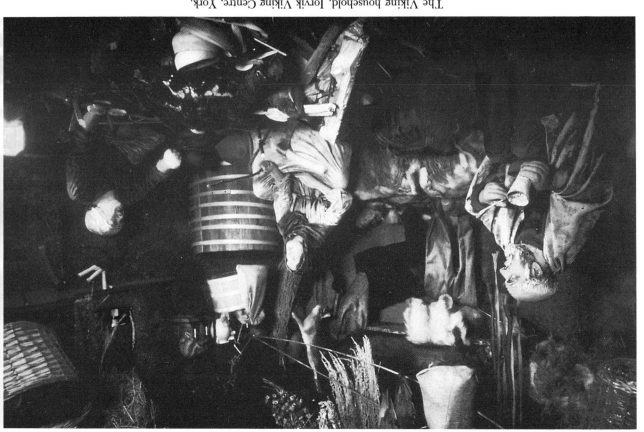

The Viking household. Jorvik Viking Centre, York.

Reconstructed Gateway of the Arbeia Roman Fort, South Shields.

> paintings and drawings of birds and flowers, an aviary, model rooms, a history of the life of Christ, a room of art processes, a gallery of the industrial arts, a gallery dedicated to J M W Turner, and another to local history . . . Horsfall began lending pictures and reproductions to elementary schools in the Manchester area.'[1]

But it was a failure in that it got little support in Manchester. The Corporation took it over in 1918, and then in 1954 the collections were dispersed and the museum demolished.

'Although Horsfall's museum no longer survives, his ideology has formed the basis of much City Art Gallery thinking over the last century,' wrote Mr Clifford. 'His museum was the first of its type in the world and anticipated by over twenty years the similar museum founded for poor children in Brooklyn, New York.'

The art collections are superb, with nearly all the greatest British artists of the later eighteenth and nineteenth centuries represented, and its Pre-Raphaelite collection is probably the finest in public ownership. Its twentieth-century arts section is also strong but specialises in sculpture, with pieces by Moore, Epstein, Hepworth, Gill and Dobson on show. Manchester City Art Gallery is more than an art gallery, in that it contains important collections of applied art such as ceramics, metalwork, and textiles.

'Most of Manchester's collections are in store because of the acute lack of display space,' wrote Mr Clifford in 1983. 'One day the Galleries will have an extension, something they have been waiting for since 1897. When that happens the stored collections, like a wrinkled brown chrysalis, will undergo a metamorphosis into that magnificent and brilliantly coloured butterfly which at present lies dormant.'

That has not happened. Instead the gallery, under a new director, Julian Spalding, has instigated an outreach programme, a system of creating travelling exhibitions using the stored material, and some material usually on display if appropriate, which go out to schools, libraries and community centres. It will also lend pictures to private individuals, pictures which wouldn't be seen otherwise, because there is no space.

A £90,000 annual grant from the Arts Council from 1985, under their 'Glory of the Garden' scheme to encourage the arts in the provinces, was matched by funding from the Manchester Corporation, and the result was a successful exhibition programme which quadrupled attendances from 100,000 to 400,000 a year.

'Manchester was the largest beneficiary in the art gallery world,' said Mr Spalding in that it got £90,000 from the Arts Council, matched by £90,000 from the city council. That resulted in the introduction of a big exhibition programme, community contact schemes and a public lending service for the public.'

The 'community contact scheme' is a system whereby thematic exhibitions are put together by the gallery and loaned, as a package, to schools, libraries and community centres, free of charge. The lending scheme means that individuals can borrow paintings from the reserve collection to hang on their own walls.

[1] Timothy Clifford, *A Century of Collecting, 1882–1982.*

Perhaps the modern star of the gallery is no longer the Duccio painting for which there was a successful appeal to raise the £1,800,000 asking price in 1984 and hangs in Room 1, but the 1987 re-creation of the the painter L. S. Lowry's Salford living room. 'It is absolutely faithful,' said Mr Spalding, 'based on photographs which we have and the actual items which belonged to Lowry and which have been generously lent to us. It is easily our most popular exhibit and it tells us so much about not only the painter but a fairly typical house in the Manchester area in the 1950s and 60s.'

So popular have the exhibitions and new displays been, not to mention the outreach programme which extends Horsfall's theme by taking the collections beyond the confines of the City Art Gallery and its branches, that between 1985 and 1987 the attendance quadrupled to 400,000.

It would be very satisfactory to be able to leave the Manchester City Art Gallery narrative there as a success story on the upward slope, but politics has intervened. Manchester was ratecapped and in 1988 had to save £40,000,000. The Corporation chose to find some of that money in a massive cutting of funds to the gallery, so that posts were lost, the exhibition programme was drastically curtailed, and the pastoral activities, though not stopped, became perfunctory.

Any thoughts of the long-awaited extension 'are very much on the back burner on a low light', said Julian Spalding, and a scheme to turn the Athenaeum's long disused lecture theatre into a restaurant has been indefinitely deferred. It is difficult to argue for an arts budget in preference to housing, or education organisation, but Manchester is one of many communities, large and small, which are having to make such insidious choices, choices which history will show to have been crazily incongruous at a time of clamourous demand for museums and galleries and a time of national growth and prosperity.

## *The National Gallery of Scotland*

If Manchester laid claim to the title of 'The Athens of the North', Edinburgh never relinquished it and the Granite City's museums and galleries would only reluctantly admit to second place to London's. It was here that Timothy Clifford went in 1984 after Manchester, to become director of the National Gallery of Scotland. It is claimed by many to be one of the most beautiful buildings in Britain, and for Greek Revival architecture it is certainly exemplary and has now been restored to its mid-nineteenth-century appearance. It was built, as so many great Victorian museums and galleries were, to be an inspiration to the artists, particularly those in the Royal Scottish Academy which it was designed to house as well.

The foundation stone was laid in great pomp and perfect weather by Prince Albert in 1850, in a wave of royal fervour which the visit of the Queen and the Consort had instigated with the return of Queen Victoria to the home of her Stuart ancestors at Holyrood the evening before. The earthen Mound above the Edinburgh–Glasgow railway tunnel had been cleared of the wooden sheds of Wombwell's Menagerie, and the architect, William Henry Playfair (part of a distinguished Edinburgh family whose kinsman, Lyon Playfair, was to be closely associated with the South Kensington projects before moving on to parliamentary high office), the president of the Royal Scottish Academy and a Treasury minister (the Treasury were to finance the project) were all gathered in harmony for the ceremony.

'United through this common purpose, it is surprising to discover that many of those present, who were officially charged with the artistic development of Scotland, had just emerged from a series of unseemly squabbles which might have been more appropriate to Wombwell's Menagerie than the lofty new purpose the Mound was to serve,' wrote Ian Gow in 1988 in *The National Gallery of Scotland: An Architectural and Decorative History*. When, after five years of rows and false starts, Playfair was at last commissioned to draw up the architectural designs, he reflected:

> So I begin to hope that I have nothing more now to contend with but architectural difficulties which are so much more easily dealt with than the passions and intrigues of men. How smooth the affairs of the world might be carried on were it not for such impediments.

The story goes back to 1760 when Edinburgh established one of the first Drawing Academies in order to improve the standard of design and thereby exports. In 1822 a Royal Institution was built, housing the academy – which became the Royal Scottish Academy in 1826 – and, among other aesthetic societies, the Institution for the Encouragement of the Fine Arts in Scotland, which received a royal charter in 1827 and whose purpose was to build a permanent collection.

The academy and the institution grew within the building, and as they grew so the squabbles became louder and more farcical, until a civil servant had to be sent from London to sort out the matter. He recommended that the Academy should be lent government money to enable them to build their own Scottish National Gallery on the Mound. The arguments did not end, however, and Playfair even resigned from the Royal Scottish Academy when a suggestion was made that a 'temporary' brick building be thrown up. The Treasury were deeply involved and asked Sir Charles Barry to act as adviser. Eventually Playfair's scheme for a combined Academy and National Gallery building, in Doric style, was accepted, but building was to take ten years.

The royal visit of 1850 was a great triumph for Playfair – 'Pluffy' to his many well-connected supporters, such as Lord Cockburn who wrote to a mutual friend: 'It was his great day and delighted, modest and amiable he was – in spite of all the laughter and parodies that I could exhaust myself in pouring out on him. The foundation stone is a great event. It greatly adorns Edinburgh and saves it from a fatal change which nothing but an ornamental appropriation of the ground could have avoided.'

The celebrity he acquired did not impress Playfair: 'Fools!' he wrote to another friend. 'Don't they see it is the architecture that is noticed and not the man. If the Queen ever were to confer any mark of distinction upon me it should surely be when the National Gallery shall be finished and found worthy which with God's aid it may be.'

But Playfair was not to see his creation completed. After a long illness he died in March 1857, two years before the National Gallery, delayed largely by bureaucratic pedantry, was opened.

While this slow-motion drama was being enacted, the collections continued to grow, and did not draw breath after the gallery was open. By the 1880s a new building was needed, and in 1889 the Scottish National Portrait Gallery opened in Queen Street, thanks to an anonymous donor who started a long benefaction with £10,000 in 1883 which, by the 1890s, was to become £60,000.

A third member of the group arrived in 1960 when the National Gallery of Modern Art was created from the collections, which finally moved to a permanent home in the former John Watson's School, a neo-classical pile built at about the time the art academics were beginning to talk about a new national gallery in the 1820s – opening in 1983.

It was the chance to rationalise the main building on The Mound, and a five year programme of restoration and refurbishment, including the upgrading of lighting and air conditioning to modern conservation standards, was begun, to be completed in 1988. It gave Timothy Clifford the opportunity to write, in *The National Gallery of Scotland: An Architectural and Decorative History*:

> The overall plan for the redecoration and rehanging of the National Gallery has been based on historical precedent. Taste and fashions change continuously, however, so no doubt what we have struggle to achieve will be altered again at some time in the future. Nevertheless, we hope the present redecoration will heighten our visitors' pleasure in an awareness of Playfair's splendid building, in which many of Scotland's greatest pictures are displayed.

Baroness Lee's unfortunate inference of the 'dead arts' may have had an element of fact in the 1960s, but does it today? Our art museums have been described by the museums writer Kenneth Hudson as the 'backward children' of the family, but he is revising that judgement in view of some of the developments happening around the country.

Take the Harris Museum in Preston, for instance, run by the local authority since it opened in 1892. Designed as one of the Greek Revival temples in what was so much the vernacular for Victorian art museums, its architect was a local man, James Hibbert, who took a deep breath and built in a central lantern going through the whole of the building's three stories, rising 120 feet. It celebrates local history as well as art, and while its recent restoration to show the late-nineteenth-century mood of the buildings design and decoration is superbly faithful, to the intricate pattern and colours of the decor, it has developed a reputation as a temple for modern art. As well as artists from Landseer to Stanley Spencer – and including the important local painter, Arthur Devis, and his family – the Harris's temporary exhibitions tackle multi-cultural new art, examine the nature of new sculpture and is almost eager to be controversial, as it was in 1988 with its Graven Images exhibition, looking at the interplay of art, religion and politics – one work work by Tony Carter made a statement about modern values with a completely blank canvas. All this is in the most serene surroundings now, a tribute to the borough and to the curator, Vivienne Bennett.

Or the Thorburn Museum and Gallery at Dobwalls in Cornwall where an enthusiast for the wild life painter Archibald Thorburn collected so many of the man's works that he almost had no choice but to open a museum of them. His name is John Southern, and he decided to make more than a biographical museum or a dedicated art gallery: his museum fulfils those functions, but it also attempts to bring the paintings literally to life but adopting the latest ploys of the Jorvik generation by evoking other sights, sounds and smells.

Or the new Ruskin Gallery in Sheffield, opened in 1985 to show the collection belonging to the Guild of St George which John Ruskin founded in the 1870s to teach the uncultured about the origins of art in nature. A listed former wine shop was converted by leading modern craftsmen to interpret the collection and philosophy in a way relevant to the present day and present public.

There is nothing dead about the way that Gillian Wolfe brings Dulwich's galleries to life for the children she teaches there, nor about the drama sessions the actress Lucy Wilson has created in galleries like the Harris, any more than there is anything dead about modern painting.

# PART FOUR

# 14. The Guardians

*We have seen how and why museums became such a big part of our national life, what they are offering and how they seem to be developing. But what of the people who run them, the curators, conservators and teachers? How have their jobs changed, and how have they adapted? In this chapter they speak for themselves.*

A hundred years ago the museum curator was an extraordinary hybrid. He was a teacher, a scientist, an historian, a librarian, often an artist and a civic figure, in the bigger museums he was often an international scholar, in the smaller ones the ultimate wisdom on the local natural history, geology and archaeology.

He was invariably a man who took his academic work seriously and pursued it as often as he could, and who performed his administrative and managerial tasks as a secondary necessity.

Those more mundane duties amounted to guiding the research work of his curatorial staff, instructing the non-curatorial staff on their manual tasks for the day, and the responsibility to the public was seen as a little more than 'getting the place open in the morning and closing it again at night', in the words of Alf Hatton, lecturer in museum studies at the Institute of Archaeology who set up the Master of Arts course there in 1986. 'At the end of the nineteenth century the curator was still a scholar/academic, a collector of objects, rather than even data – the object containing the data,' he said.

Visitors' numbers to museums which were established at the turn of the century have not changed very greatly, some are even getting fewer. What is different is that there are ten times as many museums now as there were then, and the audience has changed. And how has the curator changed? In Mr Hatton's view:

> The core philosophy that museum professionals work with hasn't changed that much. In the Victorian period it was very much 'collect, we must collect', and was based on the idea that you could represent the sum total of knowledge in a three-dimensional collection of artefacts, natural history specimens and so on. You could represent the world in this way. The collecting function became the dominant motive, and you can still see it when new museums are being set up by small communities or large bodies: the object is to collect.

It was only in the beginning of this century, as the Museums Association's network started to radiate ideas among its membership, that museum professionals started to look up from their books and their microscopes. 'They began to say "what are we going to do with this – we have to make something more specific out of it",' said Alf Hatton.

But while the theory might have been moving along, the practice was not and there was very little change. In the 1930s discussions in the new Standing Commission on Museums and Galleries there was still more intensive navel-scrutiny about what the role of museums was to be – was it to be a general contribution to the community's quality of life, or something more tangible in more modern terms? The navel took no action.

But between the wars and just after, the curator's job was being added to by other disciplines outside the traditional archaeology, ethnology, natural history and geology. He was becoming an organiser, and very often an administrator. But first priority was still the curator's own topic or speciality of study, and he was hanging on to it.

'Where it started to change in the 1970s,' said Mr Hatton, 'was that people started to talk about forward planning, the first sign of management approaching museums, and then people have started gradually to talk about management.' In the 70s it was the new independents which were showing the bureaucratic national and local authority museums what the theory meant in practice. They had no guaranteed income, and no choice but to go and negotiate for their capital. Because they had to start from new ground rules to persuade the money market to invest, they brought in exciting techniques of presentation, examples of which are chronicled in other chapters. 'What they've done,' said Mr Hatton, 'is to bring life into the museum. They've done away with the glass and the label.'

By the late 1980s, though, the average curator was still often doing no more than 'talking about' the looming essentials of financial management, customer care and business administration, much to the rage of the new school which Dr Neil Cossons, director of the Science Museum, represented. He told *The Times* in 1987:

> Curators are an endangered species, endangered by their own lack of wider knowledge. They are feeling cornered, and they ought to see themselves as professionals who have something to contribute to a team including other sorts of professionals. It's often been curators who have had to be dragged to the alter of modern presentation, and non-curators who have done it.

The Museums and Galleries Commission, as the Standing Commission had become, produced a report that year, compiled by a committee which Sir John Hale, an academic but also a trustee of both the Victoria and Albert and the British Museums, chaired. The report was unequivocating. Sir John wrote in his Foreword:

> There has never been a more clamant need to look inwardly at documentary, administrative, managerial and marketing efficiency, the burnishing away of the Old Curiosity Shop patina of some small museums, the opening of watertight compartments in some large ones to a sense of common, planned purpose, to maintain and broaden standards of curatorial scholarship.

For there is no statutory pre-training for curators, though there are various specialist courses at universities and polytechnics, chiefly at Leicester University at the start of a career, City University London for middle management and Alf Hatton's Institute of Archaeology at University College London where a two-year postgraduate course is designed to bridge the gap. In-service training has been the postgraduate Museums Association diploma course, which by 1987 had been running for fifty years.

The MGC report recommended a national training council with courses for all museum personnel, from security warders to directors, designed to be appropriate for all kinds of museums, from art galleries to hands-on science centres. 'It's never been as important as it is now,' Sir John said to *The Times* when the report came out. 'It's never been so necessary for curators really to understand the whole of the working of a particular institution. They have to cope with administrative and managerial responsibilities which are, if not entirely new, newly urgent.'

Alf Hatton represents the kind of curator who has made the adjustment within the local authority museum orbit. He spent fourteen years in provincial museums after graduating from Durham University with a degree in oriental studies – and a passion for karate (he is a third-dan black belt) which must make him unique as a museologist. After training in Sunderland Museum and Art Gallery he moved to Wales to set up Monmouth District's museum service. In 1978 he went to Ipswich to take over one of the oldest provincial museums – both in age and style – in the country. 'It was typical: a large gallery hall with a balcony around the upper floor, and very typical but very good collections. We used to talk about an embarrassment of riches, but it was moribund,' he said. 'I found a classic example of the collection function dominating. Previous curators had collected and collected *ad infinitum*, but there were galleries that had not been changed since the museum opened in 1881.'

The first Ipswich Museum, set up like so many by the local philosophical society, first opened in 1846 in a building which still stands in Museum Street. By 1863 it had outgrown the society and the council, apparently somewhat reluctantly, agreed to take over the financing of it. By the 1880s it had outgrown the building too, and a public subscription provided the new building in the High Street which opened in 1881.

'They moved the principal main gallery lock, stock and barrel from the 1846 museum to the 1881 museum, and with the exception of some newer style labels and some replacements by self-motivated staff members, the lay-out was the same when I arrived in 1978,' Alf Hatton recalled. 'I've got a slide of one gallery in 1846, another in 1881 and another in 1978, and the difference was the change to gas, then to electric lighting, nothing else.'

It was a perfect example of a collection being allowed to accumulate with the curators' giving no thought to the end product – the contribution to the cultural health of the community and its education. By 1978 the community had decided it wanted more out of it, and was making its point by not going. The town's museum services department was closed and responsibility shifted to the recreation department; things were so bad that Ipswich Museum was within an ace of being scrapped altogether, and its last chance was Alf Hatton.

> My brief was to sort out the mess and get people using the museum service before it folded up completely.
>
> But the collections weren't just local Victoriana, the sort of thing you could find without variation in museums up and down the country, it was first-rate local material and there was lots of it in high quality. The second thing we had going for us was a hardworking education officer and a very committed and able staff who hadn't had the leadership they needed to set objectives and co-ordinate things. And they hadn't had the money.

After a year of setting objectives and co-ordinating their implementation, and of negotiating with the local authority, Mr Hatton got a £25,000 development budget for conservation, cataloguing, new displays – all the classic curatorial activities which had been sacrificed for the enlargement of the collections. They hit rock bottom in 1980 with merely 18,000 people going through, but from there the only way was up, and in six years the figures had doubled thanks to new galleries, simple low-cost marketing and a changed image.

'There was a huge argument about the tip of the iceberg – "let's sell the rest of the iceberg",' said Mr Hatton. 'So we took over the gallery next to the museum for temporary exhibitions drawn from the reserve – we got the stuff out, dusted it down, and put it on show. It meant there was always something new happening, and it was a good excuse for the staff to get into the collections.'

They even made an exhibition of themselves. There were open days when boxes were got out of stores and opened before the public's fascinated gaze, revealing objects the creators themselves had never seen before, that *nobody* had seen for fifty or sixty years.

In 1896 the council had taken on what seemed something of a white elephant when the Cobbold family left its sixteenth-century Christchurch Mansion in Soane Street to the community. The council wanted to pull it down but was persuaded not to; then for a couple of years it was a school of arts and commerce. Then the museum took it over, in 1904, and started to fill the empty place with a collection of furniture and decorative arts, and it gradually became a museum of art and social history. Alf Hatton found a wasted resource, a splendid house whose potential had been missed. He set the ground floor out as domestic quarters, 'in a manner servants would have recognised round about the turn of this century'. It has a kitchen, a servants' hall and a table being laid for dinner. Next door the Wolsey Gallery became a showcase for Suffolk artists like Gainsborough, Constable, Munnings and Steer. It became so popular with a new dynamo of its own, generated by the Wolsey's temporary exhibitions as much as anything, that in 1987 it attracted more visitors than the main museum.

'The general idea was to get it into the community's mind that there was life about the place, things were happening, things were changing,' explained Alf Hatton. 'We had conservation workshops treating some of the reserve stuff in the gallery and explaining to people what was happening and why, so we were telling the public what the museum was doing behind the scenes. I think that that was the magic ingredient.'

Figures dramatically improved, sales from the shop did likewise, and the education officer was getting the kind of back-up he needed because the staff was organised and 'product orientated', the product being the service to the public.

> At Ipswich we had a classic problem of one-and-a-half-million specimens at the best estimate, not particularly catalogued, some well some not, some barely catalogued at all. The art specialist's estimate of her reserve collection was 3,000, and she knew her collections; we started computerised cataloguing and the art collection went to four million, then six, then eight, and the last estimate I heard was getting on for twenty million, including prints, drawings and so on. That's the extent of the cataloguing scene.

Curators were still being seen, and often seeing themselves, as enlightened dilettantes, experts who did the job for the love of it rather than any career expectation. Academically our curators are among our most glitteringly qualified professionals, few at the lowest grade of Museum Assistant being without a degree; in terms of pay among the professional classes they were one from the bottom, above professional dancers, in 1987.

The recognised goal is now a centralised training system out of which will develop a national career structure for curators, and just as it was celebrating Museums Year in 1989 the Museums Association was co-ordinating a development project in consultation with the government and the Museums and Galleries Commission. It was the MGC who set the ball rolling with Sir John Hale's report in 1987 which identified that a curator's training was an *ad hoc* process which depended on what sort of museum the curator found himself in. National museums are blessed with pay scales greatly in advance of the others so that, once there, staff tended to remain and get their training in-house as they went along.

The local authority sector had relied on the Museums Association diploma, which was basically in-service work with the help of a voluntary tutor attached to the student, while independent museums tended to set their own criteria for training, criteria which publicly funded museums were only starting to recognise and which were being hoisted in to the MA's thinking – business management, public relations and media skills, keyboard skills, financial management, marketing and sponsorship trawling. All this was having to be pulled together by the Museums Association, commissioned by the government to analyse the training needs for curators in the 1990s in view of the Hale Report and other evidence. The MA's report and a possible subsequent national network for training and career structure was eagerly awaited at the beginning of 1989.

A phenomenon at the top of the museums pile has been the appointment of outsiders as directors. Mrs Elizabeth Esteve-Coll had been in the V&A just two years when she succeeded Sir Roy Strong, and Dr Neil Chalmers came from the Open University to take over the Natural History Museum. Neil MacGregor had been editor of *The Burlington Magazine*, the art publication, when he was the surprise appointment as director of the National Gallery, and he had this to say:

> I think the need is very strong to restate the functions of museums, because it's quite clear that the government as a whole has been focusing simply on the management and administration without really starting from the question of what we want these (hings to achieve.
>
> What has happened in the last five years is that trustees have been made aware that the whole of the government's relationship with the institutions is going to change, and really it's a relationship that hasn't altered in the 160 years of this gallery's existence.
>
> What trustees have been confronted with is that people have been working in museums and galleries for twenty years and have habits and patterns and assumptions. Most of those habits and patterns and assumptions are no longer reflecting the reality of the government's approach, and I think that must explain why it is that several museums have decided that the person to take the museum or gallery through that change was somebody who hadn't been shaped by those patterns.
>
> Always there's a balance, and for them it's to try to find someone who is sympathetic enough to the institution to keep the ideals and ethos of the institution intact.

In the 1830s a picture restorer advised readers of his monograph that the best method of conservation was 'damping the face of a picture and exposing it to the action of a frosty night', so that 'all the foulness will be effectually loosened and removed by the subsequent use of a sponge.'[1]

Conservation was best left to the craftsmen who conducted it, and even though there were periodic public airings of the subject – like a famous row in the 1850s after two reports of House of Commmons Select Committees into the management of the National Gallery had highlighted the standard of picture cleaning – progress was slow. And the craftsmen often turned out to be amateurs.

There was a lot of debate in the 1860s when the South Kensington Museum installed gas lighting, the first museum to do so, so that it could stay open late in the winter. 'The anxious wife will no longer have to visit the different tap rooms to drag her poor besotted husband home,' *Lloyds Magazine* reported with screaming irony in 1857. 'She will seek for him at the nearest museum, where she will have to exercise all the persuasion of her affection to tear him away from the rapt contemplation of a Raphael.'

But it was taken very seriously, and Michael Faraday was one of a team of eminent scientists appointed to look into 'the possibly deleterious effect of gas lighting upon pictures'.[2] It came to the conclusion that there was no problem provided there was ventilation, but how much notice was being taken of it can be seen by the fact that the gas lighting was already installed by the time the report was published. There was more controversy in 1888 when another report into electric lighting said the South Kensington pictures were under threat from the unaccustomed glare, but nothing significant was done.

[1] *Advice to Proprietors on the Care of Valuable Pictures Painted in Oil*, Anon, 1835.
[2] John Physick, *The Victoria and Albert Museum: A history of its building*, 1983.

Pictures got a fair amount of attention, but other objects and specimens did not. It was not until 1919 that the first museum conservation department was set up, at the British Museum, and that was only intended to be temporary to investigate war damage; it is the largest conservation department in Europe now. The Courtauld Institute established a fine art conservation laboratory after the Second World War, and the V&A established its conservation department in 1960. By then there were very few other conservation departments in the country, according to a report, *Conservation in Museum and Galleries*, produced by the International Institute of Conservation in 1974.

In 1988 a National Audit Office report into the state of conservation, storage and cataloguing in our national museums highlighted the lack of conservation facilities, and although only three museums were mentioned they were typical of all British museums. The report said that conservation and storage resources were so limited that it would be years, if ever, before damage which had already taken place could be remedied, and that in some cases deterioration had been allowed to progress so far that it was beyond redemption.[3] 'It does seem to endorse what some of us have been saying for some time,' said Peter Longman, secretary of the Museums and Galleries Commission. He told the *Sunday Times*: 'It is probably the single biggest problem facing museums. The trouble is, it's the unglamorous side of museum work, it's much easier to persuade trustees or sponsors or even government to put up money for new galleries out front, and it's the unsexy things like conservation and storage that suffer.'

One of the greatest problems was conservators' pay scales. At the time of the report, the British Museum had a complement of about seventy, but there was a vacancy rate of about 15 per cent because staff were being lured away to private practice, especially in the fields of paper and ceramics conservation.

A conservator with a degree and four years training on top of that could expect a salary of about £11,500 at one of the London national museums. In private practice they could look forward to at least twice that. What also lured them away was an increasing amount of administration paperwork, diverting them from what they saw as their real work.

The big museums' conservation departments often fulfilled a pastoral role, as well, giving advice and practical help when necessary, but this was severely curtailed in the mid-1980s because of cost-cutting. Museums had been in the hands of curators who had mostly had no conservation training at all, so that the conservation requirements were often only perfunctorily met. Dr Nigel Seeley of the Institute of Archaeology (IOA) reckoned that in 1988 there was three times as much urgent work to be done as there were resources to carry it out.

The IOA launched an appeal in 1988 for £3 million to build new conservation studios in Gordon Square, London, which would provide not only laboratories but training as well, a desperately short commodity in some areas – there are no courses in stone and sculpture conservation for professionals, for instance.

[3] National Audit Office, *Management of the Collections of the English National Museums and Galleries*, 1988.

'When conservation started to make itself felt in the last ten years, people were saying, "We need high-powered scientists"; then they were up against money,' said Dr Seeley's colleague, Alf Hatton. 'It's very difficult to explain to a decision-making process like a local authority recreations department what the keeper of a museum department does if a conservator is hired to look after the collections – it's a mighty conceptual leap. That's one of the things that's got to change urgently and rapidly,' and he called for a national plan to calibrate collecting and conservation, so that objects are not left untreated in damaging basement conditions in the way that the National Audit Office showed was happening.

The Museums and Galleries Commission started its own conservation unit in 1988 under Dr David Leigh, whose job was to monitor the best conservators in private practice around the country so that advice could be given to individual collectors about where to get their treasures conserved safely. This was, of course, also available to museums and galleries who were being encouraged to use it. A new database link was set up with the Getty Foundation's conservation research establishment, which monitors the latest developments and records it for subscribers, Dr Leigh's unit acting as a sort of agent in the United Kingdom. 'But the problem in the museums is the lack of training and resources to set up their own conservation departments,' he said. 'They are very dedicated in their intentions, and there is very good work being done in some provincial museums, but the lack of knowledge and understanding in others is astounding.'

Alf Hatton had some very positive thoughts to add:

> What's been negative about museums recently, is the conservation role. Because our basements are full of uncatalogued, unconserved material, people are beginning to slow up collecting, so it's not just because of tighter purse strings.
>
> I think we're also neglectful in terms of what we actually preserve. There has to be some sort of overall rational plan of collecting for a small island nation like Britain. We cannot allow the museums themselves to decide to carry on buying yet more Italian old masters, beautiful though they are: how are they more relevant to British heritage because they've been in some stately home for the last 200 years than the general social history of the north east, Liverpool, Glasgow, places which have changed out of all recognition even the last five years even because of the decline in manufacturing industry?
>
> Chloe Bennett, the art specialist at Ipswich said to me, 'Of course Gainsborough, Constable, Smiley and so on are very very important, but they're only local artists to us, just like a dozen others.'

'We have to give value for money and a more competent framework of management for the museum. To have a lot of different department competing for funds is divisive. There has to be a strategic approach to planning,' said Dr Cossons as he outlined his ideas for redrawing the administrative structure of the Science Museum:

> The best managers are going to have started as curators. Curators are in some respects their worst enemies. A curator who thinks that his own department or his own career comes first ought not, in my opinion, to be employed. The museum must come first, and it must be run as a team effort.
>
> Nobody owes the museums a living – on the contrary, we owe our living to the public. We are what we make for ourselves.

Museums were created for an educational purpose, and while the lofty valetudinarian of Victorian times has, thankfully, largely disappeared, the educational importance of museums and galleries has never been more important with the new GCSE examination putting an emphasis on projects.

Mary Ball, keeper of education for Leicestershire Museums, told me, 'Where we're concerned we cover all the museum disciplines here except for one – technology – and we are to get a member of staff for that. We look at what's known as human history, anything from archaeology up to the present day, and archives, because the record office is part of us.' There had been a bid to hive off the county records section and with it the education department, but this had been resisted. 'The trouble with the record section is they don't keep photographs, they don't keep a lot of information that other museum departments keep, and of course they don't keep specimens,' she explained. There are, however, plans to make the records section a more integral part of the museums service in future which will complement the education programme.

Mrs Ball, a member of Leicestershire City Museum's staff since 1968 and education keeper since 1982, has a staff of seven graduates, three trained designer/technician plus four driver/handymen and one-and-a-half clerical staff. 'So we are large. We grew enormously in 1974 with the reorganisation. We also have someone who deals with multicultural education because we have a lot of ethnographic collections and a large ethnic minority population, particularly Gujerati.'

Contact with schools takes two manifestations: an object loan service, the first in the provinces, circulates the county's schools; and direct working with teachers. 'Either schools come into the museums or teachers get in touch with us saying "we're doing such and such a project, how can you help?".' A working party was set up in 1988 to examine how the art gallery, in particular, can serve the GCSE curriculum. Mrs Ball has found that, 'Like everything else, so much depends on the teacher: art and design teachers use us a lot, history use us to some degree, we have had people in for multi-cultural education, and I do have hopes for technology with our new post, especially with our new complex at Snibston [the former colliery which is being fashioned into a science and technology museum].'

As the fifteen branch museums and sites become more active under the policy of director Patrick Boylan (president of the Mueums Association), so has Mrs Ball's programme of using the county museums as outstations of the museums education programme is growing as well:

> When I first came it was very much a case of schools ringing up, wanting to visit the museum, wanting someone to take them round. I thought this was not a good use of my time, and I started counselling teachers and using teaching rooms much more where we can get material out. Youngters have a three-dimensional look, rather than two-and-a-half.
>
> Teaching and schools have changed so much, and because we are here to serve them museums must change too. What I would like is a permanent multi-cultural gallery: this is something which an enormous number of schools ask for, and it takes an awful lot of

> time to get a teaching collection out for schools to look at. But basically I must admit that we are more fortunate than many.

London has had a leading part to play in museums education, with two of the Inner London Education Authority's museums, the Geffrye Museum and the Horniman Museum, using their collections as primary teaching resources for schools. The ILEA provided Dulwich Picture Gallery with Gillian Wolfe, the education officer there who has won several prizes for her enlightened use of the gallery. About 5,000 children pass through her hands in a year, and there is a waiting list. What she does might be anathema to the custodians of the 1880s, but it works. 'We try to make the rooms come alive for the children, to give them an idea of what it was like to be Gainsborough. We act out some of the allegorical paintings so that they know why they were painted,' she told me. 'But as well as helping them understand the gallery and the paintings, we hope that from a very early age they get the idea that an art gallery can be an exciting place, not cold or forbidding as they often seem.'

The national museums have always taken their educational role seriously, now more than ever. For instance, the Natural History Museum has a plan to turn the whole of its basement into a teaching resource centre, and the National Gallery reaches children in the summer holidays with its 'Meet the Artist' feature, in which a master such as van Eyck is portrayed by an actor painting the Arnolfini wedding, on view in the galleries, in a set designed to look like his studio, and he talks about his work and answers questions.

The new director of the National Gallery, Neil MacGregor, created a new separate department of education, enticing the Open University's head of education, Erika Langmuir, to be its keeper. His plans for this particular role of the gallery were far-reaching:

> Historically, the gallery was set up largely with a view to educating artists and improving taste, and that end goes on all the time. For the rest it was accepted that people would come and look, and that was that.
>
> We've built up over the years a steady programme of free lunchtime lectures for an adult audience, and a very large schools programme which services hundreds of thousands of children a year. What we've not been able to do is organise something more in the nature of sequence instruction – up to now it's been either you come to a lunchtime lecture or you don't, it's a one off, and what we wanted to see was whether we could involve people in something much more structured. For instance, ideas of landscape painting where you would obviously want a smallish group to go on working on the same topic but applied to different pictures over, say, eight to ten weeks. Before we've been totally unselective.
>
> It seems to us that that is now what an educational role means. I think our model is actually the Open University – it's how we offer instruction to broadly a self-selected audience. We plan to start in 1989.
>
> What is clear is that the gallery's teaching must be based on the gallery's things, the sort of teaching that only a museum can do and no adult institute or university department can – teaching from the objects. People want to be instructed as well as just to look.

Education is not confined to the publicly funded museums. Independent museums take on the responsibility too, often without any subsidy or financial support for what can be a costly operation.

'Museums have always been educational and this means for any age of course,' said David Sekers of Quarry Bank Mill at Styal. 'We run courses in creative textile work for young and old, and many museums are into adult education now, but we have a schools programme and we devote quite a lot of time and staff to making sense of the whole site and its history for schools because it is such a critical part of British history.'

# 15. The Supporters

*Museums would not always admit that they depend on external support, but existence in the 1980s would be difficult and expansion impossible without the organisations, some of which have already been mentioned, and individuals which back them. While acknowledging the importance of sponsorship to modern museum life, it is a factor which affects every form of entertainment and, increasingly, education. This chapter looks at the unique support museums get.*

'THERE has long been a desire amongst Curators and others interested in the welfare and progress of Museums for a bond of union whereby the Museums in different localities could be brought into closer connection with each other, so that their work could be more uniformly and effectively carried out.' So the Museums Association ponderously explained to its founder members at its first annual general meeting in June 1890, probably as much with a view to spelling it out for posterity as for the members, although barely a third of them had had representatives the year before in York when the MA was born. 'The fact that Museums are becoming, and may still further become, potent factors in education and scientific culture, is now generally recognised, and the day when such institutions were looked upon as mere receptacles for anything curious or abnormal has gone for ever.'

By the time it was celebrating its centenary in 1989 the association had 3,000 members and, after several robust fights for survival, was experiencing a renaissance as a stanchion of the curatorial profession.

Elijah Howarth had joined the Liverpool Free Public Museum as an office boy in 1868, seven years after it had opened, and in 1875 he became the first curator of the new Sheffield Museum. It was in *Nature* magazine two years after that that he published an article calling for a museums' association for drawing 'attention to some of the advantages that might arise from mutual co-operation',[1] perhaps to match the Library Association which had come into being that year.

Those advantages did not seem to strike any chord with his colleagues, because despite his pleas nothing much happened, as he recalled thirteen years later, not disguising his bitterness at the foiling of his attempt to create professional unity:

[1] Museums Association. Report of Proceedings of the First Annual General Meeting, 1890.

'Considerable difficulty was . . . experienced in bringing this about owing to the absence of any co-operation whatever among museums.' Seven years later he tried another angle, the Library Association, suggesting at its Dublin annual meeting it extend its membership to museums; they turned him down.

Instead Elijah Howarth looked towards his home ground. He thought the gravitas of a scientific organisation, from which many museums had sprung after all, might swing the thing, and the Yorkshire Philosophical Society came up trumps. In 1888 the society invited twenty-four museums, 'Selected from amongst the best known in England', to a meeting in York, and on 3 May ten of them crowded into the back room at the home of the society's vice-president, S. W. North. This time it worked, and the meeting decided to form a Museums Association of curators and their co-workers in and for museums, which would publish papers and hold meetings in different towns around the country.

A year later all provincial museums had been invited to join, and eleven of them sent fifteen delegates to the founding meeting on 20 June, with the Rev. Henry H. Higgins, chairman of the Liverpool Free Public Museum sub committee, as the first elected president – in fact more than half those present were elected to office.

Mr North, chairman at the inaugural meeting, informally recorded the new association's aims in a letter to the Liverpool AGM, which he could not attend: 'To bring the whole of the museums of England into harmony; to establish a bond of sympathy between them – recognising no great or small museums, only the common bond of knowledge and the desire for its diffusion is a work of the highest effort.'

They were Flowerists to a man. The Reverend Higgins stepped forward to open the programme of the first AGM: 'It may be one of the most encouraging features of our fellowship, should this Association tend to confirm our conviction that the soul of the Museum is the Curator, and the kindred spirits that work with him,' he said. 'Were a museum ever so extensive, the living elements and not the specimen, must determine its real value to the community.' So already the theme of the public's participation was a matter of doctrine.

The president returned to his theme at the end, having covered such matters as Museum Appliances and Picturesque Groups with his nuggets of wisdom in the meantime, by posing what museums' task was, and, of course, answering it: 'The conclusion cannot be far away – that the highest aim of the work of Public Museums is not – however ingeniously – to multiply facts in the *memories* [his italics] of visitors, but to kindle in their hearts the wonder and the loving sympathy – THE NEW KNOWLEDGE [his capital letters] – called for every page in the remotely-reaching annals of Nature.'

The first annual meeting recorded that there were thirty member museums, and in ten years this had risen to sixty-four, which included five overseas members. It was the beginning of an organisation which was to influence the standards of museums and curatorship in one degree or another to the present time, with Elijah Howarth busily organising in the background at least until 1910. A journal was introduced periodically to present essays on key subjects, then a monthly bulletin to distribute news. In 1903 they established, in a rather higgledy-piggledy form which took four years to settle into coherence, a directory of museums (now an annual publication as the *Museums Yearbook*).

The 1911 edition of the directory recorded attendances for some of the museums which show that their popularity was apparently as great then as it is now: the V&A had nearly a million, with its East End branch, the Bethnal Green Museum, recording nearly 400,000 (the V&A had 1,700,000 for itself and all its branches in 1987); Birmingham reported 7–8,000 (but only 514,329 in 1987); Leeds had worked out an average since 1888 of 285,870 (156,000 in 1987). Little Haslemere had 10,000 and in 1987 was able to boast 24,000. In 1987 there were, of course, something like seven times as many museums as in 1911, but the figures bear testament to the enthusiasm prevailing then.

The association became a limited company and a charity in 1930, and gradually developed links not only with public and relevant private bodies in Britain but with UNESCO and the International Council of Museums.

The MA is not a trades union, it has no negotiating rights, nor is it a professional body, in the way the British Medical Association is, because it has no disciplinary powers, but it has established a Code of Practice for museum authorities and produced a code of practice for curators, and these are the conventions adhered to throughout the profession. In 1936 it created the only professional qualification for curators, the Museums Diploma, and this was under review at the time of the MA's centenary by both the Museums and Galleries Commission (MGC) and itself. In 1988 the Minister for the Arts commissioned the MA to do a study of training requirements following an in-depth report from the MGC.

The Museum and Galleries Commission is a quango which is to museums and galleries what the Arts Council is to the performing arts. It was established as the Standing Commission on Museums and Galleries by Treasury Minute in 1930 after a recommendation from a Royal Commission on National Museums and Galleries which had been appointed in 1928. Its brief was not a very well defined one. It was to keep an overview of museums across the country and advise on national museums and galleries, promoting co-operation between them and the provincial ones and encouraging public support. It was to have up to thirteen unpaid commissioners appointed by the prime minister.

The Commission produced many reports over the next fifty years which received varying degrees of notice from government and museums, but it had only a small staff, no power and only enough finance to cover its expenses. In 1981 the ballooning museum industry, which is what it had amounted to, needed something stronger to act as a statutory guiding agent, and the Standing Commission was given its new name and a new mandate. From then on it was to advise on development and take action on specific matters when necessary, and to continue promoting co-operation and public benefaction. The muscle it was given is reflected in the fact that the budget was increased from £72,000 in 1981/2 to nearly £6 million in 1986/7, and the staff from four to sixty.

The MGC took on control of the National Museums Security Adviser, the co-ordination and funding of the Museum Documentation Association, which is largely behind the introduction of computer technology to our museums, and allocating grants to the seven Area Museum Councils in England. In 1984 it established a conservation grant scheme, and the following year took over the Purchase Aid Funds to help local museums acquire objects and specimens, a fund which had hitherto been administered by the V&A and Science Museums.

In 1963 the Chancellor of the Exchequer asked the commission to do a report on the 750 non-national museums there then were, and the result encouraged the government to start putting money into what became the Area Museums Councils. The seven AMCs – there are two more for Wales and Scotland which the MGC monitors but does not fund – are important foster parents for many museums, providing capital grants for specific projects and advice (had it not been for the advice of the Area Museums Council for the South West, for instance, Guernsey Museum and Art Gallery would never have been built). They doled out more than £2,500,000 in the financial year 1987/8.

The MGC's reports have had increasing weight and scope in recent years, as well. The Hale Report of 1987 drew public debate on the whole question of training and career structure for curators, and in 1988 an even more explosive report on the state of some of our national museums brought a flurry of change within some of the institutions. In 1988 it introduced a system of museum registration, designed to establish parameters and standards. The criteria for registration were a genuine collection, a policy of objectives and collecting, a system of documentation, conservation, display of the collections, access for the public, relevent curatorial expertise, safeguards against disposal and an income dedicated to the collections.

Also in 1988, the MGC received a royal charter, the purpose of which was to dispel the fog of that original Treasury minute, as the secretary, Peter Longman, explained:

> It means we exist as a legal entity which is separate from the government. It's a moot point as to what a Treasury minute, which we existed under before, actually means in legal terms. The royal charter is just like getting a limited company, but it's the most grandiose form you can have.
>
> In practical terms it gives us the same status as the other similar bodies working in this field, namely the Arts Council, the Crafts Council, the British Film Institute and the Design Council.

But the MGC has proved to be invaluable in administering the procedures for public collections (as opposed to those in independent museums and galleries) to acquire objects in lieu of tax, a responsibility taken on in 1985 and for which a former Inland Revenue officer, Mrs Heather Wilson, was appointed to the staff.

Until 1985 the system whereby collectors could leave works of historical, artistic or heritage importance to the nation and specific approved (that is to say, publicly funded) institutions had been administered jointly by the Office of Arts and Libraries and the Department of the Environment, and not very well. From 1985, instead of the civil servants for the two ministries deciding between them what to recommend to their respective ministers, taking into account Treasury wishes as much as cultural benefits, the MGC makes its recommendation direct to the Arts Minister only. It was helped greatly by a decision alleged to have come from the prime minister that for works of outstanding importance there should be access to the Treasury's contingency reserve fund. This has meant that in the year 1987–8 works, mostly of art, worth £10 million in taxes – twice that of the previous two years put together and many times that in auction prices – were saved for the nation.

An example was the British Museum's acquisition of nine Henry Moore drawings from Lord Clark's collection. It took Mrs Wilson a year to close the deal, but the group was saved at a bargain: just one of the drawings might have been expected to raise £250,000 at auction, yet the whole collection was accepted in lieu of a tax bill of £153,000.

Lord Clark had left the drawings to his children with the request that on their death they should pass to the British Museum, but, despite the wealth of art the former director of the National Gallery had acquired, too little cash was left in the estate to pay death duties; since the Inland Revenue's is the first call on an estate the executors could have disposed of the drawings on the open market to meet the bill and made a substantial profit for the estate as well, but under the Acceptance-in-Lieu (AIL) system the family tax bill was paid from the Arts Minister's £2 million annual AIL fund and the seminal collection passed into national possession.

Mrs Wilson's knowledge of the tax system and the MGC's increased weight to provide a greater will to keep things for the national archive have made the difference. Not only will she interpret the tax rules – sometimes in ways which have surprised the Treasury themselves – she will negotiate to raise extra funds from organisation like the National heritage Memorial Fund or the National Art Collections Fund, a hybrid used for the first time to save Picasso's *Weeping Woman* for the Tate Gallery.

Just before Dr Christopher White became its director in 1985, the Ashmolean Museum in Oxford had been hoping to get Bellini's *Madonna and Child* through the AIL system. 'The day I took up my job there was a letter form the Arts Minister saying it was very sad but there was nothing that could be done about it,' recalled Dr White. 'We went on battering for eighteen months nevertheless, and finally the picture is hanging in our galleries. Things have changed for the better. Heather Wilson has been extremely helpful to us. Although she keeps to the rules she's not an absolute stickler – there's a feeling that she's working for the museum, not to some bureaucratic guide rules.'

The independent museums also have their own body, the Association of Independent Museums, and AIM's aim is to promote the purposes of independent museums, to help them survive and get better by training, 'and to speak up for them when they need to be spoken up for,' said its chairman, David Sekers. It was founded in 1977 and by 1988 had 700 members.

The Museum of the Year Award was launched in 1971 as a reward for the 'most enterprising and lively museum in the country', in the words of its founder John Letts. It is run by National Heritage, founded to run the competition and to provide an 'action movement' for museums. It is not statutory at all and is supported entirely by voluntary contributions, and winners of the main award (there are several subsidiary ones) have included all types of museums, from Erddig Hall in Wrexham to the Natural History Museum.

'Our idea,' said Mr Letts, 'was to provide something to give museums an extra spark, something to aim at. There was such a lot of innovation going on and no apparent reward for excellence, and the Museum of the Year Award was an attempt to redress that and to heighten awareness of how good our museums are, both to the public and the funding organisations.'

Indirectly, it has given a boost to the army of volunteers who often make the difference between a museum's survival and demise. In a survey of 1,330 museums and galleries carried out for the Volunteer Centre in 1984 Jenny Mattingly discovered that over 92 per cent of our museums used volunteers in one way or another. She also found that there is a general increase in the number of volunteers.

Volunteers mostly take the form of societies of Friends; most museums have them, and the section which uses them the least, university museums, are forming Friends' associations. Their work tends to be mostly cataloguing, and a surprising number of them, June Mattingly found, were involved in conservation and restoration work. Otherwise they get involved by running sales desks, providing information or acting as guides.

Volunteering is on the increase for several reasons, of which unemployment and earlier retirement are by far the most significant, and while nearly twice as many women as men join the Friends that percentage gap is narrowing; the expansion of museums which are growing faster than their ability to take on more, mostly unskilled, staff comes next.

Back in the days of Tom Moore and Elijah Howarth, voluntary work was the backbone of their museums. They were professionals themselves, but Mr Moore could not have got Liverpool off the ground without not only the spiritual and political support of the Rev Higgins, his chairman, but also Higgins's unstinting labour on behalf of the collections as a gifted naturalist. Victorian museums, especially provincial ones, were nearly all indebted in a fundamental way to the support of volunteers, often fired by a missionary zeal to bring education to the putative George Greens of Britain (see Chapter 7).

So the ethic of the Friends organisations was established almost with the founding of the museum movement, but there is no record of an actual organisation until 1905 when the Hastings and St Leonards Museum Association was formed.[2] The first

[2] B. R. W. Swinfen, *The British Association of Friends of Museums: a short history*, 1977.

actual 'Friends' were the Friends of the Fitzwilliam, founded in 1909. After the First World War the scheme began to be in vogue. There was the Friends of Norwich Museum in 1921; Wakefield, 1925; Brecknock, 1928; Leicester, 1930; Birmingham, 1931; the Whitworth in Manchester, 1933. By 1939 there were ore thirty of them.

In the 1950s and 60s Friends organisations popped up at the rate of two or three a year, and there were 110 groups by the early 1970s. In 1972 the need for some sort of parent body was obvious, and National heritage called a meeting which resulted in the formation of the British Association of Friends of Museums (BAFM), at first with a steering committee to draft a constitution. 'The steering committee had to give much thought to its definitions,' said B. R. W. Swinfen in his 1977 history of the BAFM. 'The word "museum" was deliberately given a wide meaning so as to ward off the danger that other organisations covering largely the same field might be set up. As the committee's report put it, they 'preferred to adopt a policy of holding the door open and seeing who comes in'. . . . Efficiency and economy of administration, effective interchange of ideas, and true friendship are far more likely to come about if we all shelter under a single umbrella.'

The BAFM started with a membership of 34, and by 1977 there were 82 representing something like 50,000 individuals, and by the time of the Mattingly Report in 1984 this figure had become 130 members comprising 120,000 single volunteers.

One of the world-famous collection of dolls' houses in the Bethnal Green Museum of Childhood.

Children in the garden of the London Toy and Model Museum near Paddington Station.

The Museum of the Manchesters, Ashton-under-Lyne, where the social history of the effects of being a recruiting town for a regiment are examined.

Sir Francis Bourgeois, founder of Dulwich Picture Gallery in South London.

Haggs Castle in Glasgow, once the medieval home of gentry, now a huge historical toy.

The first Royal Navy submarine, *Holland I*, restored and on show at the Royal Navy Submarine Museum, Gosport.

Dulwich Picture Gallery from an engraving after a pencil drawing by Frederick George Kitton (1856–1904).

Gillian Wolfe, award-winning teacher for her work with children in Dulwich Picture Gallery, brings paintings to life for her charges.

# 16. The Watchers

*With the growth of museums' importance there has inevitably grown a corps of writers and practitioners whose views are likely to affect the way museums develop in the next century. The final chapter looks through their eyes.*

MORE people are going to museums in this country than do anything else with their leisure time except read and watch television.

Five years after the 1845 'Beetle' Act – the nickname given to the Libraries, Museums and Gymnasiums Act which enabled towns to set up museums on the rates – there were not as many as sixty museums, and by the end of the century this had more than trebled. By 1914 there were 350, by 1928 530 or so and by 1963, says the Museums and Galleries Commission's report for that year, there were 876. By 1973 this had grown to 950, ten years later to 1,000, and now 2,500.

But nothing was exempt from becoming a museum, even though very few purpose-built ones were appearing. Archaeological digs, once the exclusive domain of the archaeologist who carried on his scientific pursuits mercifully divorced from prying public eyes behind hoardings, have become open-air museums, with viewing platforms, visitor centres, on-site lecturers and glossy leaflets.

History is brought to life, offering a theatrical presentation so successful the 'legitimate theatre' can only stand in envious awe. In Glasgow's Kelvingrove Museum, Mary Queen of Scots steps from her portrait to talk about her life; at the Jorvik Viking Centre in York, the Canterbury Pilgrims, the Oxford Story, the Edinburgh Whisky Centre, visitors ride or wander among tableaux as if they were part of the story.

In Dorchester you can enter Tutenkhamun's tomb and see everything the archaeologist Howard Carter saw – and smelt – when he opened the tomb in the 1920s. At Duxford Airfield near Cambridge you can 'take-off' in a fighter aircraft flight simulator, and at Peebles in the Scottish Borders the Cornice Museum encourages you to learn the art, or at least the difficulties, of decorative plastering by doing it yourself.

At Quarry Bank Mill at Styal, Cheshire, you learn how to weave cloth, at the Weald and Downland Museum at Singleton, West Sussex, you can buy flour stone-ground at the watermill; at Ironbridge you can buy fresh-baked bread; at Hull's Archaeology Museum you could watch as conservators restored a 2,300-year-old log boat.

Museum-going has become more than just a pastime or a tourist activity, it is fast approaching the status of a sport, so much has participation become an element.

David Sekers, chairman of the Association of Independent Museums and director of Quarry Bank Mill, believed the visitors themselves had dictated what museums should offer, and responded when the museums began to offer it. 'People are thirsty for involvement in a way they weren't a decade ago,' he said. 'New museums are aware that there is a great public interest which is not going to be harnessed if you are ltcturing to people, talking down to them and making them feel small. The barriers are being pulled down.'

Dylan Thomas went to the Royal Institution of South Wales Museum in Swansea, Wales's first museum which had not changed significantly in over a century. 'This museum,' he declared 'should be in a museum.'

Now museums are under such scrutiny that few could cause that remark. They attract so many people and can generate huge sums of money. There were more museums and more people were going to them than ever before in the late 1980s; never before had they attracted such attention from the press.

There are statutory museum watchers, such as the government departments which fund them or the Museums and Galleries Commission (MGC), an autonamous government-sponsored body; professional groups like the Museums Association (MA) or the Association of Independent Museums (AIM); there are trustees of museums, the great and the good who volunteer their wisdom to museums' use; there are writers, like Kenneth Hudson; or the curators themselves.

The government ministries are reactors, not innovators, and to find the pattern of the future it would be pointless to look to them – they are peering as anxiously as any, eager to assess the public response, the economic significance, the burden.

The MGC, MA and AIM had all girt their loins in the 1980s to go out and meet 'the challenge', as the MA's 1988 five-year plan put it. The MGC had introduced a registration scheme to give museums a minimum standard definition, a conservation unit to advise on how and where to get objects treated, and had published deeply researched reports on key issues.

The MA and AIM had their members' interests at heart first, but since their members' interests were encapsulated in their museums their goals differed little from the MGC's. The MA, chiefly and traditionally representing the curators in local authority museums, though by no means exclusively, was revitalised in the late 1980s after a bitter period of stultification and was engrossed in the problems of career structure, visitor care, interpretation of collections and a sophistication of attitude. Many of the things local museums had to learn were to do with the facts of life long ago addressed by independent museums, and AIM's aim was to help them develop and flourish and to help them get the fiscal advantages denied them as 'unapproved' – or non-publicly funded – museums.

Scotland had the Scottish Museums Council (SMC) as one of the nine area museum councils in the United Kingdom, though with more power and influence than the others because of the size of its charge and the wealth of the museums Scotland was bringing forth. The kind of things it was trying to do were exemplified in its 1988 policy statement, 'A Framework for Museums in Scotland', in a summary which could apply to museums throughout Britain:

> Because of the way museums have grown up in Scotland, certain types of collections have tended to be favoured, whilst a number of themes that are important to our heritage are as yet covered inadequately or not at all. Numerous gaps spring to mind: certain industries, certain sectors of our society, certain aspects of our cultural life. But if we see our museum collections as together constituting a major part of the record of our past and present, then we should try to achieve a balance between them.

There was a process of sifting, rationalising and asserting under way which the MA was addressing with its report *Answering the Challenge* in 1988 and the five-year plan that contained. It was all part of preparing for the MA's centenary year, 1989, which it had declared Museums Year. Research had been the watchword in the new thinking, and for this scheme the MA had carried out extensive consultation with museum staff 'from directors to attendants, prioritising from that feedback', said the director-general, Graeme Farnell (formerly of the Scottish Museums Council) in the media newspeak which was haunting the brash new world museums were having to adapt themselves to.

The MA identified ten priorities for museums in the 1990s interpreting and promoting a corporate plan; managing budgets; working with professionals outside museums (like marketing experts, PR people and designers); managing time and assessing priorities, common enough business practice in industry and commerce, but not in museums; customer care; preventative conservation; interpreting collections; marketing; contriving an interesting, simple and helpful introduction to museums; and finally, that dog-eared old Flowerism, managing collections.

'That's getting away from the more inward looking things which one might have got five years ago,' said Mr Farnell. 'Five years ago it was blockbuster, temporary exhibitions, very much more collections-orientated than now, when it is more consumer-orientated. He went on to say:

> What museums have been failing to do is maximise the potential of their collections, their role, because historically they haven't paid enough attention to that interaction between the museum itself and the community outside. It's that sort of maximising of collections we're talking about when we're talking about customer care or marketing.
>
> We've got to demonstrate, as museums are increasingly demonstrating, that they are capable of excellent management, of generating income, of generating public interest, that they are very efficient, but on the other hand almost aggressive where elements of principle are concerned such as the sale of collections. Dr Neil Cossons, director of the Science Museum would not have demurred. A few weeks before their 1988 programme was launched, he himself had launched a multi-million pound five-year programme to transform the Science Museum, bringing in shops, new galleries, restaurants, and starting with an admission charge.

'The great boom of the 1880s was of the municipal, publicly-funded museums of enormous proportions,' said Dr Cossons, who has run museums in practically every sector before going to South Kensington, notably as the first director of Ironbridge Gorge Museum. But the age of the general collection was over in 1989, he believed. 'Multi-disciplinary museums have had their day, nobody's building any more of them. The good ones still seem to be successful and people go to them, but they have to considerably revise their product.' We are in an age when objects and collections are in danger of becoming 'products' and 'stock', but it was not a peril in Dr Cossons's book. That was not the mark of the new museum age:

> The phenomenon of the 1970s and 80s boom, it seems to me, is the single theme museums which go beyond the physical constraints which the old nineteenth-century town centre municipal type of museum imposed. In other words, you can't explore archaeology very far before you need a site-based museum, you can't explore industrial archaeology at all in the context of the traditional museum.

You found your theme and built a museum on it, in Dr Cossons's view, and if the theme happened to be a site – like the Jorvik Viking Centre – so much the better. Another example would be a museum of rural life based on a farm, like Cogges Farm at Witney in Oxfordshire.

The grand old museums could not adapt easily, he told me. 'Because they are so difficult to recapitalise, and inflexible because all their expenditure's sunk into looking after the stuff they've already got, they can't respond to the new trends. So it's new museums that respond, and the interesting question will be how far those new museums survive the next change in fashion because they're not underwritten from the public purse in the main; they're paid for by the users.'

Interviewed for the *Financial Times* in 1987, Dr Cossons expanded on the theme:

> There's a link between the artefact-based museum and the site, and if you really think in terms of the mobility of people and the fact that at a weekend more and more people spend their leisure out of the town centre - they live in the suburbs but they don't go in to the town for the recreation, they go into the countryside. The rural-based or small-town-based museum has enjoyed colossal expansion leaving behind the sort of isolated, fossilised, high investment, high cost, high staff cost, town centre museums, looking after broadly unfashionable collections at ratepayers' expense.
>
> I firmly believe that the total number of new independent, single-theme museums will diminish leaving the good ones and the strong ones, and the small ones that are not so good will disappear – not necessarily a bad thing.

It is a Malthusian view not at the moment vouched for by the flourishing boom, but Dr Cossons perceived a certain weariness in the public 'who've been through any number of heritage centres, looked at any number of graphics panels and pictures of objects or audio-visuals of objects, which heightens the real thing.' We can thank the great television documentaries of the 1970s, who introduced them to the national landscape, wildlife and archaeology.

'But we hold the real thing,' said Neil Cossons. 'There's only one quality that distinguishes a museum from all other types of entertainment, scholarly, academic and recreational activities, and that is that we hold collections. Ten years ago people would have said the word museum was a marketing liability, now it's an asset so lots of places that aren't real museums call themselves museum because it's a good selling line.'

'Selling is something which tended to send a shiver up the spine of the veteran museum-watcher,' said Kenneth Hudson. A good friend of Dr Cossons's, Mr Hudson, was not entirely offering a compliment when he said the Science Museum would be the 'first thorough-going business museum in the world'.

A former BBC Radio talks producer ('I did *Any Questions?* which I always regarded as a light comedy show'), Kenneth Hudson was originally an industrial archaeologist when he was a 'things man' and graduated to museums when he became a 'people man' twenty-five years ago. Since then there have been eight museums books, countless television and radio programmes, and the European and national Museum of the Year Awards which he had been behind since their inception in the early and middle 1970s. 'I chose museums because I found them attractive,' Hudson said. 'I may have visited more museums than anybody else in the world,' and he is probably the only man with 'museologist' in the occupation box on his passport. Beamish was his favourite British museum, the British Museum itself he saw as a bad influence in giving provincial museums an ideal a century ago which they could not afford, from which they then copied the staff structure which was inflexible and inappropriate to local collections.

'I see art museums as the backward children because they don't do anything new, but they do the old things better such as their buildings, lighting, ventilation,' and he cites the Ruskin in Sheffield as a good example.

A globe-trotter who speaks at least eight languages, Kenneth Hudson likes to look at the museum phenomenon in global terms: 'If you project forward ten years, what's the picture? What you're going to see then is different parts of the world producing their own museums of influence – at least two in Japan, one or two in India, one or two in China, Africa, South America, museums which will point the way to ours.' None, oddly, in the United States, this country or even Europe.

But what of the influences that had changed things between a century ago and 1989? The answer for Mr Hudson was a one-word one.

> Motorisation. With cars the old city museums all turn out to be on the wrong site now because you can't park there. The museums with plenty of car parking miles from anywhere have got the advantage that National Trust properties have had from the beginning.
>
> Second is the entry of competition from the leisure industries, so that museums have spent so much money on the services to visitors that we've grossly neglected what the place is supposed to be about, and this, of course, is a constant danger: you go for numbers at all costs in order to survive and then you wake up one morning and say what the hell are we doing it for? The need to compete has led people into unworthy paths. The moment you say we've got to have money to survive you become subservient to your sponsor, and the growth of sponsorship is the third influence.

But the picture was not as gloomy as all that in 1989. Because of the popularity of museums, the still underpaid bright young curators were not moving out, as they were doing in the 1960s and 70s, to teaching or other more lucrative pursuits, and despite the shadow of mammon it was from the independents that the good new ideas were coming, Kenneth Hudson thought. To him, 'European museums envy us our independent museums to an extent we don't realise. The average museum in Britain is the best in the world.'

I prefer the view of Rachel Wilkins, the young curator of Hartlepool's Gray Art Gallery and Museum, who represents the curators of the next generation of museums and believes that there is a an unstoppable dynamo of improvement, especially at the local level. 'It's quite difficult to keep up with museums. I should say they've changed more in the last ten years than in the previous hundred,' she said.

Her practice was to go to the people of the community whose history she was trying to represent and bring their experience into the museum as a legitimate device – in other words, to create a community museum. 'Participation is very much the key element now – I want to be able to provide the best museum service for the people of Hartlepool, but I wasn't born here and so they know much more about it than I do. I must encourage them to tell me about the town so that I can get the story right.'

'What is also true is that museums are not in competition with each other, as other tourist attractions might be,' said Miss Wilkins. 'If you visit one good museum you'll be encouraged to visit another, but a bad one may put you off them altogether, so it's important to hear what the public say, and provide what they want.'

Jean Francois Grunfeld is the creator and organiser of the Salon Internationale des Musees et des Expositions, the biennial museums' world trade fair held in Paris's Grand Palais. He travels the world looking at museums, talking to their directors, analysing their qualification to be represented on a global stage. Towards the end of 1988 he went to London to see a new museum which may be the museum of the twenty-first century. 'It is simply the most intelligent, the most exciting, the most relevant, the most entertaining museum I have ever seen.' said this usually phlegmatic and undemonstrative former banker.

He was talking about the Museum of the Moving Image, opened by the Prince of Wales on the South Bank in September 1988. Five years in the making, it tells the story of films and television through objects, tableaux, actors, lighting and an inventive display technique that appears to owe nothing to any existing museum, yet is a natural successor to several.

'We had to tell the story in so many facets,' said one of the conceivers of the idea, Leslie Hardcastle, who is also Controller of the British Film Institute. 'It was the dream of Tony Smith, director of the BFI until recently, and David Francis, the curator. We could have gone to a well known and experienced museum designer of which there are many in Britain, but we decided to use someone young and new, and Neal Potter has given us a three-dimensional display that is completely different from anything else.'

As visitors follow a yellow brick road through nearly 5,000 years of development from the shadow plays of ancient Egypt, actors guide them on their way through zoetropes to Odeons to a television production studio.

The founders have no public money at all and have raised all the £7 million the museum cost from private benefactors. In order to survive it must attract 400,000 visitors year, and was likely to have topped 600,000 by the end of its first year. Three years ago plans were still well ahead for the area on which the museum stands to become an underground car park.

'I think that for a successful museum of this kind you need special ingredients to keep it alive,' said Leslie Hardcastle. 'We saw a lot of museums around the world in the five years' planning, and we have learned from them, but we have our own mixture of passion, business sense and imagination. Does it work? The only way to be sure is to look at the visitors.' M. Grunfeld saw a thousand enthralled people, amused by the antics of the actors, intrigued by the science, entertained by the product. It works,' he said.

# Index


Acceptance-in-lieu, 170
Adair, Lt. Col. P., 132
Addyman, P., 110
Advertising and Packaging, Museum of, 52–5
Aikenhead, Glasgow, 30
Allen, E., 61, 62
Alleyn, E., 141
*Alliance, HMS*, 131
Ancient Monuments Committee, Guernsey, 23, 24
Arbeia Roman Fort, 114–15
Archeology, 1, 63, 113–15
Archeology Museum, 174
Archeology Transport Museum, 69
Architectural Heritage Trail, 79
Army Transport, Museum of, 135
Armstrong, J. R., 42
Art Galleries, 141–53
Art Gallery, Birmingham, 20
Ashmole, E., 46
Ashmolean Museum, 2, 45–7, 58
Association of Independent Museums, 170–1, 174
Atkinson, F., 71–7, 115–17
Austen, Jane, 44

Baden-Powell, Lord, 44
Bakelite Museum, 55–7
Ball, M., 163
Banks, Sir J., 3, 45
Bassett, D. A., 15
Beamish Open Air Museum, 71–6, 115–17, 177
Beaulieu Development Company, 39
Beetlestone, J., 98–9
*Belfast, HMS*, 135
Bell, Sir Hugh, 82
Bennett, V., 153
Bethnal Green Museum of Childhood, 8, 53, 119–22
Bewick, T., 76
Bidwell, P., 114–15
Biographical Museums, 43–4
Birmingham Gun-Barrel Proof House Museum of Small Arms, 21
Birmingham Museums and Art Gallery, 19–22
Bissett's Museum and Picture Gallery, 19
Blists Hill, 87
Bluebird (1935), 41
Boat Museum Trust, 105
Boat museums, 100–8
Boffins' cupboards, 58–65
Booth, K., 83, 84
Botany, Manchester, 63
Bourgeois, F., 142–3, 144
Bowes Museum, 71, 72
Boyle, Sir Dermot, 137
BP Library of Motoring, 39, 40
Brigg boat, 69
British Association of Friends of Museums, 172
British Engineerium, Hove, 85
British Museum Act, 3
British Museum, founded, 5
Brock, C. H., 59–60
Bromhead, Sir Edward, 90
Brontë Parsonage Museum, 43
Brooks archeological dig, 112
Brown, W., 31
Bryant, J., 106, 108
Buckingham, Duke of, 45
Buildings, re-erected, 42
Bunce, J. T., 19, 21
Burns, Robbie, 44
Burrell Collection, 30
Burrell, Sir William, 29
Burton, A., 121
Bygones, 70

Cabinet War Rooms, 135
Camphill House, Glasgow, 30
Candie Park, Guernsey, 23–6
Canterbury Pilgrims' Way, 112, 173
Carlyle, T., 44
Carter, G., 41
Catalyst, 92
Challis, L., 89, 91–2
Chalmers, N., 159–60

# Index


Chamberlain, J., 20–1
Chatham Historic Dockyard, 100
Cherryburn, 76–7
Childhood museums, 8, 53, 118–28
  Glasgow, 30
Children's Discovery Centre, 97
Children's Gallery, Science Museum, 82, 84, 95
'Chinese Dinosaurs', exhibition, 17
Chinese porcelain, 58
Clegg, J., 36
Clifford, T., 147, 150
Coalbrookdale, 85–6
Coalport, 86
  China Works, 87
Coffee Houses, 2
Cogges Farm, Witney, 176
Cole, H., 1
Cole, R., 23–5
Cole, (Sir) Henry, 6–10, 19, 20, 81–2
Collecting, 1–4
Commerce and Transport Museum, 70
Compton-Hall, Lt. Cdr. R., 130–2
Concorde Museum, 83
Conder, T., 102
Conservation, 160–3
  lighting damage, 160–1
  new studies, 161
  storage damage, 161
Cook, P., 56–7
Cornice Museum, 173
Cossons, N., 96, 97, 156, 162, 176–7
  Ironbridge Gorge Museum, 85, 86–7
  Science Museum, 83, 85
Costume, Gallery of English Costume, 148
Cotton, Sir Robert, 5
Cotton spinning mills, 43
County and Regimental Museum, 135
Courtauld Institute Galleries, 58
Crackpots' museums, 45–57
Curators, 155–60, 162–3
  courses and training, 157, 159
  definitions, 155–6
  as enlightened dilettantes, 159

Dale, R., 20
Darby, A., 85–6, 87
Darwin, C., 13
  museum, 43
Derby collection, 31
Desanfans, N., 142–3, 144
Design Museum, 57
Dewsbury Museum, 127–8
Dickens, C., 44
Digging for History, 126–7
*Discovery* Centre, 106–8
Dolls and dolls' houses, 120–1
Driffield Collection, 69
Dulwich College, 142
Dulwich Picture Gallery, 142–6, 153, 164
Dundee Industrial Heritage, 106
Duxford Museum, 135, 173

Easington Tithe Barn, 70
Edinburgh Tolbooth, 112
Edinburgh Whisky Centre, 173
Education and museums, 33, 148, 163–5
Eggleton, J., 27, 30–1
Electric lighting and conservation, 160
Ellesmere Port Boat Museum, 103
Esteve-Coll, E., 159–60
*Eureka!* 95, 96–8
Exeter Maritime Museum, 101
*Exploratory*, 93

Farnell, G., 175
Faux, R., 71–2, 73
Feber, S., 97–8
Ferens Art Gallery, 69, 70
Film and Photography, National Museum, 83
Fitzwilliam Museum, 58
Flaxman Gallery, 58
Flower, W. H., 11–14
Food Gallery, Science Museum, 84, 96
Fopp, M., 136
Forty, Lt. Col. G., 132
Fowke, F., 11, 118
Fox, (Sir) Cyril, 16
Freud Museum, 44, 83
Friends associations, 171–2
Funding of national museums, 17

Gas lighting and conservation, 160–1
Gaynor, A., 110, 112
Geffrye Museum, 164
Gerald of Wales exhibition, 17
Giant, Irish, 62
Glasgow Exhibitions, 28–9
Glasgow Garden Festival, 27
Glasgow Museums and Galleries, 26–31, 125
Gloucester Dock, 54
Gordon Bennett Napier (1903), 41
Gray Art Gallery and Museum, 178
Gray, J., 11–12
*Great Britain, SS*, 101
Green, G., 89–92
  Functions and Theorem, 90, 91, 92
Green's Mill and Centre, 89–92
Greg, M., 119, 121
Greg, S., 43
Gregory, M., 93
Gregory, R., 93–4
Grunfeld, J. F., 178, 179

# INDEX


Guardians, 155–65
Guards Museum, 134–6
Guernsey Museum and Art Gallery, 22–6
Gyroscope chair, 95

Haggs Castle, 30, 125–7
Hale, Sir J., 156, 157, 159
Hands-on museums, 93–9
Hardcastle, L., 178, 179
Harley, R., Earl of Oxford, 5
Harris Museum, Preston, 152
Harrison, R., 23
Haslemere Education Museum, 33–6
Hatton, A., 155, 156, 157–9, 162
Heritage Projects, 112–13
Hibbert, J., 152
Higgins, Revd., 171
Hirst, T., 104
Hoarders' museums, 45–57
Hogarth, W., 44
*Holland I*, 131–2
Hollins, P., 20
Horniman Museum, 120, 164
Horsfall Museum, 148–9
Howarth, E., 33, 166, 171
Howarth, J., 63
Howlett, D. and S., 52
Hoyle, W. E., 15
Hudson, K., 174, 176
Hulbert, C., 86
Hull City Museums and Art Galleries, 33, 66–71
Hunterian Museums, 3, 10, 11, 58–62
  John Hunter, London, 60–2
  William Hunter, Glasgow, 59–60
Hutchinson, Sir Jonathan, 34–6, 44

Imperial College of Science and Technology, 8, 84
Imperial porcelain, 52
Imperial War Museum, 135
Independent museums, 33–44
Industrial museums, 31, 81–5
Industrial Revolution, effects, 88–9
Inval, near Haslemere, 34, 35
Ipswich Museum, 157–9
Iron Museum, 8
Ironbridge Gorge Museum, 85–9, 174

Jenner, E., 3, 61–2
Jewell, A., 34
Jewry Wall Museum, 31
Johnson, Dr, 44
Jorvik Viking Centre, 109–13, 173, 176

Keats Museum, 44
Kelvingrove Museum and Art Gallery, 27, 173
Kelvingrove Park, 29

La Varde, Guernsey, 22
Lady Lever Art Gallery, 32
Lankester, Sir Edwin Ray, 14
*Launch Pad*, 84, 95–6
Lee, J., 141
Leicestershire museums, 31
Leicestershire Records Office, 31
Leigh, D., 162
Lending scheme for paintings, 149
Letts, J., 171
Levy, A., 122–3, 124
Levy, N., 123, 124
Lewis, P., 74, 75, 116–17
Lincoln's Inn Fields museums, 47–9, 61
  *see also* Hunterian Museums
Liverpool (Free) Museum, 31–2
Local museums, 19–32
London Toy and Model Museum, 122–5
Lukis, Frederick, 22–3
Lyons, Sir Henry, 82, 83, 84

MacGregor, N., 159–60, 164
McLellan, A., 27
McLellan Galleries, 27, 28, 29
Madame Tussaud's, 109
Magnusson, Magnus, 111
Manchester City Art Gallery, 146–50
Manchester and Industrial Revolution, 88
Manchester Museum, 62–5
Manchester Regiment (The Manchesters) Museum, 139–40
Manchester Society for Natural History, 63
Martyn, T., 59
*Mary Rose*, 101
Mattingly, J., 171
Mattingly report, 172
Maxwell, Sir William, 30
Medicis, 2
Merseyside museums, 31–2
Military museums, 129–140
Milling, 89–92
Mills, cotton, 43
Mining Museum, 31
Minns, J., 85
Monk's Parlour, 49
Montagu, Baron, of Beaulieu, 37
Montagu, Lord, of Beaulieu, 36–42
Montagu Ventures Ltd., 39, 40
Montague House Museum, 10
Moore, T., 171
Moore, T. J., 31
Mortimer Collection, 69, 70
Mosesfield, Glasgow, 30
Motoring Library, Beaulieu, 39, 40

# INDEX


Motorisation and the museum, 177
Moving Image, Museum of the, 178
Mummy research, Manchester, 64
Mundaria Court, 56
Musaeum Tradescantianum, 2, 45–7
Museum(s)
  Association, 156
    Code of Practice, 168
    formation, 166–7
    journal, 167–8
    the organisation, 167–8
    priorities for museums, 175
    Report 1893, 34
    role, 174
    *Yearbook*, 168
  definition, 109–13
  derivation, 2
  the future, 176–9
  and Galleries Commission, 109, 156, 168
    acceptance-in-lieu, 170
    activities, 169
    conservation unit, 162
    establishment, 168
    gifts and legacies, 169–70
    reports, 168
    role, 174
    Royal Charter, 169
  as a living organism, 1
  of Manufacturers, 8
  of the Year Award launched, 171
  purposes for establishment, 12

National Gallery, 164
National Gallery of Modern Art, 152
National Gallery of Scotland, 150–3
National Heritage, 171
National Lifeboat Museum, 101
National Maritime Museum, 100
National Motor Museum, Beaulieu, 6–42
National Museum of Wales, 14–17
National museums, 5–18
National Plastics Museum, 56–7
National Railway Museum, 83
National Waterways Museum, Gloucester, 101–3
Natural History, Manchester, 62–3
Natural History Museum, 10–14
Naval Museum, 130–2
Newbury Museum, 35
Nightingale, F., 44
North of England Open Air Museum, 71
North West Museum of Science, 88
Nutrition Gallery, Science Museum, 84, 96

One-subject museums, 56
O'Neill, M., 77–80
Open-air museums, 42, 70, 71–7, 115–17
Opie, I., 53
Opie, R., 52–5, 100
Osler, T. C., 20
Owen, D., 104
Owen, Sir Isambard, 15
Owen, (Sir) Richard, Natural History Museum,
  10–11, 12, 62
Oxford Story, 112, 173

Packaging and Advertising, Museum (Pack Age),
  52–5
Papworth, W. A. V. S., 49
Patent Museum, 82
Pavlova, A., 44
Penn, T., 136
Percival David Collection of Chinese Porcelain, 58
Petrie, Flinders, 64
Petrie Museum, 58, 63
Physic Garden, Oxford, 46
Pickering, C., 69
Pinakothekai, 2
Pipes' Museum, 56
Pitshanger Manor, 48
Plastics Museum, 56–7
Playfair, Lyon, 6, 81–2
Playfair, W. H., 151–2
Ponsonby, L., 34
Pope-Hennessey, Sir John, 120
Portsmouth Historic Naval Dockyard, 101
Potter, N., 178
Powell-Cotton Museum, 49–52
Powell-Cotton, P., 49–52
Prince Albert, 81
  International (Great) exhibition, 7–8

Quarry Bank Mill, 43, 165, 173, 174
Queen Charlotte, 59
Queen Mary, 120, 121

Raper, E., 68
Read, R., 24
Reading University's Museum of Rural Life, 65
Redcliffe-Maude report, 71
Regimental museums, 129–30
Renoir in Guernsey, 25–6
Ridley, M., 113–14
Robinson, J. C., 21
Roman Britain, 114–15
Royal Air Force Museum, 136–9
Royal Albert Hall, 8
Royal College of Art, 8
Royal College of Music, 8
Royal College of Surgeons, 11
Royal Naval Museum, 101
Royal Navy Submarine Museum, 130–2
Ruskin Gallery, Sheffield, 153

# INDEX


Rutherglen, Glasgow, 30

Sabin, A., 118, 119
Salon Internationale des Musees et des Expositions, 178
Science Museum, 81–5
  opened, 8
Science (Museum) Library, 82
Scottish Museums Council, 175
Scottish National Portrait Gallery, 152
Seeley, N., 161
Sekers, D., 43, 165, 171, 174
Shafto, Sir Robert, 73
Shakespeare, W., 44
Sheffield Museum and Gallery, 33
Sheppard, T., 33, 66–71
Shipsides, R., 126
Shrewsbury Castle, 130
Skipper, I., 113
Sloane, Sir Hans, biographical details, 5
Soane, Sir John, 44, 45, 48–9, 144
  museum, 47–9
Social history, 52–5
Society of Antiquaries, 2
South Kensington Museum, 8
Spalding, J., 149
Springburn and its Museum, 77–80
Standing Commission on Museums and Galleries, 156
Stewards and stewardesses, 84–5
Strong, Sir Roy, 121
Support for museums, 166–72
Swanton, E. W., 35
Swinfen, B. R. W., 172

Tangye, R., 21
Tank Museum, 132–4
Tanner, J., 137
Technology museum, 81–5
TECHNIQUEST, 95, 98–9
Tennyson, Alfred Lord, 44
*Test Bed*, 96
Textiles, 165
Thompson, H. Y., 145
Thorburn Museum and Gallery, Dobwalls, 153
Thornton, P., 49
Tomb finds, 63
Toxteth Riots, 1981, 104
Toy museums, 118–28
  *see also* Childhood museums
Tradescant, J., 2, 45–7
  'Ark', 46, 47
Transport Museum, 70
Travelling exhibition, 72
  of art, 149, 150
Trenchard, Lord, 136, 137
Tutenkhamun Exhibition, 113–14, 173

University museums, 64–5

Victoria & Albert Museum founded, 6–10
*Victory, HMS*, 101
Viking Centre, 109–13
Virchow, R. C., 13
Volunteers, 171–2

Wallis, Whitworth, 22
Ward, R., 51
Ware, M., 37–42
Warhurst, A., 64, 65
*Warrior, HMS*, 101
Waterfield, G., 143, 144, 145
Waterhouse, (Sir) Alfred, 10, 11, 28, 29
Waterways Museum, 54
Waterways museums, 100–8
Watson, R. S., 73
Weald and Downland Open Air Museum, 42, 173
Wellington, Duke of, 44
Welsh Folk Museum, 17
Welsh Industrial and Maritime Museum, 17
Welsh Woollen Industry Museum, 17
Welsh Slate Museum, 17
Wesley, J., 44
Weston, Dame Margaret, 83
Wharton, T., 46
Wheeler, Sir Mortimer, 16
Wigan Pier, 74
Wilberforce, W., 69
Wilkins, R., 178
Williams, M., 96
Wilson, A., 95
Wilson, H., 169–70
Windmill, Green's, restoring, 89, 91
Wise, T., 129–30
Wolfe, G., 153–64
Woodcroft, B., 82
Woof, R., 44
Wordsworth Trust, 44
  and Museum, 44
Wrought Iron Works, 88
Wunderkämmer, 2

York Archaeological Trust, 110

Zeuner, C., 42